Atypical Child Development in Context

Janet M. Empson and Dabie Nabuzoka

with David Hamilton

© Janet M. Empson and Dabie Nabuzoka 2004
Chapter 4 © Janet M. Empson and David Hamilton 2004;
Chapter 6 © David Hamilton 2004

First published 2004 by
PALGRAVE MACMILLAN
Houndmills, Basingstoke, Hampshire RG21 6XS and
175 Fifth Avenue, New York, N.Y. 10010
Companies and representatives throughout the world

PALGRAVE MACMILLAN is the global academic imprint of the Palgrave
Macmillan division of St. Martin's Press, LLC and of Palgrave Macmillan Ltd.
Macmillan® is a registered trademark in the United States, United Kingdom
and other countries. Palgrave is a registered trademark in the European
Union and other countries.

ISBN 0–333–94935–8

This book is printed on paper suitable for recycling and made from fully
managed and sustained forest sources.

A catalogue record for this book is available from the British Library.

A catalog record for this book is available from the Library of Congress.

Editing and origination by Aardvark Editorial, Mendham, Suffolk

10 9 8 7 6 5 4 3 2 1
13 12 11 10 09 08 07 06 05 04

Printed in China

To our parents

As a flower grows concealed in an enclosed garden,
unknown to the cattle,
bruised by no plough,
and which the breezes caress,
the sun makes strong and the rain brings out;
many boys and many girls long for it.

Carmina *no. 62*
CATULLUS, *Roman poet c84–c54* BC

Contents

List of Figures

List of Tables

Preface

The plan to write this book came from teaching developmental psychology to undergraduates on a wide range of courses, notably psychology, social work, nursing and allied professions. Many of these students were working with or would go on to work with children experiencing problems in development and their families. Students generally seemed to be particularly interested in developmental difficulty, which reflected our research interests. A third-year module 'Atypical child development' was developed. This studies the relationship between normal and abnormal development, taking as a basic premise that children who are developing atypically are more like so-called normal children than they are different from them. By studying both kinds of development, each facilitates a better understanding of the other. This approach is called developmental psychopathology.

Developmental psychopathology is a relatively new discipline, but a very important one. The greater our understanding of normal child development in relation to atypical development, the more effective will be our intervention to help families in need. A rapidly expanding body of research is now contributing to an explanation of the processes involved in atypical development. Much of this research is being carried out in the USA, but there are other teams in different countries worldwide. Our intention here is to introduce the reader to the current state of the field, utilising this range of sources, emphasising where appropriate the relevance of cultural context to the experience of children and families. We should like to acknowledge the influence of the ideas of Michael Rutter, Ann and Alan Clarke, Urie Bronfenbrenner and Robert Serpell in particular, although of course many others have contributed to the substance of the issues presented here. The importance of social adversity on children's development as well as individual differences, both biological and psychological, in response to such experiences is a major theme. So also is the view of discontinuity and change in developmental pathways, especially as influenced by environmental change. Problems in childhood are very much seen as due to the environment in which the child is growing up – family, school and neighbourhood – as well as individual difficulty. But the child is also recognised as a major contributor to his or her own development. We have focused on what we think are the most frequently occurring conditions and circumstances associated with atypical development and distress in children and their families. We hope that our discussions will help the reader to understand how and why these arise. In addition to improving our knowledge of human development, some of the implications for society are also illustrated.

About the Authors

Janet Empson is Principal Lecturer and Head of Psychology in the School of Social Science and Law at Sheffield Hallam University; a Chartered Psychologist and full member of the Health Division of the British Psychological Society. Her specialist teaching area is developmental psychology with a particular interest in child well-being.

Dabie Nabuzoka is Senior Lecturer in Psychology at Sheffield Hallam University and a Chartered Psychologist. His research interests include the social functioning of children with learning disabilities, and cultural influences on chid development. He is author of *Children with Learning Disabilities: Social Functioning and Adjustment.*

David Hamilton is a Lecturer in the Department of Psychology and Disability Studies at RMIT University in Melbourne, Australia. He is co-author of *Children's Phobias: A Behavioural Perspective* (with Neville King and Tom Ollendick). He has held previous academic appointments at Deakin and Sheffield Hallam Universities, and conducts research on intellectual disability and autism.

Acknowledgements

We should like to thank all the many people who have contributed in different ways to the final version of this book. First there are those who read earlier drafts. One particular cohort of third-year undergraduates studying our modules gave us very valuable feedback from the perspective of our proposed readership. Janet's daughter, Rachel, also gave us constructive comments at an early stage. Our colleague and friend Sue McHale read various sections and gave us much encouragement. Peter Derlien read the whole manuscript and made detailed, helpful comments. We are also greatly indebted to the anonymous reviewers whose thorough reading and directive, facilitative feedback helped us greatly in improving the clarity of our discussions. In the final stages we were assisted by Dabie's daughter Tutsirai and Peter Derlien who formatted the figures in Microsoft.

Finally, Janet would like to record personal appreciation of the support given throughout the writing of this book by her friend and mentor, Dorothy Rowe.

JANET EMPSON AND DABIE NABUZOKA

Introduction

This book introduces difficulties faced by some children during the course of development that make their experiences and possibly their progress 'atypical'. Although health care for most has generally improved in the course of the last century, there are still many children coping with various forms of difficulties in development. These include physical difficulties associated with problems during pregnancy and childbirth, and psychological problems associated with, for example, child abuse. Many children (perhaps as many as one in five) have some degree of emotional and behavioural difficulty and most of these are linked with home environments. Developmental problems may also include intellectual or learning disability, which, it is estimated, affects ten per cent of children. All such children are said to be developing atypically.

Environmental factors are implicated in some if not most conditions of atypical development. For example, many children are growing up in conditions of poverty, which may also be a source of poor development in children and is associated with problems in coping for families. In some families, the relationships between parents and their children are abusive, and the development of maltreated children is associated with a wide range of atypical behaviours and considerable emotional distress. Many of these circumstances which are associated with atypical development overlap for particular children. For example, poverty, learning disability and maltreatment may co-occur in the life experience of a particular child. Overall then, the children with whom this book is concerned constitute a significant proportion of the population as a whole. Difficulties faced by these children may require some kind of specialist intervention to facilitate the possibility of optimal development and alleviate suffering.

The overall aim of the book is to introduce our readers to the psychological theory relevant to our understanding of developmental difficulties in childhood and draw implications for the practice of professionals such as teachers, social workers and nurses, as well as practising psychologists. The focus is on the context of such difficulties relating to society in general, but more especially in the context of the family, school environments and other settings in which children spend a great deal of time. Specific aims of the book are:

- To introduce the reader to some of the major theories of (and perspectives on) child development, and how these explain both typical and atypical development
- To discuss some of the major circumstances in which atypical development occurs and attempt to explain how and why these arise
- To enable the reader to arrive at a better understanding of similarities as well as differences between children thought to be developing normally and those developing atypically
- To enable a better understanding of the relationship between theory and practice.

This book is written mainly, although not exclusively, from a psychological perspective. It is based on a number of guiding principles or premises, which are based on currently available evidence and include:

- Children developing atypically are much more similar to normal children than they are different from them
- Atypical child development can be identified and described at many different levels (ranging from the biological to the experiential)
- Although the focus may be on the person, there is an acknowledgement that the psychology of the individual cannot be separated from her biological make-up or social contexts and experiences.

The emphasis of the book is therefore on dynamic systems and reciprocal interactions, which need to occur on a fairly regular basis over extended periods of time to be effective. Such interactions provide the context in which children develop and involve the children themselves as active, evolving human organisms and also the persons, objects and other aspects of their immediate external environment.

Various theoretical perspectives have informed efforts aimed at meeting the needs of children developing atypically. For example, the principles of learning established by the behaviourists and Jean Piaget's (1952, 1970) theory of stages in cognitive development have informed the development of interventions with children and families in difficulties. John Bowlby's (1969, 1980) pioneering work on babies and young children being separated from their parents gave rise to the concept of 'attachment'. This led to a recognition that enduring affectional bonds that develop between infants and caregivers – as a result of their shared experiences – are of fundamental importance to healthy social and emotional development in children. Also of significance to all aspects of development are those adults and older siblings who constitute 'models' of development for growing youngsters. Such models are considered to be important by the social learning theorists. Judy Dunn (1988) has described and analysed the whole family context in which development takes place in terms of variables critical to the child's developing sense of self and social understanding.

The wider context of human development, including the institutions of society such as school and workplace, has also been considered (by Sameroff and Chandler, 1975, in particular) to be of importance in influencing individual development. Such a view is consistent with Bronfenbrenner's (1979) ecological perspective. In all, social ecological factors are significant in typical child development and as such also have implications for development that is atypical. These factors may interact with environmental factors, as well as biological or maturational factors, to determine the course of development for a given child. Variations in developmental pathways are also influenced by the active contribution of the child as emphasised by the transactional approach. These considerations must be brought into the formula which seeks to identify ways of reducing the associated difficulties in development. It is this perspective of factors in context and in interaction that informs much of this book.

Chapter 1 introduces this perspective by first discussing some of the major conceptual and theoretical approaches to atypical development. One definition of development is 'the processes underlying changes in growth and capability in the child'. Two of the main processes are maturation (a biological process) and learning from experience and interaction with the environment. The active contribution of the individual child to her own development is emphasised in the transactional model of development (Sameroff and Chandler, 1975; Sameroff, 1991) which also includes ongoing interactions between biological and environmental influences. The importance of the context of development (for example Bronfenbrenner, 1979; Bronfenbrenner and Morris, 1998) and the reciprocal interactions between and within the systems of which the child is a part, as well as those systems which exert a more indirect influence in influencing developmental progress, are also discussed. The central importance of socialisation for developmental outcome is also described with particular reference to attachment theory. Development is described in terms of normative change (both continuous, and discrete jumps) and normal variations, which are influenced by both individual maturation rates and experiences. Inherited behaviours, instincts and reflexes give way to voluntary control. Deviation from 'normal' development may be qualitative or quantitative and examples are given of each. An approach which has informed much theorectical and empirical research regarding atypical development is that of developmental psychopathology. This approach assumes that normal functioning of children can be better understood by studying 'abnormal' conditions in childhood. Likewise, by studying normal conditions, we can learn more about atypical development.

Chapter 2 outlines and discusses some of the risk factors for atypical development. Risk factors are classified into biological, such as genetic and chromosomal abnormalities and the effects of illness and injury, and environmental, for example stress during pregnancy and in childhood. Pregnancy and childbirth are considered as times of high risk and the main perinatal risks are described. Psychosocial factors, with a particular emphasis on interpersonal relationships, are important mediating variables whereby the wider environmental influences have their effects. The short and long-term effects of some of these factors and the interactions between them are related to the transactional model of development.

Chapter 3 focuses on the issue of child abuse, which has been a feature of society throughout recorded history, although its nature and prevalence have changed in different eras. Child abuse is a culturally defined construct. Some cultures appear to have no abuse because, it has been argued, there is no physical punishment of children; the possible link between the use of physical punishment and physical abuse is considered. Distinctions are made between different forms of maltreatment of children: between neglect and abuse, and between physical, emotional and sexual forms. The frequency with which abuse occurs is very difficult to assess, however, it is agreed that rates of abuse are higher for girls than boys and rates vary for different ages.

Models of how abuse arises, incorporating risk factors at different levels, are presented. These are linked with different theoretical explanations of the causes of child abuse – psychiatric, social learning, attachment and multifactorial. Possible effects of abuse are considered in terms of stress and developmental perspectives. It is concluded that the best explanations of child abuse will incorporate many factors interacting at different levels. It is argued that a developmental or longitudinal perspective is also necessary. Such explanations can be summarised as an application of the transactional and ecological approaches.

Chapter 4 focuses on emotional and behavioural difficulties as an aspect of atypical development. It is argued that children who show developmental difficulties/problems must be viewed in the context of the 'systems' of which they are a part. Examples of such systems are the family and the school. The child's circumstances may be eliciting the 'symptoms', which may be demonstrations of normal child reactions to inappropriate parenting. It is argued that the family is a common source of difficulty for children. Most children show isolated symptoms of 'abnormality' at some time and most conditions defined as 'abnormal' differ quantitatively but not qualitatively from 'normality'. The criteria used to assess whether a particular difficulty is serious enough to merit professional intervention are discussed and the main types of disorder described. The main dichotomy into 'internalising' problems and 'externalising' behaviours is analysed. The impact of conduct disorders is considered in relation to the work of Webster-Stratton and Herbert (1993) in particular.

Possible causes of emotional and behavioural difficulties in children are discussed in the context of risk factors in development, Bronfenbrenner's (1979) ecological theory, especially the family circumstances of the child. It is concluded that social-ecological factors are of particular importance in the genesis and maintenance of conduct disorders.

Chapter 5 discusses learning disability as another type of atypical development in children. 'Learning disability' is a term used to describe difficulties faced by children whose intellectual abilities differ from those of the general population. Such children have also been described as having 'intellectual impairment'. These may include having specific difficulties with academic subjects in school but it also includes children who may have difficulties arising from low intelligence as measured on standardised intelligence tests. Examples of such conditions that are discussed in this chapter include children with Down's syndrome and some with autism. Such children have problems that interfere with the normal course of development and often lead to difficulties of adaptation. Two main explanations of such conditions include one that takes a biological view and another that focuses on the child's environment and how she responds to it. The biological view focuses on deficits within the child, while the other position takes a largely behavioural approach and examines tasks and situations faced. However, most people do not take one or the other position but take into account factors to do with both the individual child, her environment and interactions between them. In the particular case of generalised intellectual disability, both the individual's level of functioning and adaptation to demands of the social environment are emphasised. Thus, the social context is considered to be as important as the individual's level of functioning in determining the presence or absence of disability.

Various aspects of the social context are then identified. These include the society in which the child lives, including the local culture and its values and expectations. Within a given society there are also different levels of contexts that provide different environments for the developing child. These may include the home or school or, within the school, the classroom or playground. Each of these contexts presents different tasks for a child. Her ability to perform any of these tasks may indicate the presence or absence of difficulties. An assessment of the presence or significance of a disability therefore requires taking into account the tasks at hand and the social expectations regarding their importance. Social and behavioural expectations constitute social ecological factors, which provide contexts through which learning disability can be understood.

Chapter 6 considers different kinds of intervention derived from different theoretical bases, such as behavioural or systems theory. Various intervention approaches are discussed as they are applied to children who have developmental difficulties in general, and as specifically applied to particular problems – child abuse and neglect, conduct problems, anxiety disorders, learning disability and autism. Most of these problems are expressed in the context of families who are experiencing difficulties and there is growing evidence that, in general, intervention will be optimised through the adoption of a combined approach which focuses on both the child and other members of the family, in appropriate contexts. The importance of empirical validation of the effectiveness of different interventions – evidence-based practices – is stressed so that controversial practices can be identified and avoided in future. Social validation is explained as an approach to the evaluation of interventions. Evaluations tend to show that the families with the most serious problems also seem to have the lowest success rate in response to treatment.

Chapter 7 presents an overview of the main issues raised in earlier chapters regarding explanations of atypical development in relation to particular problems and different theoretical approaches. The role of the context in atypical development is emphasised, including the further elaboration of the role of sociocultural, family and social structural factors, including the availability of resources. Issues related to the impact of child-rearing perspectives and practices on the incidence, prevalence and manifestation of developmental problems are discussed. Here examples from cross-cultural research are used to illustrate various experiences related to the role of the context in children's development.

A further discussion is presented of the role of the context in atypical development, although not at the expense of ignoring individual or biological factors. There is a focus on two main areas – health problems in children and issues relating to parenting practices. An integration of the ecological and transactional (ET) perspectives is used in explaining the relationship between violence and aggression in neighbourhoods in relation to child maltreatment. The ET approach is also applied as a possible explanation of the development of aggression in individual children. In addition, the ET approach is discussed in relation to malnutrition.

The chapter also discusses some implications of considering atypical development in context. Some general areas for research questions are identified aiming to refocus our attention in ways that can further enhance our understanding of atypical development. Some implications for the practices of professionals working with children and their parents are discussed. Finally, it is concluded that individual child variables and environmental ones, including social-ecological factors, may not in themselves be sufficient in determining the course of individual development. The ways in which they interact and mutually influence each other over time need to be incorporated into efforts aimed at amelioration of atypical child development. By considering such interactions within the frameworks discussed in this book, particularly the ecological-transactional, we are now at least part of the way to understanding some of the processes underlying the multiple causes of atypical child development in context.

1

Conceptual and Theoretical Approaches to Atypical Child Development

Janet Empson and Dabie Nabuzoka

Introduction

Each and every child is a unique individual and identifiably different from all others. Differences between individuals can be seen in babies from birth onwards. Indeed, expectant mothers perceive differences between successive babies prior to birth. At conception we all, with the exception of identical twins, inherit our own particular genetic endowment from our parents. This constitutes the biological basis of differences between people. Then, throughout the period of development in the womb, each child is exposed to an environment, which also is unique. From the start, the influences of 'nature' (biology) and 'nurture' (environment) interact in the growing individual. As these both differ between children, the developmental outcome of each child is identifiably different from all other children. But, there are undoubtedly similarities in the changes that occur within individuals during the life course, from conception to old age. So, parents and others involved in the socialisation of children can expect a predictable pattern of physical and psychological changes, which is similar across the world, in all 'normal', healthy children, in the course of growing up. This universal sequence of change, which enables the child's adaptation to his environment, and all its variations, constitutes the developmental process.

This chapter discusses the underlying bases for change in the individual associated with development. The biological process which determines the universal sequence and pattern of changes in abilities and behaviour as a function of age is 'maturation'; genetically determined differences in maturation rates can also explain variations in rates of development. Individual differences in development can also be accounted for by 'learning'. Opportunities for learning will vary between children depending on the circumstances of their upbringing – their relationships and material circumstances. Other principles of development are presented to facilitate an understanding of developmental processes and their influence on the regular ways in which physical and psychological competencies change behaviour from simple to more complex with age.

The distinction between children with 'normal' and those showing 'atypical' development is then discussed. The range of 'normal' variation in rates of development can be distinguished from that which can be described as 'abnormal' or statistically unusual, that is, development which is unusually advanced or unusually delayed. Such quantitative differences in behaviour can also be described in terms of severity, exaggerations of, or deficits in, expected behaviours and accompanying social impairment. Decisions as to whether such deviations from normal development constitute significant problems will depend on a range of characteristics of the behaviours such as their frequency, intensity, duration, age and gender appropriateness, the number of different contexts in which they occur and their association with problematic social relationships and suffering. Behaviour problems also involve underlying emotional difficulties. These may also differ quantitatively or qualitatively from normal, for example specific fears may be inappropriately intense, anxiety may differ in kind from how it is usually experienced. The different kinds of emotional and behavioural difficulty will be described and discussed further in Chapter 4.

There then follows a description of a number of different theoretical approaches to the explanation of normal development. These are attachment theory, ecological theory, the transactional and the developmental psychopathological approaches. All these can provide possible explanations for the occurrence of different kinds of atypical development associated with circumstances of risk for abnormal development such as child abuse. The application of these theories where appropriate will be made clear in subsequent chapters.

Characteristics of development

The study of child development concerns the changes in behaviour and competencies that occur as a function of developmental processes. A sequence of behaviour change, characterised by the emergence of new behaviours which change in predictable ways over time, reflects the underlying biological process of maturation. Human beings are also very varied and flexible in their behaviour in different circumstances, and this reflects their adaptation due to learning from experience. The processes of development – cognitive, social-emotional and biological – transform environmental input into output by the individual, which is characterised by new competencies and behaviours. The concept of 'growth' is usually used to refer to physical growth, which forms the basis for behaviour change. Myelination, or the laying down of a fatty sheath for the neurones (nerve cells) in the brain, occurs during the first two years of life and facilitates a more rapid transmission of information (via nervous impulses) and is the basis of more controlled behaviour. The growth of bones and muscles is necessary for the development of physical skills such as sitting and walking. Thus, there is a predictable pattern to growth as it is genetically determined.

The term 'maturation' refers to a genetically determined sequence of physical growth changes that influences the development of behaviour in an orderly way, and is relatively independent of learning or experience. It provides a 'readiness to learn' certain skills at a particular time. No amount of practice can cause a child to walk, for example, until his nervous system is ready, but lack of opportunity to practise walking may retard the emergence of this ability. Distinguishing features of behaviours based on maturation are that they constitute a relatively fixed sequence of events, such as the sequence of gross motor development in the first year or so of a baby's life – sitting, crawling, standing then walking. Although these behaviours require bodily control, such as control of the bladder and bowel when children are two years old, other behaviours form a particular sequence, such as the stages of speech development. Using the first word with meaning is followed by two-word phrases, then simple sentences, or the stages of the acquisition of grammar as described by Chomsky (1969). Such stages in the development of particular skills are acquired in the same order, independently of gender, socioeconomic status and cultural differences, in all children at approximately the same ages. This is called the 'ages and stages' view of development.

Development, as directed from within, by the action of the genes, that is, maturation, is fundamental to Gesell's theory of child development (Gesell, 1950; Gesell and Ilg, 1943). Gesell established the principles of how maturation happens, such as sequences of change which occur relatively independently of environment and experience. There is evidence from studies of identical twins (Gesell and Thompson, 1929) to support the maturational view. The twin who had had practice at such activities as stair-climbing and the manipulation of cubes did show some initial superior skill but the other twin soon caught up, with much less practice, and performed the skills at the ages at which one would expect them to be acquired. There is an inner timetable determining the readiness to do things so the benefits of early training are only temporary. This suggests that efforts should not be made to teach things ahead of schedule. At the right time children will begin to master tasks. Attempts to teach skills too early can put pressure on the child, lead to conflict between caregiver and child, and ultimately a failure to perform skills such as, say, bowel and bladder control.

This view has its limitations, particularly as there is a wide range of individual differences between normal children in the ages at which they acquire different capabilities. So, for example, the normal range for the development of walking is from 8 to 20 months in 'normal' children. Such differences may be due to differences in maturation rates. Late development of walking may be the result of an interaction between slow maturation rate, a particular body build – a very plump infant may prefer to sit rather than crawl or walk – and aspects of the baby's temperament, such as fearfulness.

There is a sequence of development within each developmental field. These are motor (gross and fine), communication, self-help, adaptive (intellectual) and social-emotional (Gesell, 1950). Development in one field does not necessarily run parallel with development in another. For example, a child with cerebral palsy may be late in walking but average in manipulating objects and in intellectual development. Sometimes a child may appear to be delayed in one or more domains of development when no progress is apparent for a period of weeks, but this frequently occurs in normal children and is often followed by a sudden advance. So the rate of development is not constant. Sometimes, however, there is an overall slowing down of development across all domains, which is the result of abnormal functioning. Children with Down's syndrome are less developmentally delayed in the first year than in subsequent years, when communication and cognitive skills are usually developing rapidly; a tragic deterioration in an apparently normal child may result from severe emotional deprivation or a metabolic disorder (Illingworth, 1987). Slowness, or retardation, in all domains generally indicates learning disability but could be due to slow maturation, which often runs in families. Although developmental norms are used to suggest to professionals when a child may have developmental problems, no child is deemed to be learning disabled on the basis of delay in only one developmental domain. Usually, the most indicative area is that of language development, but even that may be delayed for a number of normal reasons. What is more important is not when a particular skill starts but the rate at which it proceeds once it has started, for example, language acquisition.

When a baby is born, it is equipped for survival with a range of different behaviours. There are many different reflexes or simple patterns of reaction to specific stimuli, which serve a biologically useful purpose. Examples include the rooting reflex whereby the baby obtains food by moving his mouth towards the stimulus stroking his cheek, or the grasp reflex in which the infant holds onto a finger placed in the palm of his hand, which enables the child to maintain contact with a carer. The testing of such reflexes indicates the health of the newborn baby; premature babies have exaggerated reflexes, and particular abnormalities in reflex functioning indicate different kinds of disorders of the nervous system (Illingworth, 1987).

The stepping reflex is elicited in infants by lowering them on to a flat surface. When their feet touch the surface, they reflexly move them in a rhythmic stepping motion that resembles walking. Zelazo (1983) studied the development of this reflex by giving a group of infants daily practice in using the reflex. The disappearance of the reflex was slowed and the emergence of the voluntary actions of walking was speeded up so that these babies walked earlier than usual. How this can be explained in terms of the usual principles of maturation is problematic. The process is not yet understood.

These reflexes disappear at specific ages in the course of normal development, to be replaced by voluntary control. When reflexes persist beyond the usual age, this again can be an indication of abnormality in the nervous system influencing development. Babies universally show other more complex behaviours, which are biologically adaptive. They are very socially oriented and curious about the world around them. Social behaviours such as eye contact and smiling facilitate the development of attachment or bonding between infant and caregiver(s) and crying elicits concern and attention from carers.

There are other principles of development shown in the regular ways in which physical and psychological competencies change from simple to more complex behaviours. The first principle is that behaviour becomes increasingly controlled with age. This happens in a number of ways. Coordination increases as in hand–eye coordination of reaching. There is inhibition of certain muscle groups when others are active, for example the infant laughs with the whole body, whereas the older person controls associated bodily activity. The direction of attention becomes more controlled – children are less distractible when older.

Behaviour also becomes more organised. There is greater integration so that longer sequences of behaviour lead to a long-term goal; behaviour becomes more planned and purposive. This can be because we have more knowledge of the world and can predict events and plan how to reach goals, for example playing with bricks and building towers and bridges.

All the different ways in which behaviour changes as a result of practice, or experience, depend crucially upon the use of memory, which improves in functioning with age in a number of important ways. Short-term memory increases in capacity as the child grows older and working memory becomes more efficient. This enables more to be learned and the child benefits more from past experience. The nature of storage in memory will change from images in the pre-language stages to the additional use of verbal codes once the tools of language are available for use. The child additionally develops new strategies in remembering, such as the use of rehearsal and organisation of material into categories. Different kinds of learning also become available to the child as he develops. Learning becomes more volitional, flexible and generalisable to new situations. It involves ever-more sophisticated kinds of thinking; problem solving becomes less tied to the perceptual and reasoning uses abstract thought (Piaget, 1960).

Additional principles of development are that behaviours become finer and more differentiated (for example the nervous control of the muscles facilitates the development of skills such as accurately directed reaching and oppositional finger and thumb for grasping small objects and holding a crayon for drawing) and, at the same time, integration of behaviour develops so that experience and behaviour become more of a coherent whole. An example of this is in intersensory integration where, for instance, the infant relates the smell of the mother to the sound of her voice and then to the sight of her in the distance so that visual recognition becomes possible. Also, perceptual–motor integration allows the development of skills such as catching a ball.

Figure 1.1 illustrates four early conceptual models of development. As already mentioned, the 'stage model' views development as occurring in step-like, discontinuous stages, each of which is qualitatively different from earlier ones. They follow a particular order, which is universal in all children.

The 'linear' and 'continuity models' both see development as constituting incremental growth. In the linear view this reflects continuous, cumulative and regular increases in skills and abilities over time, while the continuity view sees the increments as being more variable over time, reflecting growth at different rates at different ages. Developmental change is primarily genetically programmed and directed by processes of maturation.

The 'interaction model' sees development as the product of individual characteristics interacting with environmental influences. The factors in the individual and the environment and the

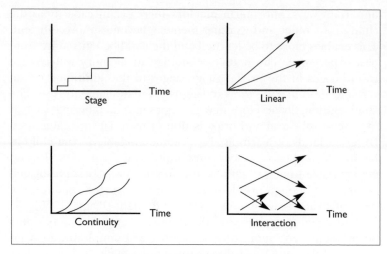

Figure 1.1 Models of development

ways in which they reciprocally influence each other may well differ at different points in time. This view forms the basis of the transactional and ecological approaches to development.

All models conceptualise developmental change as occurring at different rates in different individuals, with variability about an average for the achievement of each skill or competence.

Continuity or connectivity in development has long been emphasised by Western developmental psychologists and this stresses the importance of early experience for later development. The transactional approach (Sameroff and Chandler, 1975) has directed attention to the dynamic nature of development, which allows for the possibility of a change in the trajectory of development, whenever there is significant environmental change or change in the individual. This idea of discontinuity in development allows for greater flexibility in individual development so that progress may be made from an inauspicious start to a very positive outcome or vice versa. So a child whose development is problematic in the preschool years may have a definite change in status (possibly following intervention) resulting in normal development later on. In support of the discontinuity view is the evidence that the correlation between early measures of intelligence and later measures of developmental status is very low

(Ceci, 1990). Therefore the predictive ability of assessments on children is poor. Such ideas will be developed further in later sections and chapters.

One of the important developmental achievements is the gradual increase in autonomy and independence in the child as a function of age, which is made possible through the acquisition of motor and cognitive skills and the development of social competence. Such abilities enable the child to adapt to an ever-widening social world. Key figures in the child's life help him to develop these competencies through the process of socialisation in interacting and forming relationships with others. Socialisation is a reciprocal process whereby parents and other significant people in the child's life, such as siblings and peers, help the child to acquire the skills necessary to become a competent and able member of the society in which he is growing up. The child is an active participant in this process, influencing other people's feelings and behaviours towards him. The child also learns the values and beliefs of the culture, not just through the family, but also from other people at school and in the community, and through the media and other cultural tools. Through the processes of development the young child begins to develop a sense of identity, purpose and achievement in life. Thus, development is a complex process of influence involving the child, immediate family and the wider society.

'Normal' and 'atypical' in child development

We have already noted the wide range of normal variation in rates of development and the age at which particular skills are acquired. There is greater variation in the development of psychological skills than physical skills, and variation increases as the child grows older. Within this context of normally occurring differences between children, it is very difficult to identify genuine and important delays in development, which may be indicative of significant problems for the child. There is an average level of development for a particular age (although there is no such entity as the 'average child') but it is impossible to draw a line between normal and abnormal achievements for that age. There is a statistical notion of abnormality which considers that children whose scores on a measure of assessment lie more than two standard deviations from the mean, that is, the extreme 5 per cent at the ends of the distribution, are unusually far from the mean or norm for that age. So the concept of 'deviance' arises, a term which in statistical use is impartial but comes to have a negative connotation when used to describe human behaviour.

All children show some considerable deviation from the norms of behaviour at some time in their development and this is usually in one particular aspect of development, or in one environmental setting. Such deviation is often termed 'abnormality'. Again this word frequently has negative connotations and implies that action needs to be taken to reduce or eliminate such differences from the norm, as they are 'undesirable'.

Being different from other children may create developmental difficulties for the child and those close to him. Research into bullying, for example, has shown that children at risk of being bullied are those who are different from most of the others, in terms of physical appearance such as being fat, or personality characteristics such as shyness, or background circumstances such as being fostered or having some developmental difficulties (Whitney et al., 1992).

Johnnie is very small for his age, having been born as one of twins. His twin died when only a few days old. Johnnie has always been seen as very vulnerable by his parents as he has had frequent periods of illness, which resulted in him missing many weeks of school. Johnnie is also very short-sighted and has to wear thick-lensed spectacles, another cause for worry for his parents. Johnnie has been unable to form close friendships at school and is rather socially isolated. Recently he has become the target of a group of boys who bully him whenever they get the opportunity. At school Johnnie has no one to turn to for support and has never needed to stand up for himself before. Consequently he is afraid to defend himself or let anyone know and is becoming more and more unhappy.

Children who are particularly vulnerable to abuse by parents are also frequently 'different' in some way, for example those with physical or learning disabilities. Further discussion of this can be found in Chapter 3.

There is abnormality at both ends of the normal distribution of different characteristics and behaviours in children – the extremes at both ends are usually equally infrequently occurring. (In the case of the distribution of intelligence, there are more individuals at the low end of the range, which can be accounted for by those with congenital conditions.) But the negative connotations are usually associated with one end of the range – very low intelligence, for example, is viewed as more problematic than very high intelligence, although it has been recognised for a long time that both can be associated with major difficulties in development. High intelligence is however generally associated with good adjustment in social-emotional domains.

As shown in Figure 1.2, there are more individuals with a very low IQ than would be predicted from a normal distribution curve. The reason usually given is that in addition to the normal variation in IQ, which generates some very low scores, there are other individuals whose very low intelligence is the result of biological conditions resulting from genetic abnormalities and other biological causes.

Children of very advanced cognitive development may have difficulties because their intellectual development is far in advance of their development in other domains such as social-emotional development. Also, they may experience frustration at being held back and not being allowed to work at the pace they want, or they may be put under pressure for high achievement. In many countries there are government initiatives aimed at improving provision for the able and talented in schools, which illustrates the ongoing need for progress in this area (Department for Education and Employment, 1999).

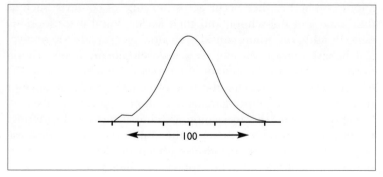

Figure 1.2 Normal distribution of IQ

Criteria of 'abnormality' or 'atypicality' in development

The criteria which define abnormal, deviant or atypical behaviour in children are social ones and are therefore relative. Behaviours which are atypical and considered to be undesirable by one social group, as they violate the social norms of acceptability, may be considered perfectly acceptable by another, for example the use of foul language by children or physical fighting between peers. Those constellations of behaviours which co-occur and are viewed as deviant constitute childhood behaviour problems. These are, by and large, exaggerations, deficits or handicapping combinations of behaviours common to all children. Usually problematic conditions differ quantitatively from normal in terms of severity and accompanying impairment as, for instance, in the difference between an assertive child and a bully.

The description of a behaviour as normal or problematic will of course depend on the context in which it occurs – children learn from their exposure to different contexts, for example that shouting, laughing and giggling are an acceptable part of playground behaviour but not of behaviour in church.

It is common for *observable behaviours* to be used as criteria of normality or difficulty, and assumptions are made that these reflect particular internal difficulties or conflicts, the description of which will differ depending on which perspective or theoretical viewpoint is preferred. The decision as to whether particular behaviours are abnormal will reflect their age and gender appropriateness, how intense the child's reactions are, how persistant as the child changes developmentally, how specific to particular situations or whether they occur across a range of contexts, such as the home and the school, and their sociocultural inappropriateness. In addition, when considering how problematic these atypical behaviours are for the child's development, other criteria need to be taken into account: the severity, number and diversity of undesirable behaviours, the type of behaviour (disturbance of relationships is more problematic than minor indications like nail-biting or tics) and the association with impairment and suffering. If unusual behaviours are part of the child's repertoire but cause neither stress, distress nor adverse effects on development, then they are not considered to be problematic. Behaviour problems by definition involve emotional difficulties, pain and stress in the child himself and others, they restrict the child's social activities and relationships, and development will usually be hindered. Emotional and behavioural problems always occur in a social context and the extent to which this elicits the problem needs to be taken into account. The different kinds of emotional and behavioural difficulties which occur in childhood will be discussed in Chapter 4.

So-called problems in development frequently occur and it could be argued that a child is abnormal when they show no signs of any developmental difficulty throughout their childhood. So the perfectly adjusted child is a myth and the concept could be attributed to an ideal of conformity which constrains individuality. It is very difficult to find a division between normal and abnormal in child development and behaviour, but the needs of societies such as ours require that this endeavour is pursued so that help and special provision can be provided where it is needed. The pitfalls of quantifying and categorising children and their abilities should not, however, be ignored.

Most emotional and behavioural disturbances are 'quantitatively' rather than 'qualitatively' different from normal. It can be seen from the criteria listed above that most of them refer to behaviours which occur in most or all children but differ only in number, amount or degree, that is, quantitative differences. Qualitative differences are more difficult to identify and often amount to professional judgement or interpretation. There are many theoretical explanations of qualitative and/or quantitative differences in the development of children and some of the major ones are described next.

Theoretical approaches which provide an explanation of atypical development

Figure 1.3 illustrates the relationship between different approaches to atypical child development and their associated theories, models and interventions. Those that are particularly focused upon in this chapter are the 'developmental psychopathological approach' and 'attachment theory' and examples of systems theory as exemplified by the 'ecological' and 'transactional approaches'. The associated interventions are described in Chapter 6.

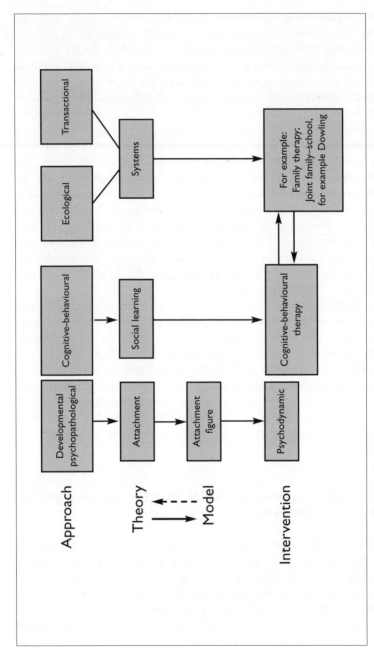

Figure 1.3 A taxonomy of approaches to atypical development

The developmental psychopathological approach

Until the 1980s child development and child psychiatry were separate fields of research. Then it was realised that developmental issues were important in psychopathology, the expression of emotional and behavioural problems in children of clinical severity. So the developmental psychopathological approach came into being (Rutter, 1996). This approach involves the study of children whose development is atypical, or is likely to be so because of the risks they are exposed to, the premise being that understanding of the causes and course of psychopathology will inform our current theories of normal development (Cicchetti, 1984). This argument is an old one, also expressed by Cicchetti (1989), that 'we can learn more about the normal functioning of an organism by studying its pathology and, likewise, more about its pathology by studying its normal condition' (p378). So, developmental psychopathology studies:

- mechanisms and processes involved in the origins and course of psychopathology in children
- individual differences in response to developmental challenges and transitions
- individual differences in psychological development.

The approach uses abnormal situations or cases, such as blind children, to investigate the role of specific processes, such as visual perception, in development (Rutter, 1996). Rutter also points out that we must take care not to assume that normal and abnormal development do or do not share the same mechanisms or exhibit the same qualities. We should expect that both will be found. So specific developmental competencies may be reached by both sighted and blind children but by different routes; language development in some children with learning disabilities follows the same sequence of stages as in normal children but the vocabulary acquired is different.

The study of developmental psychopathology puts the issue of continuities (quantitative differences) and discontinuities (qualitative differences) as a key issue. Traditionally, developmental psychology has stressed continuity and the similarities between children deemed to have some form of pathology and those without, while child psychiatry has emphasised difference and the identification of categories. Both need to be taken into consideration, taking into account the characteristics of a particular child and his circumstances and the purpose for which assessment is being made. It is important to note that continuity may be of two types. In 'heterotypic' continuity the form may change while the process underlying it is the same, for example the childhood precursors of adult schizophrenia are to be found in attentional deficits and social difficulties rather than in hallucinations and thought disorders; while in 'homotypic' continuity both form and process stay the same, as in aggression and anxiety (Rutter, 1996). Those conditions that have a biological cause are more likely to be identifiable as discrete categories and those which are interpersonal and psychological in origin are more likely to be represented on a continuum (Rutter, 1996).

Cicchetti (1989) discusses the study of child maltreatment as a good example of the application of the developmental psychopathological and transactional approaches, which, combined, produce a sound theoretical framework for understanding the negative effects of abusive parenting (the 'continuum of caretaking casualty', Sameroff and Chandler, 1975).This framework also facilitates the development of models of child maltreatment which incorporate a developmental dimension, with the contributions of risk factors at different levels. These are described in full in Chapter 3.

Overall, the research areas of the developmental psychopathological approach encompass all the aspects of atypical child development discussed in this volume. It is not a theory, or even a body of knowledge, but is a set of research questions and strategies that utilise developmental variations (including pathological) and are designed to aid understanding of the processes of normal and atypical development (Rutter, 1996). This involves empirical research into the different problematic conditions of development themselves, in addition to the study of normal development, and these conditions form the substance of the following chapters. As Weinert and Weinert (1998) put it:

> Psychopathological development ... frequently cannot be fully understood from the context of normal development. Rather the particular phenomena, symptoms, possibilities for change, spontaneous remissions, and interventions must be explicitly studied. (p31)

The research findings arising from this approach inform the application of theories of normal development, such as attachment, ecological and transactional, to the development of explanations of atypical development in different circumstances.

Attachment theory

It is widely accepted that the quality of parent–child relationships is important for the development of personality and the self-concept in infants and children. When these relationships are stressful and frustrating, they tend to be associated with the development of problem behaviours by the child. As Rutter (1996) pointed out, abnormalities in relationships are significant in the development and maintainance of many types of psychopathology. Also, abuse and neglect of children always occur in the context of relationships. Attachment theory is a relationship-based theory of personality development. Attachment relationships are those stable, loving bonds which normally develop in the early weeks and months of life between infant and caregiver(s). Such relationships provide protection, security, relief from distress and opportunities for learning for the infant (Howe et al., 1999). Within attachment relationships babies first organise their expression of emotion and behaviour, later taking other people's affective states into account.

Attachment relationships develop out of particular behaviours on the part of both caregiver and infant. Firstly, the attachment figure, who is often the mother in the first instance, needs to be psychologically as well as physically available. Attachment is fostered by the expression of four positive maternal qualities, described by Ainsworth et al. (1971) as:

1. sensitivity (rather than insensitivity) to the infant's needs
2. acceptance (not rejection) of the whole person in all respects
3. cooperation in supporting the baby's developing autonomy (not interference)
4. accessibility or availability to the infant (rather than ignoring).

These dimensions were identified as a result of observations by Ainsworth and colleagues of mother–baby interactions. Behaviours on the part of the infant which promote attachment are part of the repertoire of biologically based activities present in all normal infants. Babies are very socially oriented from birth and from an early age they show signalling behaviours, such as smiling or vocalising, inviting social interaction. At times of distress they show aversive behaviours like crying which elicit concern and attention from the mother whose aim is to terminate the behaviour she finds aversive. When the child is developmentally able, he shows active behaviours, for example crawling, to gain or maintain proximity to the attachment figure. When separated from the mother, anxiety in the baby increases; this activates attachment activites and the re-established closeness between the infant and caregiver reduces the anxiety. Thus, the normally occurring attachment behaviours of caregiver and child are reciprocal and biologically adaptive; they protect the child from harm and help to ensure his survival. Attachment also serves very important functions in social and emotional development.

In addition to providing security and a safe base for exploration, the attachment relationship also facilitates opportunities for the infant to experience personal control and the beginnings of effectiveness in dealing with self and others. This is achieved through those sensitive, accepting and cooperative behaviours on the part of the mother or other caregivers. These qualities are incorporated into the infant's 'internal working models' – mental representations or schema – of self, others and the relationship between self and others. The models contain expectations and beliefs about their own and others' behaviour which will guide perception and memory to aid more efficient behaviour in dealing with new social situations. The internal working models also represent developing cognitions about the worth and acceptability of oneself, and the emotional availability of others (Howe et al., 1999). Out of close relationships come enduring patterns of thought, feelings and behaviours, expressed in different circumstances, which constitute personality. Internal models influence the choice of subsequent relationships, and help us to organise and self-regulate our own emotional experiences. The ways in which these happen are influenced by the infant's particular style of attachment. Different attachment patterns were first demonstrated in the classic 'strange situation' studies of Ainsworth and her colleagues (1978). These studies examined mother–infant interactions in the context of a strange (unfamiliar) room in which the infant experienced brief separations from the mother and the periodic presence of a stranger to both mother and child. Howe et al. (1999) describe four different working models (see Table 1.1) based on the three main patterns of attachment originally described by Ainsworth et al. (1978) – secure, avoidant and ambivalent – plus a 'disorganised' pattern identified by Main and Solomon (1986).

Ainsworth et al.'s study (1978) of how infants behaved in the 'strange situation' demonstrated different attachment patterns. For the securely attached infant, the mother is a safe base from which to explore, so the baby plays actively with toys. When the mother goes, the child stops playing, shows distress and often tries to follow the mother, to maintain proximity. When the mother returns she is greeted eagerly, baby calms down and starts playing again.

The insecure-disorganised attachment pattern is associated with the infant having had negative experiences with the parent(s). The baby makes no attempt to maintain proximity to the caregiver who clearly does not provide a secure base. Reactions by the child to the parent include apprehension, confusion and freezing which are frequently found in abused children.

TABLE 1.1 CHARACTERISTICS OF DIFFERENT PATTERNS OF ATTACHMENT AND THEIR FREQUENCY OF OCCURRENCE

Attachment pattern	Characteristics of self	Characteristics of others	Frequency in population (from van IJzendoorn et al., 1992)*
Secure	loved, effective, autonomous, competent	available, cooperative, dependable	55%
Avoidant	unloved but self-reliant	rejecting, intrusive	23%
Ambivalent	low value, ineffective, dependent	neglecting, insensitive, unpredictable	8%
Insecure-disorganised	confused, bad	frightening, unavailable	15%

* van IJzendoorn et al. conducted a meta-analysis of 'strange situation' classifications in non-clinic samples

Positive views of the self related to secure attachments early in life seem to be associated with sound development of social competence and relationships with peers in the preschool years (Waters et al., 1979) and better performance in academic tasks at school later on.

There is much empirical evidence (Campbell, 1995; Keisner et al., 2001) implicating parent–child relations in the development and maintainance of conduct problems. Mothers of children with behaviour problems are less warm and less positively involved than those in comparison groups. Positive parenting attributes – sensitivity, acceptance, warmth and responsiveness – are associated with secure parent–child attachment and so attachment may serve as a useful global variable describing the history of caregiving quality. However, Waters et al. (1993) note that attachment correlates with other family variables such as stress, marital relations and parental psychopathology so the relative influences of each need to be determined.

Overall, for many years the central importance of early relationships to concurrent and later development – social, emotional and cognitive – has been acknowledged. Problems in relationships are crucially implicated in the development and maintainance of atypical development. Connections between various attachment patterns and the main topics covered in this book – risk factors in development, child abuse, learning disability and emotional and behavioural difficulties – have been indicated here and will be developed further in later chapters.

Ecological theory

The ecological perspective is associated with Bronfenbrenner (1979). The approach has implications for our understanding of atypical development as it emphasises studying human development within the context of various environmental systems. Each of these systems contributes to developmental outcomes in various ways but also in relation to each other. The approach therefore provides a comprehensive attempt to explain the ways in which interactions among social structures affect the content and course of human development, including atypical development.

According to Bronfenbrenner's (1979) perspective (Figure 1.4), the ecological environment consists of an interrelated series

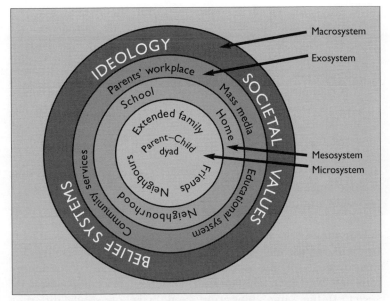

Figure 1.4 Bronfenbrenner's (1979) systems model

of environmental structures, each nested in the next 'like a set of Russian dolls' (Bronfenbrenner, 1979):

1. The basic unit is the dyad, the parent–child relationship. This is itself intimately related to the larger interpersonal systems, especially the nuclear family but also other prominent social contacts of everyday life including the extended family, neighbours, friends, and others with whom the dyad interacts on a face-to-face basis.

   These complex interrelationships form 'microsystems'. Each microsystem comprises a pattern of activities, roles and interpersonal relations that are experienced by the developing person in a particular setting with particular physical and material characteristics.

2. Microsystems are themselves nested within 'mesosystems'. A mesosystem consists of the interrelations among two or more settings in which the developing person participates, such as the home, school and neighbourhood.

3. Mesosystems are in turn nested within an 'exosystem'. The exosystem consists of social settings that do not themselves directly involve the developing person as an active participant, but do provide contexts that affect the mesosystem and microsystem.

   Components of the exosystem include the extended family, parents' workplaces, the mass media, community services and the educational system; the availability and quality of each of these may have implications for how a given family and its microsystems are organised.

4. The outer shell is the 'macrosystem', the belief systems and ideologies of the culture, which constitutes a pervasive set of values around which societal life is organised.

An important aspect of Bronfenbrenner's model is that it cautions against making assumptions about the universality of a macrosystem, or the developmental contexts and experiences afforded by it. Even among similar societies (for example Western societies) the same 'blueprint' could take on subtly different meanings. On a wider plane are very different systems of social organisation with very different consequences for development. Another important aspect of the ecological perspective is that it moves away from the idea of linear effects assumed in much of behavioural science (that is, the idea of cause–effect relations among social variables) to a broader conception of the interrelations among systems.

Thus, an ecological perspective emphasises the need for a multidimensional consideration of atypical development. For example, rather than focusing on a static categorisation of the child's current level of functioning, what would be required is an appraisal of the child's behavioural repertoire in dynamic relation to the developmental potential of various interrelated systems. These include caregiver–child microsystems, family and friendship networks, instructional programmes and career paths. These systems exist at various levels and each has certain implications for the development of the child. For example, at the macro-level the child is situated in a given society and culture. Any presenting difficulties are defined within the context of that culture. Similarly, risk factors, including the strengths and vulnerability of the individual child and other family members, can only meaningfully be defined in their social-ecological context. The latter also applies to the opportunities for addressing the presenting problems. Thus, at the micro-level are the personal contacts and relationships that exist. These are largely in the context of the family or immediate neighbourhood, but may also include relationships in other contexts such as the school – linking with the meso- and exosystems.

The transactional approach

Sameroff and Chandler's (1975) model of development presents development as a two-way process involving reciprocal interactions over time between an active child in an active environment. Child developmental progress could be predicted by considering a combination of influences such as those given in Figure 1.5.

According to this model, risks to healthy child development derive from:

- internal influences (biological and psychological characteristics of the child)
- external influences (physical and personal aspects of the child's environment).

Longitudinal studies can identify and follow up at-risk groups to identify the range of outcomes shown by different children and how these may be related to conditions of upbringing.

The extent to which there may be causal relationships between particular risks and specific disorders can be identified as, for example, in foetal alcohol syndrome (FAS). In FAS there is an

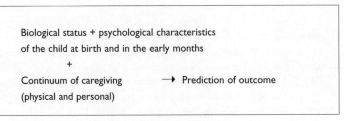

Biological status + psychological characteristics
of the child at birth and in the early months

+

Continuum of caregiving   → Prediction of outcome
(physical and personal)

Figure 1.5 A diagrammatic summary of Sameroff and Chandler's (1975) transactional model of development

identified link between excessive drinking by the mother during pregnancy and physical and developmental abnormalities in her baby (Rosett, 1980).

Foetal alcohol syndrome (FAS) often occurs in children born to mothers who have consumed large quantities of alcohol throughout most or all of their pregnancy. The infant has particular physical characteristics including slow growth and facial features of widely spaced eyes, small nose and thin upper lip. The head is small showing that the brain has not developed fully. Physical abnormalities of internal and external organs may also be present. Mentally, the child is likely to have learning difficulties, poor attention, memory, language and problem solving. Motor skills are probably poor. Brain damage caused by the effects of the alcohol experienced prior to birth is permanent.

Sameroff and Chandler take a 'transactional' view of development as dynamic and constantly changing, so that discontinuity between developmental stages can be expected. Early factors that have enduring consequences do so because of persistant influences across a lengthy period of time rather than at discrete times in development. So, for example, children who have been brought up in isolation for many years, as in the case of 'Genie' described by Clarke and Clarke (1998) who was kept in solitary confinement in a bare room until she was 12 or 13 years old, have very long-term effects on all aspects of their development, whereas those who were similarly maltreated for shorter periods and then enjoyed good child-rearing environments from the age of two years overcame their early developmental problems (Rutter et al., 1998b).

Following a period of enormous political and social upheaval in Romania, a large number of children who had been living in the dreadful conditions of Romanian orphanages were adopted by English families. The 324 children studied by Rutter and his associates (1998b) were less than 42 months old when they came to England. Most of them had entered institutional care in the neonatal period. They had been mainly confined to cots, had no personalised care, little talk from caregivers and few if any things to play with. A comparison group of UK adoptees was used. As they had all been adopted by six months, the Romanian children who were adopted by this age were analysed separately. The children from Romania were found to be severely mentally impaired, with many physical problems. Those children who came to the UK before six months were found to have caught up developmentally by the age of four years, despite the nature of their early experience. Those who were older when they moved here showed an impressive amount of developmental catch-up but it was not complete. The strongest predictor of cognitive functioning at four years was the age at which the children left the conditions of deprivation. Thus, the conditions of subsequent caregiving were able to compensate for most, but in the older children, not all, of the earlier deprivation. The remaining cognitive deficit was probably the result of early psychological privation in the Romanian orphanage.

Sameroff (1987) further explained the transactional view of development to which the child and the environment both make independent contributions. Both child and environment can provide the impetus for change and hence discontinuity in development. So early atypical development can be overcome if the child is brought up in a favourable home environment. When children are born prematurely or of low birthweight for other reasons, they start life with a lower growth rate and a lower baseline of developmental competencies. However, children of middle-class families overcome the developmental delay which is evident in the early months and perform as well as full-term children by the age of three. On the other hand, children brought up in conditions of socioeconomic disadvantage continue to show developmental delays throughout childhood. Further examples are provided in the following chapters.

The ways in which individuals and environments contribute to development may be restricted by different factors (Sameroff, 1987):

- individuals are constrained in the contribution they can make by their physical and psychological stage of development
- environments are structured and organised so that the rules of the culture and particular social groups prescribe particular

behaviours, achievements and roles for individuals at different
phases in development
- thus, both the child and his environments are constrained and
  the child has to find or adjust to the best fit between his own
  abilities and motivation and the opportunities offered within a
  structured environment
- over time, the child can, by its previous behaviour, be a strong
  determinant of his own current experience
- in part he does this through influencing the kinds of interactions he has in developing relationships with other people.

Bronfenbrenner (1979) also emphasised reciprocal transactions between the child and different aspects of the environment
in child development, thus the importance of studying the child in
context, the ecological approach. Both the transactional and the
ecological approaches include the individual (physical/biological
and psychological), interpersonal and sociocultural processes in
explaining development. They provide a framework for investigating the mechanisms whereby risks may influence child developmental outcome.

Evaluation of theoretical approaches

All the theoretical approaches described above have their limitations and differences in explaining atypical development. Taking
each in turn, attachment theory could be said to be the most
limited in scope. It can be criticised as placing too much emphasis
upon the importance of the primary relationship with the main
caregiver, usually the mother. Although nowadays attachment theorists do acknowledge that young children have multiple attachments, the importance of family dynamics is still insufficiently
recognised. It has been demonstrated that marital quality is more
closely related to aspects of fathering than of mothering: when a
marriage is in difficulties, the father's relationship with his child
became more negative while the mother's seemed to be affected
little (Belsky et al., 1991). Dunn (1988) has shown the significance
of *all* the relationships between different family members, and in
particular, that the mother's relationship with her second-born
child differs in association with her relationship with the first-born.

Attachment theory also stresses continuity between early and later development whereas Clarke and Clarke (1976, 1998, 2000) take issue with this. They present a large body of evidence which shows that the development of the child follows the direction of any environmental change; continuity in development could only be expected if the child experiences similar circumstances for very many years. There are so many changes in children's circumstances while they are growing up, and so many influences on the child – home, school, teachers, peers and siblings – that continuity in development would seem unlikely. The situation in which attachment was originally studied, the 'strange situation', has also been much criticised as being atypical of the child's usual experiences. It is not usually recognised, however, that most of the participating children's reactions were checked out in the home (Bretherton, 1991). Bretherton also presents powerful arguments that the concept is centrally useful to an understanding of developments and relationships across the lifespan, and in the area of developmental psychopathology. Overall, it seems that the concept of attachment and its application to atypical development is useful, and offers a partial explanation of the interpersonal processes involved in development in atypical circumstances such as those of child maltreatment.

The transactional and ecological approaches both offer wide-ranging and complex explanations of development which take into account many variables operating at different levels. Both emphasise the reciprocal influences between the child and his environment. The transactional approach places more emphasis on the child's active influence upon his own development, a dynamic longitudinal approach, and discontinuities in development. All these explain why early risk factors have adverse effects on development in some children, but not others. The transactional approach does acknowledge cultural influences as prescribing particular behaviours and roles at different phases of development but these are not well articulated. The ecological approach, on the other hand, does give these wider influences on child development more attention. The ecological approach also has a view of development as dynamic, with reciprocity between the child and other elements of the systems of which he is a part. But the ecological approach could perhaps be criticised as being rather 'top-down', with more emphasis on how the child is influenced rather than influencing. The non-linearity of this approach is attractive, and emphasises understanding *how* development occurs rather than answering questions as to *why*. So the transactional and ecological approaches are complementary and are relevant to an explanation of atypical child development in a wide variety of circumstances. Whilst acknowledging the role of environmental factors such as culture in defining and explaining atypical development, neither of these approaches offer an elaborated account of cultural influences. These will therefore form a major focus of the final chapter as together they form the main theoretical framework for this text.

The developmental psychopathological approach is described not as a theory but as a set of research questions designed to aid our understanding of the processes of normal and atypical development. This leads on to a questioning of the relevance of theories of normal development in application to atypical circumstances and encourages the delineation of exactly how the processes of normal and atypical development may differ. If the questions raised by this approach are examined in the theoretical framework of the transactional and ecological perspectives, then an explanatory model, appropriate to particular circumstances, may be developed. The evidence arising from research on attachment theory could also be incorporated in such a model. This will be elaborated in the final chapter.

Conclusion

This chapter described the characteristics of child development with a discussion of some of the key features of the essential processes of development. Development is defined as 'the processes underlying the change in growth and capability in the child'. The main processes are maturation and learning. Maturation defines a common pattern to developmental change but there is a wide range of differences between children. Some of these differences may be due to variation in individual attributes such as temperament, but most are the result of experiences in the different contexts in which they are growing up. Atypical development also arises through these different mechanisms. Atypical development is usually associated with abnormality, which has negative connotations implying the need for intervention. The criteria for defining abnormality are social and therefore relative. However, those criteria most used by professionals are based on a statistical notion of deviance from the norm. So, emotional and behavioural problems in children are exaggerations, deficits or handicapping combinations of characteristics which many children may have in common. Problematic conditions, then, in the main only differ *quantitatively* from normal in terms of severity and accompanying difficulties. *Qualitative* differences tend to result from specific biological conditions.

There are various theoretical approaches to explaining atypical development. These include attachment theory, which emphasises the importance of early interpersonal relationships. These are said to have implications for the social and emotional adjustment of the developing child. Problems in childhood, and subsequently, inevitably occur in the context of relationships. Another perspective is represented by ecological theory. This emphasises the influence of mutual relationships within interacting systems with varying degrees of proximity to the child. These systems represent different contexts in which the child is developing. The importance of context to the emergence and maintainance of atypical development is stressed in this approach. Different contexts may also influence the outcomes for development of specific conditions.

The active contribution of the child to his own development is emphasised in the transactional approach. This includes dynamic interactions between biological and environmental factors which across time result in continuity or discontinuity in development. Thus, the effects of early biological risk factors may be increased or decreased by transactions with the caregiving environment in which the child is growing up. The concepts of risk factors for development and individual differences in susceptibility to their influences provide the basis for explanations of atypical development in a variety of situations – child maltreatment, mild learning disability and other developmental problems.

The developmental psychopathological approach takes the view that our understanding of normal development will be advanced by the study of abnormality or atypicality in development. The approach uses situations or cases considered to be abnormal, such as autism or visual impairment, to tease apart variables that usually go together so that the importance of specific processes in development can be understood. The developmental psychopathological approach comprises research questions and strategies that utilise individual differences in providing explanations of child development in different circumstances.

The main principles of the transactional and ecological approaches form a framework which is used throughout this text for understanding atypical child development.

Discussion topics

1. What is your definition of development?
2. How can 'normal' be distinguished from 'abnormal' development?
3. What are the basic principles of attachment theory?
4. How do attachment theory, ecological theory and the transactional approach account for atypical development?
5. What is the value of the developmental psychopathological approach to understanding atypical development?

Recommended reading

Bronfenbrenner, U. (1979) *The Ecology of Human Development.* Cambridge, MA: Harvard University Press. This is a classic introduction to the ecological theory of child development.

Cicchetti, D. (1984) The emergence of developmental psychopathology. *Child Development,* **55,** 1–7. A straightforward introduction to the developmental psychopathological approach as a way of investigating and explaining atypical child development.

Rutter, M. (1981) *Maternal Deprivation Reassesed* (2nd edn). Harmondsworth: Penguin. An evaluation and critique of Bowlby's original ideas about attachment.

Rutter, M. (1996) Developmental psychopathology as an organising research construct. In D. Magnusson (ed.), *The Lifespan Development of Individuals.* Cambridge: Cambridge University Press. A more current restatement of the use of the developmental psychopathological approach as a research tool.

Sameroff, A. and Chandler, M.J. (1975) Reproductive risk and the continuum of caretaking casualty. In F.D. Horowitz (ed.), *Review of Child Development Research,* Vol. 4. Chicago: Chicago University Press. The classic paper explaining the transactional approach.

2

Risk Factors in Child Development

Janet Empson

Introduction

Many influences on children are adverse. They may be related to
the occurrence of atypical development, which is shown by developmental difficulty and disorder. Influences may be:

- biological, such as genetic or chromosomal
- environmental, for example violence in the home or the neighbourhood
- an interaction between the two, such as stress.

Examples of these major groups of influence and the mechanisms
through which child development may be affected are described
in this chapter.

Individual children react in different ways to similar environmental circumstances. This reflects differences between children
in their 'vulnerability' to harm or 'resilience' with which they
overcome difficulties, when faced with negative circumstances. In
addition, children can create their own experiences and
contribute to the direction of their own development. This may
change course as the child grows up, and how and why this occurs
needs to be explained. A model of development, which predicts
discontinuity, is the transactional model. This conceptualises
development as the product over time of transactions between an
active child and an active environment – a number of different
ecological contexts and the people in them. The course of devel-

opment is also seen as influenced by a wide range of biological and psychosocial risks.

So, the major aims of this chapter are to explain the concepts of risk and protective mechanisms, vulnerability and resilience in child development. These will be illustrated with reference to the major risk factors in development – biological, environmental and psychosocial – and possible ways in which they interact. In terms of biological risk, there is a focus on genetic and chromosomal abnormalities, the risks associated with the prenatal and perinatal periods, and examples of illnesses and injuries, all of which may have negative effects upon development. The main environmental influences on development to be described are those of stress during pregnancy and in childhood, the effects of maternal drug-taking (including alcohol) and of living in poverty. Psychosocial factors are described separately as they constitute a discrete topic for research and theory, although they are implicated as a process through which other factors exert their effects.

The main theoretical explanations of the influence of risk factors on development to be presented are the transactional and ecological approaches.

Definitions of risk and protective mechanisms, vulnerability and resilience

Sroufe et al. (1996) define risk factors as describing any character-istic, condition or circumstance which may increase the likelihood of developmental difficulty or disorder, in a direct or indirect way.

Risks include influences at many levels:

- genetic conditions, such as microcephaly in which the baby is born with a very small brain and head, with associated severe mental impairment
- familial circumstances, such as an alcoholic father or a depressed mother
- socioeconomic conditions, such as living in poverty
- cultural experiences, such as living in a subculture where the accepted patterns of behaviour are different from those of the dominant culture which may create difficulties in integrating into society

- developmental risk where poor early development can provide a context which has a negative influence on the course of later development.

Case 2.1 demonstrates a few of the risks that may come with pregnancy and childbirth. Can you identify those factors which could create difficulties for Chloe's early development?

Case 2.1 The story of Jayne and Chloe

Jayne was a small, slightly built girl who looked younger than her age of 15 when she became pregnant. It was only three months before the baby was due that Jayne realised that she was expecting a baby. Jayne told no one. She was no longer in contact with the father of her baby and her own mother was too depressed and preoccupied with her own worries to be supportive to her daughter. Chloe was born four weeks premature after a difficult birth, was underweight for her age, and needed care in the special baby unit for a time. Jayne was apathetic and did not want to have anything to do with her baby.

For Chloe, those aspects of her circumstances which could increase the likelihood of developmental difficulty are the age and physical build of her mother which constitute risk factors for prematurity and low birthweight; the lack of antenatal care, attention to diet and so on for most of the pregnancy meant that special care was not taken to provide the best circumstances for the baby's development; the lack of social support; birth difficulties, prematurity and low birthweight; separation from her mother in the early period after birth, coupled with apparent lack of care and attention from Jayne could give rise to problems in developing attachment between mother and child.

This combination of risk factors may seem to amount to overwhelmingly adverse circumstances for Jayne and Chloe to contend with, but the concept of risk is a statistical one, which applies to a whole group of people. The outcome for any one individual cannot be predicted (see Case 2.2).

Case 2.2 The story of Jayne and Chloe continued

Jayne and Chloe both received excellent care in hospital. Chloe became alert, interested and fed eagerly. Jayne began to feel more positive with more sleep and good food. She was also greatly helped by talking with a counsellor and the prospect of living for a time in a group home for young mothers in which she would be given help and support in caring for Chloe and herself. Her usual independence and determination reasserted themselves. Three years later Chloe was in local authority daycare while Jayne worked as a word-processor operative. They lived in a small flat of which Jayne was very proud, with friends close by. They formed a close and affectionate unit. Chloe's development was normal in every way.

From the continuation of Jayne and Chloe's story, you can see that the difficult situation of Chloe's birth and the period following it changed with professional help and Jayne's determination to be independent and care for her baby. The combination of improved environmental circumstances and Jayne's personal characteristics led to a positive outcome. These constitute 'protective factors' which Sroufe et al. (1996) defined as any characteristic, condition or circumstance that offsets, or makes less likely, the effects of a risk factor and promotes healthy development.

Jayne could be said to have 'resilience' to adversity and stressful circumstances so that potential difficulties for Chloe's development were avoided. Resilience is a characteristic of individuals which makes them less likely to develop problems when they have experienced difficult circumstances to which other, more vulnerable children respond with disturbance in development. Some individuals have more resilience to adversity than others. This may be because resilient children have personal characteristics, such as those of temperament, which mean that they react in a more positive or stable way when faced with difficulties. Processes within the child function as mechanisms operating between the risk and the outcome, which may enhance or reduce the likelihood of negative effects. Examples of such processes which develop in children from the early years onwards are:

- self-esteem
- self-efficacy and self-control

- self-motivation and autonomy
- cognitive appraisal and interpretation of situations.

These vary between individuals to influence the likelihood of developmental difficulties emerging. Exposure to a risk may help the individual to learn ways of dealing with it and some children will learn and adjust more quickly than others, and those who are more adaptable will build up resistance more easily. This does not mean that children should be exposed to major environmental stressors so that they can learn ways of coping with stress. They can learn how to cope with stress from everyday experiences such as peer relationships. In these there will be disagreements, arguments and falling outs. Children need to find ways of dealing with these less agreeable aspects of friendship. In school there are educational challenges which do not always result in success but rather in disappointment, and maybe inferiority, and these must be faced up to and coped with.

Different kinds of negative circumstances create a vulnerability to different developmental difficulties (Sroufe et al., 1996). For example, aggression and conflict between parents or amongst peers is particularly upsetting to maltreated children (Rothbaum and Weisz, 1994). They are more likely to have difficulty in establishing positive and secure interpersonal relationships with adults and peers, and are more likely to use aggression as a way of dealing with difficulties (Howe et al., 1999). However, even in groups of children who have been abused, studies have found that some children show no evidence of harm (Kagan, 1983). This may be associated with the age of the child, the child's previous relationship with parents or current good relationship with a non-abusive parent. Relationships between child maltreatment and child development will be discussed further in Chapter 3.

Thus, a close relationship with an adult can be a 'protective' factor for children, not just in situations of maltreatment but also in other circumstances. For example, Quinton (1988) demonstrated that when children are brought up in care they show better parenting as adults if they had a supportive long-term relationship with an adult while they were growing up. Protective factors act as 'buffers' to reduce the likelihood of risk factors being related to difficulties in development. For instance, Rutter (1979) showed that if children experience three or more risk factors for behaviour problems, then there is a 75 per cent likelihood of problem behaviour occurring, but if a child has 'a loving relationship with a dependable caregiver' the risk is reduced to 25 per cent. So, 'a loving relationship' in this case is functioning as a protective factor.

Protective factors may promote healthy development through a number of possible psychological or interpersonal processes or mechanisms. Rutter (1987) argued that it is necessary to find out what protective mechanisms there are and how they create resilience in individuals, so that the possible negative effects of risk situations do not occur. Such protective factors can operate at a number of different possible levels, that is, within the individual, between individuals or in the form of wider social influences. Garmezy et al. (1985) described the possible protective characteristics of stress-resistant children:

1. within-individual personality features, for example self-esteem, temperament
2. interpersonal factors, such as family cohesion and absence of discord
3. external systems of wider social influence that support the child's coping efforts, such as social groups of which the child is a member.

When considering the possible influence of risk factors on development, it is important to consider the *totality* of the child's experience and *combinations of factors acting together*, rather than considering the effects of individual risk factors in isolation.

Different risk behaviours are often associated in life. For example, drug-taking and criminal behaviour and drug-taking and emotional neglect are frequently linked. While a single risk factor is unlikely to be predictive of disorder for a particular child, a combination of risk factors makes it much more likely that an individual will be adversely affected. Thus, having an alcoholic parent is a risk factor for the children themselves growing up to become alcoholics, but having two alcoholic parents has a 'multiplier effect', making it much more likely that an individual will become an alcoholic.

The work over many years in the field of criminal behaviour by Farrington and associates (1990; Loeber and Farrington, 1998) indicates that the risk factors for the development of criminal behaviour in young people include:

- having a father who is a criminal
- being of low intelligence
- living in a subculture in which juvenile delinquency is the norm
- maternal depression
- parental substance abuse.

If children are exposed to three or more of the risk factors for criminal behaviour, there is a 75 per cent chance that they will be arrested for an offence more serious than a traffic violation by the age of 32 years (Sroufe et al., 1996).

When attempting to predict the way in which development will progress in a particular group of children, individual circumstances as well as differences in the personal characteristics of individuals must be taken into account. Different mediating mechanisms for protection from risk may operate in different circumstances and also have differential effects on individuals. Rutter (1987) described these as follows:

- Situations may be created which reduce the impact of risk, the nature of the risk itself may be altered, or exposure to it reduced. For example, parents may keep control of their children so that they do not come into direct contact with delinquents in the neighbourhood. Some children may react positively to restrictions on their movements by entertaining themselves happily indoors, while others may respond with negativity and defiance and find other ways of getting to know the young people who the parents consider to be a bad influence.
- A series of negative chain reactions which may follow an initial negative situation can be interrupted as in interventions in families with negative patterns of interaction.
- The establishment and maintenance of self-esteem and self-efficacy may be developed through sound personal relationships or task accomplishment. Again, differences between children in their intelligence and abilities may make feelings of self-efficacy more or less likely.
- Opportunities may open up at turning points in the child's life, such as when the child goes into foster care or when the young person leaves school, and these are times when protective processes can act to influence a developmental trajectory for the better and thus have long-term effects.

Duration of exposure to risk

The circumstances of risk for children's development usually last
for extended periods. Frequently the experience of negative
circumstances is ongoing and may escalate due to events being set
in motion which exaggerate the initial difficulty. For example,
marital discord – arguments and fights – or parental drug-taking
may elicit acting-out in the child. A parent in a heightened state
of arousal may react with less patience and attempt a more
controlling style of interaction with their child. This may result in
more negativity, perhaps aggression, on the part of the child and
ultimately a spiral of negative behaviours towards the other by
both caregiver and child. Or, a child with a different temperament may react to unpleasant home circumstances by with-
drawing from interpersonal interactions with parents and
becoming progressively more isolated and withdrawn as time goes
on. Intervention may then be necessary to change the family
dynamics or family situation in an effort to influence the course
of development for the better. More longitudinal studies (which
follow the same individuals over time) are necessary to find out
how experiences at an earlier period of development may influence reactions to events later on. The use of longitudinal studies
allows the reciprocal functioning of individual and environmental
factors over time to be measured. The implications of longitudinal studies for our understanding of, for example, reactions to
child abuse will be illustrated in Chapter 3.

Child's age at exposure to risk

There are some influences which have particularly damaging
effects when they occur at particular times in a child's development. These were originally called 'critical period' effects. For
example, if a mother contracted rubella (German measles)
between 8 and 12 weeks of pregnancy, the likelihood of damage to
the sensory systems, vision and hearing, which were developing
rapidly, was very high. If the mother caught rubella before or after
that 'critical period', it did not have the same negative effects.

A classic illustration of critical period vulnerability is provided by the case of the tranquilliser thalidomide, developed in the late 1950s by the German firm Chemie Grunenthal. Pregnant women who took thalidomide in the first trimester, when the limb buds of the foetus are developing, gave birth to children with catastrophic limb deformities. Some 8000 children across the world grew to adulthood having to cope with the consequences of this experience (Derlien, 2001, personal communication; Sunday Times Insight Team, 1979).

An important aspect of early interpersonal relationships (see Chapter 1) to later child development is that first, loving and lasting relationship between caregiver and child, known as 'attachment'. Different types of attachment relationship have been described which are associated with different kinds of developmental progress. Optimal socio-emotional development is related to secure attachment(s) in the first year of life, whereas less positive social behaviours are associated with insecure and disorganised attachments early in life.

When Bowlby (1951, 1969) first investigated attachment in human infants, he thought that it could only happen within a constrained period of time (the first six months of life). It is now recognised that even if an infant does not have access to a continuing, secure and loving relationship with a particular caregiver early in life, but is provided with this later on, it is still possible for an affectionate bond or attachment to be established. This was demonstrated in studies of children who formed attachments later in childhood when moved from care to a stable adoptive home (Tizard, 1977; Hodges and Tizard, 1989).

Later, the concept of 'sensitive periods' with respect to human development came to be preferred to that of critical periods, in that the limits of critical periods were not as fixed as first thought (Schaffer, 2000). Hinde (1963) had described the phenomenon as one of changing probabilities of certain forms of learning, with the likelihood being related to the time in the individual's life at which particular stimuli, or learning opportunities, occurred. So, the 'sensitive period' is that at which the person is maximally susceptible to particular environmental stimuli and is the optimum time for specific kinds of learning to take place.

The idea of sensitive periods has been shown to be a valuable one in studies of many aspects of development including the development of gender role identity and language acquisition (see Schaffer, 2000). These show that particular types of learning do take place more readily at certain phases of development. Some learning will take place because the child is maturationally ready. An example is that of learning bladder and bowel control which can only take place when the nervous system is sufficiently mature for effective voluntary control of bladder and bowel function. However, maturation of the nervous system is not the only possible mechanism to underlie the working of sensitive periods. Much variation in learning and development is due to environmental stimuli which will have different levels of importance in different domains of development. For example, gross motor development will be less affected by variations in the social environment than verbal development.

Early ideas about human development were therefore based in part on the notion of the 'irreversibility of early learning'. Clarke and Clarke (1998, 2000) argue that effects of early learning have been found to be variable; irreversibility is *not* characteristic of most of human learning Some forms of learning are more easily reversible than others and some effects of early experience are long-lasting. In each instance we need to determine how and to what extent particular early experiences limit later learning and adaptation to circumstances.

It should be noted that risk factors have been found to have differential influence in the development of behaviour problems in children at different developmental periods. For example, attachment may play an important part in the development of oppositional behaviour in early childhood, while peer relations may be more important to the development of antisocial behaviour later (DeKlyen and Speltz, 2001). Such age differences in susceptibility to particular risks are discussed further in the chapter on emotional and behavioural difficulties in development (Chapter 5).

Summary

The concepts of 'risk', whereby an individual exposed to particular influences may experience problems in development, and 'protective mechanisms', which offset the effects of risk factors, have been explained. Possible relationships between risk factors, and difficulties in development were discussed in relation to *combinations of risks* and possible *mechanisms* through which they may have their effects. The importance of individual differences in *susceptibility* (vulnerable children are more susceptible; resilient children less so) to adverse influences on development, together with differences in the circumstances of different children, was emphasised. The age of the individual when exposed to risk was considered in relation to the ideas of critical and sensitive periods, and irreversibility and change in the direction of development.

The next section examines some of the main biological risk factors for atypical development to which children may be exposed.

Biological risk

In this section some of the major biological risk factors for poor development will be discussed. The basis for all development lies in the genetic material passed on from parents to children and this will be described in terms of some of the conditions that follow from abnormalities in this process. During the period of pregnancy, birth and early postnatal life, the child is particularly susceptible to adverse influences upon development which commonly arise, such as lack of oxygen and low birthweight. These influences are discussed in relation to the transactional model of development. Possible negative effects of illness and injury to the child are also presented.

Genetic and chromosomal abnormalities

It is estimated that two out of every three conceptions are spontaneously aborted in the early months of pregnancy. In the majority of cases, the embryo is found to have genetic or chromosomal abnormalities (Fogel, 1991). These abnormalities can also account for two-thirds of deaths of newborns. They have been termed 'nature's way' of limiting the number of handicapped children growing to adulthood and possibly reproducing the abnormality. The more severe the extent of the damage to the foetus, the less likely it is that the baby will survive to term or will survive the trauma of birth. The total number of genetic disorders is unknown, but at least 3000 have been recognised so far, of which the gene(s) responsible have only been identified in a small number of instances. All of us are likely to be carriers of genes for a number of different genetic disorders. This means that despite natural abortions, and terminations when foetal abnormality has been detected from the amniotic fluid in the womb, a significant number of children are born with some kind of genetic abnormality. In most cases the parents are normal and there is no expectation of any problems.

Genetic effects may be due to genes acting in a number of different ways:

- *single gene* effects may be due to the action of a 'recessive' gene in which both parents are carriers of the gene and pass it on to the foetus at conception. The probability of having a child with a disorder due to the action of a single recessive gene if both parents are carriers is 1 in 4. It is only when an individual inherits genes from both parents for such a disorder, for example phenylketonuria (PKU), that the genetic effects are shown. An infant with PKU has an inability to metabolise a particular component of protein. In the days before the condition was recognised, it was associated with severe mental handicap in the developing infant. Today, however, PKU is identifiable at birth (in approximately 1 in 25,000 births), appropriate dietary restrictions are put in place and developmental difficulties avoided (Mazzocco et al., 1994).

- *dominant gene* conditions are much rarer than recessive gene conditions. Because the condition will always manifest itself in all carriers, it is easy to identify. Often such conditions are associated with death in infancy or childhood, or infertility if adulthood is reached. In conditions due to dominant gene effects, the probability is 1 in 2 that the offspring of carriers will be affected. One of the best documented examples of the latter is Huntington's disease (Simpson and Harding, 1993). The effects of Huntington's disease usually do not become evident until after child-bearing age. So the symptoms of Huntington's disease most often show when carriers are in their forties or fifties; the affected person becomes clumsy in her movements, a butterfly rash appears on the face and progressive mental and physical deterioration sets in.

Genetic counselling can limit the reproduction of this fatal condition by providing knowledge of individuals' heredity and associated risks, so that would-be parents can make informed choices about whether or not to have children.

- *multiplicative* effects of many genes. Psychological characteristics, such as intelligence, which vary along a continuum, have a basis in the action of many genes.

Chromosomal disorders arise due to abnormalities in one or more of the pairs of chromosomes which are present in every cell of the body. Chromosomes carry the genetic material which determines heredity. Disorders resulting from abnormalities such as extra parts to chromosomes include those associated with the sex chromosomes. Some of these affect females, others affect males and they may bring about abnormal sexual development and other problems. Certain disorders resulting from abnormality of the sex chromosomes apparently do not affect sexual or mental development in any way (see Moore and Persaud, 1998). There are sex differences in the incidence of particular disorders where the relevant gene(s) are carried on the sex chromosomes. Thus, haemophilia, for example, affects males but is carried by females (Berk, 1996).

The most frequently occurring form of chromosomal disorder is that of Down's syndrome, occurring in approximately 1 in 1000 individuals, in which there is typically an extra chromosome 21. The condition of Down's syndrome is described in the box below.

Children with Down's syndrome have moderate to severe learning disabilities and a similar physical appearance of short stature, flabbiness and folds of skin over the eyes. They often have respiratory, circulatory or glandular problems. Down's syndrome occurs most frequently in mothers over the age of 40 years, with the incidence in mothers between 45 and 49 years being 74 times greater than those less than 30 years of age. It has been hypothesised that this increase in occurrence in older mothers may be due to decreased oestrogen production or the age of the ova when fertilised. However, the father's age is implicated also, with an increased risk due to a mutation of unknown causation (Phillips and Elias, 1993). Down's syndrome is one of the many conditions where the nature of the environment in which the child grows up can make a considerable difference to developmental outcome, particularly when parents make special efforts to involve the child in her surroundings (Harris et al., 1996).

The factors which may place the child at risk of poor development often involve the interaction between biological factors and environmental circumstances. The transactional model explains this interaction. This was described at length in Chapter 1. The key features are revisited below.

Transactional model of development

Sameroff and Chandler's (1975) model of development, described in Chapter 1, presents development as a two-way process involving reciprocal interactions over time between an active child in an active environment. Child developmental outcome could be predicted by considering a combination of influences such as early biological status and the continuum of caregiving experienced during childhood. Sameroff (1987) further explained the transactional view of development to which the child and the environment both make independent contributions, so that the rate of child development can be constrained by the attributes of the child, the child-rearing environment or both. The wider culture prescribes ways of behaving and rules for socialising their children for parents, and presents models of appropriate behaviour to be imitated. Within the organisational framework of the culture are different rules and patterns of behaviour for different social groups and child development is further constrained by these. Expectations for child behaviour such as obtaining employment and contributing to the family income will differ between the social classes, where professional parents will expect a longer period of financial dependency for their children. Within the constraints of the social group, parents within a group differ widely in terms of their attitudes towards child-rearing and their actual child-rearing behaviours, for example the desirability of using physical punishment.

The child, too, can be a strong determinant of her own development through her own personality or other characteristics which influence the way others behave towards her. Thomas and Chess (1977) developed the concept of 'goodness of fit' to describe the relationship between the type of child and the kind of parenting to which they were best suited. Behaviour problems and other kinds of atypical development can occur when there is a poor fit between the specific needs, motivations and interests of the child and behaviour of the parents and the structure of the environment they provide. In addition, if the child is born with a physical or mental impairment, perhaps due to a genetic or chromosomal abnormality, their lack of developmental progress may violate the expectations of the parents, so that the parenting is inappropriate to the developmental stage of the child. This creates problems for development and for the relationship between parent and child.

Prenatal and perinatal risk factors

The main risk factors for infant development are:

- prematurity with associated low birthweight
- small for dates
- experience of some kind of trauma during the birth process, such as lack of oxygen (asphyxia).

There is much evidence that the main cause of severe impairment stems from prenatal problems (the period prior to the baby's birth) but most of these problems do not show up until the perinatal period (the period around and including the time of birth) (Kopp and Parmelee, 1979). About 85 per cent of severe developmental problems in the preschool years are due to prenatal and perinatal causes.

Lack of oxygen (asphyxia) during the birth process

Robertson et al. (1989) examined a group of children aged eight who had all shown clinical evidence of perinatal asphyxia. All the children who had experienced severe lack of oxygen had either died or had developed severe mental impairments, whereas none of those with the mildest degrees of oxygen lack developed any major developmental difficulties. Those in the middle, who had experienced moderate perinatal effects, were significantly worse than a comparison peer group who had not experienced lack of oxygen and the group with mild perinatal effects on measures of IQ, reading, spelling and mathematics. Thus, in middle childhood there seems to be a continuum of effects of brain injury due to perinatal asphyxia which exists when other perinatal and demographic effects are controlled for.

Effects of low birthweight

Low birthweight and preceding growth retardation in the foetus account for most deaths at birth and more than 50 per cent of long-term neurological problems (Goldenberg, 1994). These deaths and neurological abnormalities are particularly likely in infants who weighed less than 2500 grams at birth. Low birthweight is known to be an indicator of difficulties in middle childhood such as lower IQ scores, more motor difficulties, more neurological problems and more behavioural problems than control populations (Illsley and Mitchell, 1984). The lowest birthweight children perform least well.

However, low birthweight is associated with many different circumstances, in the periods preceding conception, or during pregnancy and childbirth. In particular, the socioeconomic circumstances of the mother, her age and state of health and nutrition are important. Low birthweight and prematurity are particularly a feature of poor social and environmental conditions, although they do occur in other social groups.

Application of the transactional model of development

Low birthweight and prematurity can provide illustrative examples of the transactional model in practice, as early biological and later environmental characteristics interact over time to influence child development.

The majority of studies (summarised by Hack et al., 1995) have found an interaction between low birthweight and adverse sociodemographic characteristics across the range of low birthweight. The environmental factors associated with disadvantage had more important effects on long-term cognitive outcomes than the biological risk factors. For example, the longitudinal study of Illsley and Mitchell (1984) found, in comparisons between low birthweight children and normal birthweight controls, that conditions of child-rearing were a better predictor of developmental status at ten years than low birthweight. So, the continuing caregiving environment throughout childhood appears to be a more important influence on development than the initial risk for development associated with low birthweight. (It should be borne in mind, however, that very low birthweights of less than 1000 grams are linked with permanent damage to various organs and severe and continuing problems in development – see the study by Sykes et al., 1997, described later in this section.) Also, as the children aged, the negative effects of social or environmental risks became more pronounced. Thus, the developmental trajectories of the children in the highest and lowest socioeconomic groupings increasingly diverged the older the child (see Figure 2.1).

Illsley and Mitchell's study (1984) found that the possible long-term effects of low birthweight, such as poor performance in school, seem to be overcome by the benefits of the environment (such as a healthy diet, parental stimulation and encouragement at school) for children brought up in the best socioeconomic conditions. For children growing up in conditions of socioeconomic deprivation, environmental factors (such as poverty, poor health and parental neglect) and the physical characteristics of low birthweight children act together to adversely influence development. These findings fit well with the ideas of reproductive risk and the 'continuum of caretaking casualty' (Sameroff and Chandler, 1975).

Not all studies found an interaction between environment and birthweight. For example, Sykes et al. (1997) in a large study in

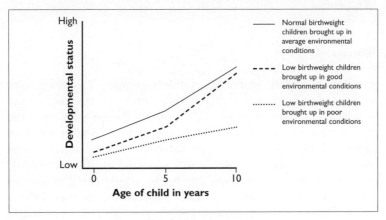

Figure 2.1 Diverging developmental pathways of low birthweight babies brought up in different environmental conditions

Northern Ireland found that very low birthweight children had more teacher-rated behavioural problems, poorer adjustment to school, worse learning and were less happy than control children *across all social classes.* Sykes et al. explained this in terms of physiological differences between below-average weight babies as considered in the studies described by Hack et al. (1995) and the very low birthweight babies who took part in Sykes et al.'s study. Sykes et al. suggested that very low birthweight babies have difficulties in 'state regulation' of physiological systems. This would affect emotional regulation and patterns of feeding, waking and sleeping.

The care of babies with such problems would place extra demands on caregivers and the interpersonal interactions between the two could constitute the source of developing behavioural problems. The stress experienced by caregivers in parenting could operate equally across social groups. Difficulties in self-regulation could account for the major difference between the very low birthweight group and the normal weight group, which was in school achievement. This was associated with attentional difficulties, hyperactivity or withdrawal. Following the earlier finding of similar problems in a group of very low birthweight children (Szatmari et al., 1993), Sykes et al. concurred with Szatmari et al.'s suggestion that very low birthweight children have a 'pure' form of attention deficit/hyperactivity disorder (ADHD) arising from their early physiological problems which accounts for their later difficulties in school.

Illness and injury

The infant is particularly susceptible to damage resulting from illness during the first month after birth, when severe illness occurs in 1 in 100 and death in 1 in 1000 infants. Those who are most at risk may have encounted trauma in the womb or during the birth process. The likelihood of prenatal and birth complications leading to conditions of illness and injury varies with social class, with the most socioeconomically disadvantaged being at greater risk. Oxygen deprivation may lead to cerebral palsy, especially in low birthweight or premature babies, and brain haemorrhages occur most often in premature infants. One of the most dangerous and frequently occurring bacterial infections is meningitis. Rhesus incompatibility between mother and child occurs when the mother has rhesus negative blood and bears a child who is rhesus positive. The mother develops antibodies to the child's blood, which is insufficient usually to affect a first child but may cause severe jaundice and later mental retardation in subsequent children unless the mother has been given gamma immunoglobulin following the birth of the first child. Nowadays, in developed countries, rhesus incompatibility is not much of a risk, although it still is in developing countries. In all these examples, we can see an interaction between the risk factor, the environment in which the child is growing up and the likelihood of occurrence, and severity, of atypical development in the child.

Summary

The effects of biological risks range from the potentially very severe, as in some genetic disorders and extreme lack of oxygen in the birth process, to those less damaging effects which are modifiable by the experience of a favourable environment. So, for those children brought up in good socioeconomic conditions, the possibly harmful effects of conditions such as prematurity and low birthweight are offset by environmental influence and have disappeared by mid-childhood. This provides an example of the transactional model in practice.

Environmental factors

Here we consider some features of the environment which may affect physical and/or psychosocial development of the child. Such influences may act via a number of different processes. These may range from:

- psychological, such as coping strategies or cognitions
- interpersonal, for example relationships with others
- physical, for example poor diet affecting physiological development
- sociostructural, such as aspects of living in poverty, including overcrowding, which creates stress and difficulties in learning.

Stress during pregnancy and in childhood

Stress during pregnancy

Stress in pregnancy may result from physical stimuli or psychological experiences which constitute an assault on the person, perhaps causing injury, but in any event requiring adjustment and coping on the part of the affected individual. The process of pregnancy itself is a stress on both physical and mental capabilities and may be accompanied by other conditions such as high blood pressure and the frequently occurring nausea and vomiting. All these can contribute to feelings of anxiety about the developing foetus as well as the mother's concern for her own health and well-being. So, pregnancy itself features in scales of stressful life events. In addition, while pregnant, the woman may be subjected to a range of other stressful circumstances. There is evidence that stress experienced by the mother may impact upon the development of her child.

Major damage may be done to the developing foetus if the mother is subjected to physical violence during pregnancy. The foetus may be injured directly or harm to the mother's physiology can affect the placenta and nourishment for the infant. Psychological stresses encountered by the mother may also have detrimental effects on the baby. Many teenage mothers come from poor socioeconomic conditions associated with the high stress of poor family relationships, lack of medical care and poor general health (Gunter and LaBarbera, 1980). All these conditions are associated with an increased likelihood of low birthweight, prematurity and other possible damage to the baby. (See also the case example of Jayne at the start of this chapter.)

The age of the mother constitutes a risk factor for the developing foetus, both when the mother is very young (less than 17 years) and when she is considerably older than the norm (over the age of 40). The very young mother has an immature reproductive system and often high levels of social stress, and most premature babies are born to teenage mothers; the older mother has more medical problems and is more likely to give birth to a child who has a chromosomal abnormality.

Altogether, there is some evidence associating the well-being of mother and child with a range of circumstances in pregnancy. Knowledge to date is, however, not conclusive and more studies are needed.

Stress in childhood

Since the early and influential work of Sigmund Freud (1954), it has been widely recognised that the experiences of early childhood may be implicated in the aetiology of later psychopathology. Freud specifically linked trauma such as child abuse with later emotional problems. Cannon (1928, 1929) showed that external stimuli associated with emotional arousal caused changes in basic physiological processes – the reaction to stressful occurrences. People will differ widely in their reactions to the same experience, because of differences in temperament which affect their reactivity, their previous experiences which may have prepared them to deal with particular types of stress and their present state which could affect their appraisal of the situation. Some experiences, such as the effect of divorce of a child's parents, bring about long-term life changes which may then constitute ongoing, chronic stresses. Others, such as a minor accident, may be over and done with very quickly with no long-term effects.

Goodyer (1990) described some of the most frequently occurring chronic stressors in children's lives. In Western society, the physical environment in which many children grow up is not conducive to optimal development. Lack of space due to overcrowding, lack of amenities for bathing and cooking, and lack of safe places to play constitute adverse factors in the ecology of the environment that contribute to family stress (Quinton, 1988). Living in flats, high-rise buildings and tower blocks predisposes to increased rates of psychiatric disturbance in preschoolers and depression in mothers (Brown and Harris, 1978). It seems that the effects of city life influence children's development via the family and so constitute an indirect effect. Generally, rates of family adversity are higher in urban, particularly inner-city, environments. But, when family adversities are held constant, there is no difference in the rates of emotional and behavioural disturbance in children from rural and urban environments. So various stresses within the family are associated with living in poverty. But, which came first, the family adversity or the poverty? Those families who have the least resources for coping with negative life events such as unemployment may be the ones that move into the spiral of poverty. Peter's family, described in Case 2.3, is leading a life characterised by multiple stressors, both structural (the physical environment) and functional (interpersonal relations).

Case 2.3 **Peter**

Peter is the youngest of five children and lives in a three-bedroomed council house with his brothers and sisters, grandmother, mother and her unemployed boyfriend. The small garden is piled high with refuse of various kinds, bedsteads, an old cooker, car parts, and the house is on a main road, all these circumstances restricting Peter's activities to the house. This is sparsely furnished, damp and smelling of urine and tobacco smoke. All three adults are heavy smokers, spending much of their time watching TV with cigarettes in hand. Peter suffers from asthma and bronchitis and frequently misses school. He is small for his age, undernourished and listless. There are no toys or books. Peter's mother is taking Valium and is too preoccupied with keeping the family together to pay attention to Peter's needs.

EXERCISE: *What features of Peter's environment constitute possible stressors for Peter and which may have adverse effects on his development?*

The lack of space in the house, its smokiness and damp will constitute negative factors for Peter's health and physical development. His well-being is also likely to be affected by the lack of fresh air and outdoor play. The facilities for indoor play are non-existant, which will impair his cognitive development and deprive him of other opportunities for fun and enjoyment. The adults appear to provide little stimulation for Peter's learning.

Goodyer (1990) described within-family factors of chronic adversity. These are associated with an increased incidence of conduct disorder in children (Rutter, 1985b). Both structural stresses, such as unemployment of father, large family size and children having been in care, and functional stresses, such as maternal psychiatric disorder and ongoing marital discord, contribute to the likelihood of occurrence of the disorder. The presence of one of these factors does not increase the level of risk of disturbance in the child, but the presence of two or three has a multiplicative effect.

Societal stresses, such as war, obviously affect large numbers of people including children over extended periods of time. Experience of sustained conflict, with bombings, lack of food and breakdown of the normal routines of life, coincide with events of major loss, such as separation from family, death or injury of family members, malnutrition, illness or injury to self and loss of home through destruction or evacuation (see Machel, 1996). When children have witnessed terrible events, such as deaths of friends or family members, they show signs of acute stress – anxiety, fear, insomnia, fatigue and psychosomatic complaints – and these are followed by longer term effects of the trauma, in the form of repeated experiencing of the event, nightmares and panic attacks. This constellation of symptoms constitutes post-traumatic stress disorder (PTSD). The available evidence highlights the importance of the social consequences of the event and that family and friends can, by their own behaviour, maintain the consequences of the events in the child's emotional state and behaviour (Goodyer, 1990). Also, the physical effects of living through war and its aftermath, such as malnutrition and refugee status, will also contribute to continuing psychological effects.

Overall, without belittling the effects of disaster on young children, it seems that they may, in some ways, and in some individuals, be protected from long-term adverse effects by the coping behaviours of the adults caring for them. A continuance of the social structure they knew before the event helps, as does a good level of family adjustment (Goodyer, 1990).

Drug effects

If a birth defect arises due to an environmental agent, the agent responsible is called a 'teratogen'. The effects of teratogens such as drugs, which are taken by many women, depend on a number of factors. One is the period in pregnancy at which the drug is taken, with most birth defects arising in the first trimester (first three months). Generally, the earlier in pregnancy the drug is taken, the greater the risk, but the effects are moderated by the size of the dosage, the duration of exposure and the type of drug taken. Most drugs appear to move from mother to child through the placenta and so potentially have an effect upon development. So, pregnant women are generally advised to avoid antibiotics, analgesics such as aspirin, stimulants such as amphetamines and nicotine (tobacco), tranquilizers and hypnotics such as alcohol, and narcotics like heroin, cocaine and marijuana (see Fogel, 1991). As research continues, other substances are becoming suspected of causing harmful effects. These include such commonly consumed substances as cafeine (coffee), antidepressants, antacids and antihistamines.

Illicit drug use is becoming an endemic problem in some sectors of Western society. Intravenous drugs such as heroin, and, increasingly, 'crack' cocaine are the most frequently used. The use of these types of drugs by the mother means that the baby will be born a narcotic addict and will have to go through the experience of withdrawal from the drug at an age when its immaturity and vulnerability makes this possibly fatal. Affected children are usually of low birthweight with a range of problems in physical and mental development. Frequently, mothers who are addicts will not have looked after themselves well during pregnancy, so are likely to be malnourished and have other health problems. Increasingly, drug addiction may be linked with the AIDS virus which is associated with a range of risks to the newborn child. She is likely to be of low birthweight and susceptible to infection such as pneumonia in the first year of life. Babies infected with HIV by their mothers may develop problems related to the disease soon after birth or they may remain free of physical symptoms for years. There may also be psychological or behavioural effects, expressed in learning difficulties and behaviour problems. The developmental status of the infant over the years will be influenced markedly by the family situation and other socioeconomic factors.

Effects of maternal drinking

In the Western world, alcohol is the most frequently used drug, and the consumption of alcoholic drinks is condoned or even encouraged by society. The research findings in relation to the consumption of alcohol by pregnant women are somewhat equivocal.

Moderate drinking, one to two drinks each day, during pregnancy has not been found to have detectable effects upon the neonate, but by age four years, the children of mothers who drink moderately were found to have below-average physical growth and varying degrees of learning difficulty (Abel et al., 1983). This has been termed 'foetal alcohol effects'. The condition of an infant which can result from mothers drinking heavily during pregnancy is called 'foetal alcohol syndrome' (FAS) (Rosett, 1980). Affected babies may have facial abnormalities, hyperactivity, slower physical growth, mental retardation and a range of other problems .

However, the extent of the true risk to the developing foetus of the consumption of alcohol by their mothers during pregnancy has recently been called into question by Koren et al. (1996) and Whitten (1996). These authors point to the millions of infants born worldwide each year who have been exposed to mild alcohol consumption by their mothers without apparent ill effects. The results of many studies testify to this. There is no agreed consensus of opinion as to how much alcohol is needed to produce foetal alcohol effects or foetal alcohol syndrome. Given the prevalence of alcohol consumption in Western society, it is surprising that the number of abnormal births associated with alcohol is only 0.4 per cent of all birth defects. In addition, FAS has only been consistently observed in chronically malnourished populations of women who had consistently consumed large quantities of alcohol during pregnancy (Whitten, 1996). So, again, *all the circumstances* of the pregnancy and birth need to be taken into consideration when evaluating the degree of risk. Individual risk factors rarely operate in isolation.

Alcohol can have direct, primary effects upon the developing foetus as a result of maternal drinking, which then causes FAS and continuing adverse effects upon development. Alcohol can also have indirect, secondary effects upon a child's development via the effects of alcohol consumption on the parents' behaviour. So, older infants and children are also at risk when their parent(s) drink heavily, and especially when one or both parents is an alcoholic. This condition is associated with child neglect and also with physical violence (see also Chapter 3). Eiden et al. (1999) demonstrated a relationship between parental alcohol problems and lack of sensitivity and more negativity to the infant in interaction. In both mothers and fathers this was mediated by their depression. The infants were found to be less responsive than control infants which, the authors suggested, could be a precursor of later maladjustment, which is higher in the children of alcoholic fathers.

Poverty

In the last 30 years the number of children living in poverty in this country has trebled, so that now, at the start of the twenty-first century, 1 in 3–4 children is growing up in impoverished circumstances. Poverty is a personal and social condition, as well as one where there is such a lack of physical resources that the basic human needs cannot be satisfied (Kumar, 1993). The personal development of children suffers through a poor diet and associated ill health and low self-esteem; lack of variety and stimulation in everyday life means low motivation, poor cognitive development and educational achievement. Families living in in-adequate housing, often cold, damp, inaccessible and over-crowded, are frequently socially isolated. They spend much of their time at home, as there is no money to spend on transport or entertainment. Long-term unemployment and ever-greater numbers of children growing up in one-parent households add to the difficulties for individuals lacking the support of a partner, friends or workmates.

So what does a life in poverty mean for those experiencing it? The impoverished circumstances of Paul and Sue are described in Case 2.4.

Case 2.4 Paul and Sue

Three-year-old Paul and his mother, Sue, share a one-bedroomed flat on the tenth floor of a high-rise block in south London. Their lives are charac-terised by monotony and isolation. They spend much of their time in the flat as there is insufficient money for transport and entertainment. Once a week they have an outing to the post office to collect Sue's benefits and then to the supermarket to buy food for the week. Their staple diet is cut-price, sliced white bread and economy baked beans. Fresh fruit and vegetables are not often on their menu as tinned food keeps so much better. Also, Sue never learned to cook. Neither did she do well at school. Her education had been disrupted by much illness in childhood and a home life that was so chaotic that it led to periods in care for Sue. Sue is depressed about her life and her lack of family and friends; she often stays in bed for large parts of the day. Paul is pale and anxious; his appetite is poor and he frequently wets himself.

As in the example above, those living in poverty are likely to be accommodated in the most unpopular dwellings such as high-rise flats. Women who live in such flats, especially when they have several very young children, are more likely to experience depression and anxiety, feelings of isolation, concern for their children's safety and day-to-day difficulties because of broken lifts, keeping children quiet, inadequate heating, damp, and insufficient money to buy food.

Impoverished neighbourhoods typically have limited resources for the residents. Shops are expensive and have a limited choice of goods so that food for a healthy diet is difficult to obtain; the housing is run-down, with many boarded up properties covered in grafitti. There is lack of open space for outdoor pursuits; an accumulation of rubbish in the streets; higher than usual concentrations of children and the elderly and a lack of stability, community and support for one another (Korbin et al., 1998).

Such environments are associated with a host of social problems such as juvenile delinquency and high crime rates, linked with drug addiction and the threat of, or actual, violence. Violence in the community is correlated with violence in the home, so that physical child abuse and neglect are at higher levels in socioeconomically deprived environments than in the more affluent areas (Helfer et al., 1997). In addition, there are higher than average levels of sociocultural intellectual difficulty which is linked with inadequate coping strategies.

Overall, then, families growing up in poverty experience continuously high levels of stress, both structural (physical aspects of the environment) and psychosocial (interpersonal relationships) which create an ongoing strain for people with poor personal resources for coping (Pearlin and Schooler, 1978). In addition, the chronic stress associated with 'daily hassles' (Kanner et al., 1981), everyday examples of minor irritations and set-backs, creates a further burden. These disadvantaged families are likely to have experienced a number of negative life events, such as loss of partner or loss of job, which constitute an acute stress to be adjusted to. Such life events may have contributed to a lowering of income and the move into the poverty trap. In addition, the conditions of living in poverty may lead to marital conflict and then marital breakdown. All types of stress have been associated with later physical and mental ill health (Lazarus, 1999). Maternal depression, for example, creates ongoing strain, and possibly subsequent breakdown in relationships. So, marital discord, marital breakdown and psychopathology impact adversely on the well-being and development of the children. These negative effects on the children associated with parental problems occur in all sectors of society but tend to be amplified by living in circumstances of poverty. For many families these circumstances and consequences constitute a spiral of increasing difficulty and deprivation.

Children's education also suffers when the children are growing up in poverty. If the parents are stressed and depressed by the demands of everyday living, then they cannot take as much interest in their children's education and their attainment is constrained. There is a lack of educational resources in the home, computers, books and a quiet place to work. Inner-city schools tend to have a high turnover of staff and other difficulties to contend with, and children may have to keep changing schools as they move from one temporary accommodation to another. Education may also cease because of adolescent pregnancy, for which there is an elevated risk in communities with high rates of poverty, dependency on benefits and single-mother households (Wilson, 1987). Those at risk of adolescent pregnancy do not perceive its costs, as it is viewed as an escape from alienation from school and lack of career prospects (Luker, 1996).

It is often difficult to determine to what extent the adverse effects of living in poverty result from the conditions of poverty themselves or are due to associated factors such as lack of maternal education (Brooks-Gunn et al., 1999). Most research has found that maternal education and family income are equally predictive of children's ability and achievement (Duncan and Brooks-Gunn, 1997). Income seems to be more predictive of ability and achievement than family structure (for example lone mother) but family structure influences emotional well-being more.

There are a number of possibly causal mechanisms implicated in the relationship between low income and child outcome (Brooks-Gunn and Duncan, 1997):

- Poor diet and ill health often co-occur and are associated with lack of attendance at school, poor motivation and concentration, apathy and lack of involvement. One result is poor educational attainment.
- Parenting behaviour in conditions of poverty has been shown to be less supportive and involved, and more punitive. The children (especially boys) are more likely to receive severe

physical punishment. This is likely to affect child self-esteem and feelings of competence.

- Parental mental health suffers in conditions of poverty. Psychological distress means that stressful life events and chronic stress are not coped with well and relationships deteriorate, for example if a parent is depressed or anxious. Poor mental health can be both a cause and a consequence of stress and failure to cope. For example, maternal depression can accentuate marital difficulties or can result from a loss of partner through marital separation. Such family stresses are associated with behaviour problems and poor intellectual development in the children.

- In the home environment, a lack of resources, both physical and interpersonal, restrict opportunities for learning and having fun. Children's cognitive development and emotional well-being may both be affected.

- The lack of amenities in impoverished neighbourhoods, such as good schools, limits opportunities for mental growth and physical development; social disorganisation characterised by a lack of support from neighbours and the threat of, or actual exposure to, violence can influence the well-being of both parent and child (Brooks-Gunn et al., 1999).

Thus, the pathways through which a relationship between poverty and poor child development may be mediated are numerous. They differ in terms of how close they are to the child and the extent to which they involve personal, interpersonal and structural factors (which relates to Bronfenbrenner's systems model of influences on development). All need to be included in any overall model of risk factors for children growing up in poverty. Such multifactorial and reciprocal influences can be utilised in a transactional interpretation of the effects of poverty on atypical child development.

Summary

Some of the main environmental factors – stress, drugs and poverty – associated with developmental difficulties have been discussed. All of these may co-occur and interact in their effects.

For example, maternal illicit drug-taking is associated with deprived socioeconomic conditions, poor health and pre- and perinatal problems in their infants. So the origins of difficulties may be environmental but operate through biological and interpersonal processes such as psychopathology and associated behaviours in the mother. These fit well into a transactional model of risk to development. Psychosocial risk factors are described in the next section.

Psychosocial factors

Interpersonal relationships

As described in Chapter 1, the first important interpersonal relationship is the attachment between caregiver and child. Attachment can be described as an emotional bond that endures in time and space and in which both find satisfaction. Within attachment relationships, babies first organise their experience and expression of emotion, later taking other people's affective states into account in their developing understanding. Since the influential work of Bowlby (1951, 1969), the importance of the quality of parent–child relationships for the development of personality and the self-concept of the child has been recognised. When children experience stressful and frustrating interpersonal relationships, there is an increased risk of the development of problem behaviours in the child. Abuse and neglect of children always occur in the context of problematic relationships. As Rutter (1991) puts it, abnormalities in relationships are important in many types of 'psychopathology'. This is discussed further in relation to emotional and behavioural difficulties in children in Chapter 4.

Problems in attachment in infancy are associated with poorer later development – a greater likelihood of relationship difficulties with peers in the preschool years and worse social adjustment in primary school (Sroufe et al., 1993) which is itself a predictor of worse educational achievement.

There are different ways in which the establishment of secure attachment relationships may be hindered, as described next.

Characteristics of caregivers

Specific groups of mothers may be at increased risk of difficulty in establishing a warm and enduring bond with their infants over the first months of life. Research has shown that those mothers who did not experience a secure attachment relationship with their own mother or other caregiver in infancy have more difficulty in relating to their own child (Parkes et al., 1991), as do depressed mothers and, possibly, very young mothers who have unrealistic expectations of motherhood and the behaviour of their babies, and are struggling with their own developmental needs (Chase-Lansdale and Brooks-Gunn, 1994). These kinds of attachment difficulties may also be exacerbated by living in impoverished environments which makes people more susceptible to mental disorder, and is also associated with a higher incidence of young and lone mothers. The relationship between attachment difficulties, risk of child abuse and poor development in children are discussed further in Chapter 3.

Characteristics of children

There are also characteristics of individual children which can make it more difficult for sound emotional relationships to be developed with them. If the child is very premature, of low birthweight or handicapped, then their early days may be filled with parental anxiety about whether they will survive and what their future is likely to be. Parents may restrain themselves, or find it difficult to provide their child with the love and security the attachment relationship requires, and the child is likely not to show the range of behaviour patterns such as eye contact that facilitates positive parental bonding behaviours (Oates, 1994). So, for these children, the establishment of a secure attachment relationship may be problematic. In addition there is a group of children described by Thomas and Chess (1977) as 'difficult'. Their behaviours are characterised by negative moods, overreactive, lacking in rhythmicity, with difficulties in feeding and sleeping, which can create difficulties in forming rewarding relationships with them. Parents have to be very dedicated to understanding the child's needs, mindful of the child's difficulties and very patient in order to avoid the behaviour problems which

Thomas et al. (1968) described as occurring in more than 50 per cent of 'difficult' children in late childhood.

Quality of relationships

Marital discord is another factor in the interpersonal environment which is associated with stress and distress in the child and adverse effects upon development. There are established links between marital discord and depression in the adults which impacts upon the children in the family; there are also links between discord in the family, isolation of the family and child abuse (Peterson and Brown, 1994; Helfer et al., 1997). The adverse effects on the children of separation and divorce of their parents is related to the degree of discord, quarrelling and violence between the partners prior to separation. Amato and Keith (1991) analysed the results of 93 studies involving 13,000 children of divorce and found that these children of divorce scored lower than children from intact families on measures of academic achievement, conduct, psychological adjustment and the quality of parent–child relationships. Further, Jekielek (1998) found that children had better emotional well-being if their parents separated than if they stayed together in a situation of marital conflict. Few studies have been carried out recently into the effects of living in a conflict-ridden environment, but Jekielek's study suggests that it is harmful to children.

There are differential effects of marital discord, separation and divorce according to the gender of the child. Quinton et al. (1991) have described how boys have an elevated rate of disorders (twice as frequent) when they have experienced open family discord and hostility and there is also a personality disorder in the parent; the situation for girls is that rates of disorder are elevated if a parent is disordered whether or not there is family discord. Thus, there may be different mechanisms whereby boys and girls are affected by abnormalities in the home environment.

Summary

Many kinds of developmental difficulty – intellectual, emotional and behavioural – in children can be linked with abnormalities in the child's close relationships. Among the processes which have been implicated in these risks to child development are problems in attachment, negative relationships between family members and mental health problems affecting parents' ability to be warm, attentive and positive with their children. The association between these interpersonal factors and child maltreatment will be considered in the next chapter.

Conclusion

This chapter has presented examples of risk factors for poor development in children. They have been described in such a way as to illustrate the development of the child as influencing and being influenced by their participation in a number of different systems which constitute the ecological context. The processes which contribute to both atypical and normal development operate at the physiological level, involving, for example, the immune system; at the psychological level, such as self-esteem or self-efficacy; and at the interpersonal and community levels. Characteristics of the developing child (both biological and psychological) interact in a dynamic, ongoing process with characteristics of the family, such as maternal drinking; the relationship between the parents; and social and structural features of the wider community, to influence developmental progress.

The possible influence of individual risk factors cannot be considered in isolation; risks to development often co-occur, such as poverty and low birthweight. In addition, the age of the child when exposed to adverse influences, their intensity and duration also need to be taken into account when considering their likely effect.

There is a wide range of outcomes possible for those who have experienced biological and/or psychosocial risk in childhood. This is partly due to individual differences in vulnerability and resilience – a dynamic process of protection from negative influences through developing personal characteristics such as personal resources, cognitive maturity, self-esteem and ego control – and partly due to the caregiving environment which the child experiences throughout the course of her development. The environment may constitute a powerful force for change if it changes at any stage in the child's development.

Discussion topics

1. What do you understand by the term 'risk factor'?
2. Why are risk factors important to an understanding of atypical child development?
3. Discuss the role of psychosocial factors in the aetiology of atypical child development.
4. What are the processes through which biological factors may be involved in the development of disorder in children?
5. Discuss some examples of atypical development which involve biological and environmental interactions.

Recommended reading

Clarke, A.M. and Clarke, A.D.B. (2000) *Early Experience and the Life Path*. London: Jessica Kingsley. This text is particularly useful with reference to the issue of reversibility of early learning, sensitive periods in development and case examples illustrating different developmental pathways in relation to environmental change.

Goodyer, I.M. (1990) *Life Experiences, Development and Childhood Psychopathology*. Chichester: Wiley. An excellent analysis of the relationship between psychopathology and stress in childhood.

Rutter, M. (1987) Psychosocial resilience and protective mechanisms. *American Journal of Orthopsychiatry*, **57**, 316–31.

Sameroff, A.J. and Chandler, M.J. (1975) Reproductive risk and the continuum of caretaking casualty. In F.D. Horowitz (ed.), *Review of Child Development Research*, Vol. 4. Chicago: University of Chicago Press. The classic paper explaining the transactional approach.

Schaffer, H.R. (1996) *Social Development*. Oxford: Blackwell. Chapter 2 provides a clear explanation of the biological foundations of child development.

Schaffer, H.R. (2000) The early experience assumption: past, present and future. *International Journal of Behavioural Development*, **24**, 5–14.

Sroufe, L.A., Cooper, R.G. and DeHart, G.B. (1996) *Child Development. Its Nature and Course* (3rd edn). New York: McGraw-Hill. A clear and readable introduction to child development which explains the concepts of risk, vulnerability and protective mechanisms in relation to problems in child development.

3

Child Abuse

Janet Empson

Introduction

Child abuse, or child maltreatment, occurs in up to five per cent of families in the UK and thus constitutes a major problem for society. Most of the children who are abused develop behaviours that are atypical for their developmental stage. Many have long-term developmental problems characterised particularly by low self-esteem and difficulties in interpersonal relationships. It is necessary to understand how and why abusive relationships develop in families so that appropriate interventions can prevent reoccurrence, and the possible transmission of abusive behaviours to the next generation, so that abused children do not grow up to abuse their own children. Many individuals who were abused as children do not grow up to abuse their own children and some who have not been abused themselves do become abusers. The possible mechanisms underlying these differences need to be understood.

This chapter documents a brief history of child abuse and the difficulties of estimating the incidence of abuse. Definitions of different kinds of abuse – physical abuse and neglect, emotional abuse and sexual abuse – are examined, with the attendant difficulties of distinguishing between harsh parental treatment and actual maltreatment. Risk factors for different kinds of abuse are considered in relation to such factors as the conditions in which families are living, different family structures and characteristics of perpetrators and victims. Many of the risk factors for child abuse were introduced in Chapter 2. A number of different models which predict the occurrence of abuse are presented, such as those of Belsky (1980) and Peterson and Brown (1994). It is gener-

ally agreed that only multifactorial explanations of child abuse
which incorporate sociocultural risk and personal and interpersonal risk factors can possibly explain such a complex phenomenon. Some of the processes (such as social learning and
attachment) which may be implicated in the development of
abuse are also discussed, followed by a consideration of the main
short- and long-term effects of abuse in relation to atypical child
development. An appropriate model based on a knowledge of the
relevant processes and effects on the child are all necessary for the
formulation of interventions to help child and family.

History of child abuse

Child maltreatment has been a feature of human society
throughout recorded history (see Zigler and Hall, 1989). The
Bible has descriptions of instances of infanticide in the ritual sacrifice of babies, and a wide range of societies have practiced infanticide for centuries. Those who were killed were, in the main,
disabled in some way, female, children of the poor or later born
children of large families. As children were seen as chattels, such
events were accepted by society. In the Middle Ages there was
widespread poverty and children were mutilated to make them
effective beggars.

Zigler and Hall also described how, in the Industrial Revolution, children were exposed to long hours of hard work in awful
conditions. There were widespread industrial diseases affecting
the young, such as testicular cancer in chimney sweeps. Until
recently, corporal punishment was widely used in schools (Aries,
1962) and parents were advised to use harsh, physical discipline
well into the twentieth century. Even today many parents in countries such as the UK and the USA believe in physical punishment
as a suitable way of disciplining their children, even those who are
very young (Leach, 1993).

It is only in the last forty years or so that society has awoken to
the reality of the way in which children have been so badly treated
for centuries, and research has been directed towards understanding the causes and effects of such maltreatment of children.
Maccoby (1980) reported that such treatment 'had its roots in
three factors: Puritan religious values, a lack of medical know-

ledge, and a perception of children and childhood as a mirrored replica of adults and adulthood' (quoted in Garmezy and Rutter, 1988, p50). Children have for centuries been subjected to physical and sexual abuse, perhaps largely through ignorance, the prevailing attitudes of the day and their status as powerless. Nowadays, when children's rights are enshrined in a UN Charter, and society's responsibility for the care of its young is part of every political party's manifesto, it is therefore more shocking that on average one to two children die each week at the hands of adults responsible for their care in the UK (NSPCC, 2003).

It is only relatively recently that research has documented the different ways in which adults may maltreat children, and their incidence. The phenomenon of physical abuse was brought to public attention by Kempe et al., who, in 1962, described the 'battered baby syndrome'. The context was a medical one but since then the concept of 'child abuse', or child maltreatment, has become more holistic, incorporating cultural, social and psychological dimensions to the problem.

The phenomenon of child abuse is very much in the public consciousness today, with constant headlines concerning the latest victim. An example is the recent death in the UK of Victoria Climbié, sent by her parents to England from Ivory Coast to give her the opportunity of a better life. Victoria suffered terribly at the hands of her great aunt and the aunt's partner who beat her, stripped her naked, bound her and kept her all night in a dustbin bag in the bath in an unheated bathroom. Victoria was not removed from their 'care' even though she had been seen by numerous professionals, so clearly there are still problems in identifying even serious child abuse. One reason may be that the perpetrators of child abuse are often thought to be different from other people and Victoria Climbié's guardian did not appear to be 'mad' or 'bad' (Hinsliff, 2003).

That fatal cases of child maltreatment are still occurring today because these children have been failed by the institutions of society – social services, the police and the health service – is a severe indictment of our provision of social care. Thousands more children are abused every year. This too is a reflection of the inadequacy of our social structures and social provision. Child abuse must be seen as the result of interactions between social structures and the social processes and dynamics within families, where most abuse occurs. Abuse in families occurs within a wider social context of institutional and structural abuse and we need to attend to the wider social processes associated with poverty, deprivation and exploitation (The Violence against Children Study Group, 1990). Finkelhor (1983) has suggested that abuse is carried out to compensate the abusers for their perceived lack of, or loss of, power, which is particularly evident in socioeconomically disadvantaged homes, characterised by low income, unemployment and lack of choice. There is a clear association between the frequency of occurrences of physical abuse and neglect and social class (Pelton, 1978), but also a lack of relationship between the incidence of sexual abuse and the social class of the family in which the victim grew up (Parton, 1990). Both can be seen as an act of the strong against the weak. In the former case this is an expression of a lack of control, or anger, against the state which is vented upon the child or children; sexual abuse seems to stem from a need to compensate for a sense of powerlessness in other interpersonal relationships. So all kinds of child maltreatment may be interpreted as a political issue.

The frequency of occurrences of abuse is influenced by government policy which brings about extrafamilial social change; this, in turn, affects intrafamily relations. The stresses of parenting, associated with certain forms of abuse, are intensified by poverty, racism and isolation (The Violence against Children Study Group, 1990). To understand abuse as a prerequisite for reducing its occurrence, we need to examine the relationship between social problems, such as poverty, isolation and unemployment, combined with individual propensities. The role of statutory agencies, such as social workers, also needs to be borne in mind. The social worker has a dual responsibility to families in need which is for both social care and social control. Problems may well arise through conflict between these two duties, and also because the client is often viewed as the parent rather than acting in the best interests of the child. Social workers must take into account both the rights of parents to bring up children with as much freedom from state interference as possible and the rights of children to be protected from any harm which may be inflicted on them by their parents (Frost, 1990). This often seems to lead to what has been termed the 'rule of optimism' (Horne, 1990), whereby the parents' story is believed and hope is maintained that they will put things right. Such families often experience an array of problems and there is a failure by the social worker to prioritise suspected child abuse. Social workers are at the front line of social problems like child abuse and the inadequacies of their practices are often exposed in cases of very severe abuse. But child abuse is more than a problem for social services, it is one for which society as a whole must take responsibility. Child abuse as a major social issue has been hidden in the past, perhaps because of power relations and structured inequalities within society and the family, and, in relation to child sexual abuse, because of the 'incest taboo'. It is only recently that the extent of the problem of abuse has been recognised, and this is a step in the right direction towards addressing the problem.

The problem of child abuse is a difficult one to explain, as such behaviour is neither adaptive nor functional. It is uniquely human, in that there are no parallels in the animal world. It is to be hoped that the more that becomes known about the causes and consequences of different kinds of maltreatment, the more able society will be to effect changes to reduce the occurrence of abuse. Research into child abuse is of major interest today and is shedding light on some of the common myths associated with it:

- that intergenerational transmission of abuse is inevitable
- that child abusers are psychologically different from other parents
- that abuse is restricted to particular socioeconomically disadvantaged groups.

Evidence is presented later in this chapter which relates to these suppositions.

Definitions of child abuse

Child abuse is a socially defined construct, a product of a particular culture and context (Corby, 2000). Within a particular society, what is considered abusive changes over time, and what is considered abusive in one society is not considered to be so in another. Korbin (1981) describes cultural practices in the southern hemisphere which would be considered abusive in Western societies:

extremely hot baths, designed to inculcate culturally valued traits, punishments such as severe beatings, to impress the child with the necessity of adherence to cultural rules: and harsh initiation rites that include genital operations, deprivation of food and sleep, and induced bleeding and vomiting. (Korbin, 1981: 4)

But Korbin also points out that some of our own child-rearing practices, such as isolating a small child in a room alone at night or withholding food even though it is available, until the feeding schedule determines that the child should be fed, would be considered to be maltreatment by people in other societies (Corby, 2000). There are, however, common standards across virtually all societies in that none tolerate the battered child syndrome, for example. Some cultures appear to have very little or even no abuse which, it has been argued, is because there is no physical punishment of children in these cultures (Gil, 1970).

It is very difficult to assess the prevalence of abuse as, quite apart from problems of definition, it is still, as stated earlier, a hidden problem. Assessments will depend on how general and inclusive the definition of abuse is, the child-rearing practices of the society or subgroup within that society, and how different professional groups within a particular society perceive individual cases.

Underlying abuse and connecting all its forms is the destructive element – child maltreatment (Becker-Lausen et al., 1995). Steele (1997) describes child maltreatment as a large, complex group of human behaviours characterised by traumatic interactions between parents or other caregivers and the infants and children of all ages in their care, as well as between strangers and children during casual contact. Physical, emotional and sexual abuse and various forms of neglect often co-occur.

The above definition does not take into account that abuse also takes place between older and younger children, wherever there is a difference in power, and need not involve someone with responsibility for the other.

Child abuse and neglect is 'any interaction or lack of interaction between family members which results in non-accidental harm to the individual's physical and/or developmental states' (Helfer et al., 1997). In relation to Helfer's definition, the following should be noted: abuse may involve unrelated people but less often than between people who are kin; and evidence of harm is not always easy to identify.

In constructing an appropriate definition of child abuse, a number of conditions need to be taken into account:

- definition depends upon context in which the definition of abuse is being used, such as legal or medical
- intention – non-accidental incidents are usually considered as abusive but what about 'accidents' and failure to protect from harm? Identification of situations where the abuse results from inadequacy of a parent to nurture his child (Newberger, 1973)
- distinguishing between acceptable and unacceptable practices as, for example, in hitting a child
- the developmental status of the child
- differing interpretations of how serious different kinds of abuse are.

With reference to this last, Giovannoni and Becerra (1979) found that different professional groups differed in how serious they considered different examples of abuse to be, with lawyers rating incidents as less serious than the other groups – police, social workers and paediatricians. This may reflect the stereotypical cautiousness of lawyers. However, there was general agreement amongst the groups in their rankings of the seriousness of different kinds of abuse. Those were as follows, from most to least serious: physical abuse, sexual abuse, fostering delinquency, lack of supervision, emotional maltreatment, alcohol/drug use, failure to provide physical necessities and educational neglect.

Frequency of occurrence of abuse

Despite the difficulties inherent in establishing criteria for different kinds of abuse, various organisations do calculate reported incidents. In 1996, Childhood Matters (cited in Hobbs et al., 1998) provided figures for the UK, with the caveat that many more children are abused than represented in the figures. Annual occurrences are:

- at least 150,000 children suffer extreme physical punishment
- up to 100,000 have a potentially harmful sexual experience

- 350,000–400,000 children live in an environment low in warmth and high in criticism, which constitutes emotional neglect.

Of 160,000 children referred to the services in 1992, only 24,500 were finally registered as at risk. In 1995 there were nearly 35,000 children on the child protection registers in England (Hobbs et al., 1998). These comprised:

- Physical abuse   37%
- Neglect   32%
- Sexual abuse   26%
- Emotional abuse   13%
- More than one category   9%

These figures add up to more than 100 per cent because individual children can be on the child protection register as experiencing more than one type of abuse. It is also important to note that there will be more visible signs of some types of abuse than others, which can lead to an underestimation of the incidence of some forms of abuse, such as emotional abuse. In addition, *single registration*, which happens in a number of countries, obscures a much higher incidence of co-ocurrences.

The referral rate in the USA is three times that of the UK as a percentage of the population (Cicchetti and Carlson, 1989). Moreover, there are differential rates of reporting of suspected child maltreatment between different neighbourhoods, ranging from less than 10 per 1000 children to more than 20 per 1000 children. There are also different rates of reporting between urban and rural communities, the latter being consistently lower. These rates of reporting may not reflect actual incidence. In communities with a high population density, the activities of neighbours will be more visible (and audible) so others are alerted to possible malpractice; distance between dwellings may account for the difference between rural and urban rates. Also, middle-class families may find it easier to hide abuse from others, if the abuse is less likely to be physical, which is more easily noticed.

Child abuse represents such a serious problem in society today that it is estimated that approximately two children die as a result of abuse each *week* in the UK (National Society for the

Prevention of Cruelty to Children, 2003), and that one to two children die per *day* in the USA (see Clarke-Stewart et al., 1988). Most of these children die as the result of injury and neglect by their parents.

Types of abuse

Physical abuse

Gil (1970) defined physical abuse as:

> the intentional, non-accidental use of physical force or intentional, non-accidental acts of omission, on the part of a parent or other care-taker interacting with a child in his care, aimed at hurting, injuring, or destroying that child. (p6)

The Department of Health (2000) specified the kinds of behaviours which would constitute physical abuse as involving:

> hitting, shaking, throwing, poisoning, burning or scalding, drowning, suffocating or otherwise causing physical harm to a child. Physical harm may also be caused when a parent or carer feigns the symptoms of, or deliberately causes, ill-health to a child. This situation is commonly described using terms such as fictitious illness by proxy or 'Munchausen syndrome by proxy'. (p5)

Although more specific than previous definitions, it does not address the issue of when a behaviour becomes serious enough to require intervention. However, there is general agreement that:

- there is a consensus in society as to what are acceptable and what are unacceptable child-rearing practices
- there is an agreed view that interpersonal relationships should not involve harm to either party.

It is clear that the term 'child physical abuse' covers a wide range of actions and circumstances, from the relatively minor bruise, as when perhaps a parent restrains a child too forcefully in grasping him by the arm, to life-threatening or even fatal injury.

Views differ as to whether different kinds of abusive actions should be thought of as categories containing discrete units which are qualitatively different or whether abuse should be seen as positioned on a continuum of caregiving, ranging from the very positive, loving and nurturant, to the very negative featuring severe physical and mental harm to the child, as has been proposed by Zigler (1980).

Whichever view is taken, it does not alter the fact that physical abuse is widespread, occurring in 2/3 in 100 families in the USA (Zigler and Hall, 1989). Given the possible severity of the effects of physical abuse, it is clearly a major problem for society to deal with. The case of Judith's physical maltreatment of her family is illustrated below.

Case 3.1 Judith

Judith is a 20-year-old lone parent with three children, all under the age of five, by three different fathers. Judith first became pregnant at the age of 16 just after she had left the care of the local authority. As she has no family to help her, she spends her time feeling anxious, angry and depressed, struggling to make ends meet and bring up her children, the youngest of whom is only nine months old. All the children are failing to reach developmental norms, are uncooperative, defiant and temperamental. They clamour for Judith's attention. This frequently comes in the form of screaming at them to shut up, accompanied by verbal insults and severe beatings. All the children are badly bruised. John, the eldest, had a dislocated shoulder from being forcibly moved to his bedroom as a punishment. This problem was not taken to the doctor for a week, so caused a lot of pain and took a long time to recover from. Jim, the middle child, had a fractured forearm from being hit so hard that he fell. The baby is smacked if he squirms while his nappy is changed and if he drops food on the floor when feeding himself. The eldest child was expected to look after the younger ones; because Judith was failing to cope. She showed many stress symptoms including eating and sleeping difficulties, a negative mood and lack of patience. She was drinking heavily. So she failed to satisfy the children's developmental needs. They reacted to her negativity and severe physical punishment with emotional outbursts which created more problems. When Judith finally went to see her GP, she admitted that she felt completely overwhelmed but that her disciplining of the children was for their own good and to keep things under control.

Risk factors for physical abuse

Emery (1989) describes stresses arising from medical disorders, financial burdens, marital discord, problematic living arrangements, and an environment of much change or threat. In addition, there are characteristics of individual parents with limited child-rearing knowledge who, for example, use excess force on their offspring (Burgess and Conger, 1978). Risk factors at the wider cultural level include the cultural tolerance of aggression and a social history of violence in the family (Pogge, 1992).

Emotional abuse

Brassard and Hardy (1997) describe emotional abuse as incorporating cognitive, affective and interpersonal conditions which constitute

> a repeated pattern of caregiver behaviour or extreme incident(s) that convey to children that they are worthless, flawed, unloved, unwanted, endangered, or of value only in meeting another's needs.

Psychological or emotional abuse has been described by Garbarino et al. (1988) as a concerted attack by an adult on a child's developing self-esteem and social competence. They delineated five forms of destructive behaviour:

1. *rejection* – the adult systematically ignores the child and the legitimacy of his needs
2. *isolation* – cutting the child off from others
3. *terrorising* – exposure to bullying and frightening verbal assaults
4. *ignoring* – stifling the child's emotional and intellectual growth by depriving him of stimulation and response
5. *corruption* – forcing the child to engage in destructive antisocial behaviour or other deviant acts.

Any or all of these adult behaviours may occur in the same family. They all deny the child full satisfaction of those 'psychosocial needs' (Pringle, 1971) which are essential for optimal development. These are:

- love and security
- new experiences

- praise and recognition
- opportunity to develop responsibility.

The denial of these psychosocial needs may lead to lack of basic trust (see Erikson, 1963) and difficulties in future relationships. An example of emotional neglect is given below.

Case 3.2 Emotional neglect

Twins Robert and Rachel, aged nine years, live with their parents in a comfortable, detached house with two garages and a very neat garden, complete with decking and a water feature. Their father, Mike, works away from home much of the time and their mother, Mary, also works full-time in a demanding post in the Civil Service. She commutes quite some distance each day and brings work home with her in the evenings. So she has little time for the twins, who let themselves into the house after school and fend for themselves until Mary comes in from work. Mary has always been a private and reserved person with no friends. She suspects that Mike is having an affair. She has never really related emotionally to the twins, perhaps because their birth was so long and arduous. From an early age they were kept in their bedroom. Mary has always needed to keep the house exceptionally clean and tidy and could not tolerate the disruptions to orderliness which babies bring. At first the twins had baby toys to play with but were never given any new playthings, so those they had became increasingly inappropriate as they grew older. Even now, the twins have to eat and entertain themselves in their bedroom. They receive no help with homework and they spend most of their time at home with no company other than each other. Mike and Mary are unaware that their lack of involvement with their children is so unusual. They were both brought up in strictly regulated homes with distant parents. The teachers at the twins' school have become concerned because both children are so pale, withdrawn and depressed. They have very poor language and social skills and are falling further and further behind in their school work.

Risk factors for emotional abuse

According to Roberts (1988), when parents have experienced an unhappy childhood, with the features of separation, rejection and being abused, there may be a vulnerability to relationship problems throughout development and into adulthood. These may be expressed in marital difficulties and problems in their relationships with their own children which may be abusive. If parents are young and immature and have few resources for coping with stress, they are more likely to take drugs and/or consume excessive amounts of alcohol; they may be vulnerable to social isolation and have diffuse social problems which may not be easy to identify. Such parents often have unrealistic expectations of the child – the children who are not abused tend to be those who are more intelligent and achieving.

Neglect

The severe neglect of a child was defined by the Department of Health (2000) as:

> The persistent failure to meet a child's physical and/or psychological needs, likely to result in the impairment of the child's health or development. It may involve a parent or carer failing to provide adequate food, shelter and clothing, failing to protect a child from physical harm or danger, or the failure to ensure access to appropriate medical care or treatment. It may also include neglect of, or unresponsiveness to, a child's basic emotional needs. (p6)

Polansky et al. (1976) provided additional examples of situations which demonstrate neglect:

- if the child is left unattended
- if the child fails to attend school regularly
- if he is exploited or overworked.

The above definition emphasises that the effect on the child is important, but can be criticised as being vague in its terminology regarding the failure to meet the 'child's physical and/or psychological needs' and 'impairment of the child's health or development'. A definition of 'good enough' parenting and conditions of child-rearing, including minimum acceptable standards, needs to be added. The definition goes some way towards explaining the circumstances of neglect, but does not include a notion of cultural relativity and the material or personal resources available to caregivers in relation to minimum acceptable standards. These are described in the next section. Case 3.3 is an example of child neglect.

Case 3.3 **Child neglect**

Lee and Sharon are heroin addicts in their mid-twenties. They have two children, Lee and Mel, aged eight and six, who have a very poor record of attendance at school. The school has informed social services that they think there are problems at home. Lee and Mel are small and underdeveloped physically for their age, dirty and unkempt, with poor, unwashed and inadequate clothing. Although eligible for free school meals, they bring lunch with them of bread and margarine. They both suffer from poor concentration and hyperactivity. Also, their facial expression is often one of wariness and distrust. They suffer from perpetual colds and never have a handkerchief. Both children have had bronchitis several times, scabies and frequent diarrhoea. When a social worker visited their home, she discovered both parents in a very poor state of health, with a complete disregard of their children's needs. The house was cold, damp and dirty, with inadequate furnishing and a lack of toys and books. All available money, much of it illegally obtained, is used to feed the parents' drug habit.

Risk factors for neglect

These are similar to those for emotional abuse as the two kinds of maltreatment frequently occur together. Pre-eminent are the conditions of social inadequacy (parents with physical and mental health problems and few resources for coping with stress) and social deprivation (poverty, poor housing, undernutrition and lack of social life and cultural opportunities) (Garbarino et al., 1988).

Sexual abuse

Child sexual abuse was defined in the Department of Health (2000) guidelines as:

> forcing or enticing a child or young person to take part in sexual activities, whether or not the child is aware of what is happening. The activities may involve physical contact, including penetrative (e.g. rape or buggery) and non-penetrative acts. They may include non-contact activities, such as involving children in looking at, or in the production of, pornographic material or watching sexual activities or encouraging children to behave in sexually inappropriate ways. (p6)

This definition is useful in that it states that sexual abuse need not involve physical contact, and includes various activities associated with pornography. This latter seems to be becoming an increasingly significant problem, as there are so many new ways of producing and disseminating pornographic material involving the internet and other aspects of new technology.

Hobbs et al. (1998) state their preference for the definition of Schechter and Roberge (1976) which is that sexual abuse is

> the involvement of dependent, developmentally immature children and adolescents in sexual activity that they do not fully comprehend and to which they are unable to give informed consent or that violate the taboos of family roles.

This second definition emphasises the involvement of family members who are contravening the accepted child-rearing practices of care, protection and encouragement of physical and mental development. Sexually abused children are frequently exploited by those who should be protecting them, thus violating trust in these relationships. The children have their sense of control over their bodies and their relationships taken away; such events are often associated with abnormal expressions of sexuality, bodily disturbance expressed later in self-mutilation and eating disorders and problems in establishing mature adult relationships (Hobbs et al., 1998). The example of Meg in Case 3.4 illustrates some fairly typical features of sexual abuse.

Case 3.4 Sexual abuse

Meg is an attractive 18-year-old student from a professional family who attends the student health service very frequently. She suffers from asthma and eczema, problems with control of her appetite and bouts of bulimia. She agrees to see a counsellor who uncovers the family secret of incest. Starting when she was a young girl, Meg's father had sat her on his knee, stroked her and gradually began sexually stimulating her. This progressed to further incidents at bathtime and bedtime, with Meg being required to become more active in stimulating her father. By the time she was in her teens, full intercourse was carried out on a regular basis. Meg was sworn to secrecy by her father who said that if she told her mother it would destroy her. Her mother was already on medication for emotional problems. The family had always been socially isolated. Also, Meg felt guilty because she had done what she was told and she thought that perhaps this was just an expression of her father's genuine love for her.

Incest occurs between members of the same family, the most frequent being father–daughter relationships. Often the young girl is coerced into keeping the activity secret by means of threats or bribes or both. The father may lead his daughter to believe that she is responsible by emphasising her attractiveness and involvement, while the motivation and power is all his. He is gratifying his sexual needs at the expense of the needs for security and self-esteem of his child. It is therefore not surprising that the child develops a destructive confusion about her self-worth and a distortion of her relationships with other people.

Molestation refers to acts by people outside the family, who are often known to the child but who may be strangers. Such acts are much less common than within-family sexual abuse. It is, however, very difficult to estimate the actual incidence of sexual abuse, as it is associated with such shame, guilt and fear on the part of the child that it is highly likely that it will not be disclosed.

Incidence of child sexual abuse

Estimates vary with the method of investigation used. Disclosure is more likely the closer the relationship between researcher and participant, so questionnaire studies elicit lower rates than face-to-face interviews (Finkelhor, 1986). Finkelhor estimates that at least 10 per cent of the female population have experienced some form of sexual exposure before the age of 16, the figure for males being somewhat lower at about 5 per cent. Finkelhor also points out that these are conservative estimates, as people may not remember, or choose not to report, incidents of sexual abuse.

The signs and symptoms of abuse are of two main types – physical and behavioural. The frequency of penetrative abuse is high at all ages, being mainly anal or oral in younger children. Hobbs (1990) reports that in one study of sexually abused children, 27 of 30 boys and 40 of 85 girls reported penetration.

Physical symptoms of pain, soreness, swelling, bleeding, herpes and difficulty in urinating or defecating frequently result. Common behavioural signs are fear, anxiety, withdrawal, anger and passivity, and inappropriate sexual behaviour. When physical and behavioural signs occur together, diagnosis is more likely. Developmental delay often co-occurs.

Difficulties in diagnosing sexual abuse

Any of the above signs can occur for other reasons, so it is the overall effect upon the child which has to be considered. The incidences reported vary markedly in studies using different types of populations and definitions of abuse which are more or less inclusive. There is a general agreement among professionals that reported cases of child sexual abuse, of different types and differing degrees of severity, merely represent the tip of the iceberg. Many studies ask for retrospective reports, sometimes of events of a very long time ago and those recalled will probably not be representative of the actual incidence of different events. Then there are unknown cases, never reported, and the prevalence of these will be influenced by the societal attitudes which prevail at the time. For example, the acceptance of sexism and pornography, and other forms of exploitation of women and children, will make it less likely that the victim of sexual abuse will reveal the fact to others, for fear of stigmatisation or other negative reactions.

Although different types of abuse have been described separately for the sake of clarity, it is evident that different forms of abuse often occur together. Physical abuse and physical neglect co-occur, as do physical and emotional abuse, and in 10 per cent of cases Hobbs found that sexual abuse coexisted with physical injury.

Risk factors for sexual abuse

Finkelhor (1984) described the risk factors as including having a stepfather, living for a period without a mother, not being emotionally close to the mother, having a mother who is poorly educated and punitive about sexual matters, and having fewer than three friends in childhood. Therefore the vulnerable child is isolated, easily exploited and living in close proximity to an adult who did not form an early close relationship with the child.

Perpetrator characteristics include a history of any kind of abuse, having a criminal record, having limited social skills and poor self-esteem, and under- or overcontrol of aggression (Williams and Finkelhor, 1995). The only kinds of mental illness associated with engagement in child sexual abuse are personality disorder or paedophilia, and neither of these are present in the majority of perpetrators.

When other factors are controlled for, there is no association of sexual abuse with particular socioeconomic (Russell, 1983) or ethnic groups.

Summary

The abuse of children at the hands of adults is not a recent phenomenon. Historical study shows that for centuries various abusive practices have been widespread in many societies. Children have even been deliberately killed, particularly as young infants. Different groups of children have always been particularly at risk, the most vulnerable often being those who were unwanted, perhaps because they were female, imperfect or disabled. Today, child abuse is still widespread and is argued to arise and be maintained by a number of factors, varying from the societal level to interpersonal and intrapersonal characteristics. Explanations have focused on interactions between social processes associated with poverty, deprivation and exploitation of those who are powerless and the dynamics of family life. Society as a whole has a shared responsibility for the perpetuation of child abuse.

It is very difficult to estimate the frequency of occurrence of abuse as reporting rates vary in different sectors of society and between different societies. The very definition of what constitutes abuse is socially defined and varies between cultures and contexts. Different kinds of abuse have different degrees of visibility, emotional abuse being especially hard to detect. Also different kinds of abuse very frequently co-occur, but there is single registration in official statistics in the UK. When suspected cases of abuse are investigated, a relatively small percentage are verified, with the child placed on the at risk register or other outcome.

The different kinds of abuse – physical, emotional, sexual and neglect – have different definitions, as their focus is on different aspects of the relationship between perpetrator(s) and victim. The identifiable features of the abuse may be physical, for example in bruises and burns; emotional, when the child may be very withdrawn, frightened and unhappy; sexual, where inappropriate sexualisation of child behaviour or damage to the child's genitals may occur. In neglect the child may be ill-clad and emaciated. The risk factors for the different types of abuse also differ. In physical abuse, there is often a family history of violence and belief in physical punishment, combined with problematic living conditions. In emotional abuse, the parent was often abused as a child, had poor attachment and relationship problems throughout life; social isolation of the family also features. The risk factors for neglect are similar to those of emotional abuse (they frequently co-occur), with social inadequacy and social deprivation pre-eminent. In situations of sexual abuse, a distorted marital relationship, lack of attachment by a parent to the child, and isolation of the child are important factors. Overall, there is evidence that interactions between interpersonal processes and sociostructural variables are significant in the aetiology (origin) of all kinds of abuse.

Explanations of child abuse

Listed below are some of the factors that have been associated with child abuse. It should be noted that the degree of risk of abuse depends upon the type of abuse under consideration.

1. *Poverty.* There is a strong correlation between poverty and physical abuse and neglect, whereas sexual abuse is spread across all strata of society to a much greater extent (Corby, 1993).
2. *Age of parent.* Physical abuse has a stronger association with younger parents, while sexual abuse is more likely to be attributable to older offenders.
3. *Adolescent perpetrators.* Adolescents of both sexes are often violent or aggressive towards younger siblings, and 20 per cent of all sexual abuse has been attributed to adolescent offenders (Davis and Leitenberg, 1987).
4. *Sex of offender.* Adult males are much more likely to be abusive than females. It is estimated (Cicchetti and Carlson, 1989) that, in two-parent households, two-thirds of physical abuse is by males and that in 90 per cent of sexual abuse cases, the perpetrator is male. Different studies have different findings for gender differences in abusiveness. They often fail to take into account how much time each adult spends in contact with the children.
5. *Sex and age of the child.* In many families, only one child is the victim of abuse and the other children may even be cared for

well. Girls are more at risk than boys, particularly for sexual abuse, where the ratio is 4/5 to 1. The risk of being sexually abused increases with age, whereas that of being physically abused decreases.

6. *Physical characteristics of the baby or young child.* Prematurity and associated problems, for example with feeding; disability, either physical or intellectual and birth injuries; ill health in the child and a personality characterised by irritability, inconsistency, irregularity of functioning, lack of adaptability and a tendency to cry a lot. In many cases, the child is seen by the parent as unlovable. The pregnancy may have been unplanned, the mother deserted by the father during pregnancy, there may be lack of support for the mother before and after the birth, pre- or postnatal illness. All these circumstances would increase the stresses upon the parent(s) (see Kempe and Kempe, 1978) and make the likelihood of abuse greater.

7. *Family structure.* Different family structures seem to be associated with different probabilities of different kinds of abuse, with the incidence of physical abuse being overrepresented in lone-parent and reconstituted families (for example Creighton and Noyes, 1989). On the other hand, sexual abuse is more likely to be instigated by stepfathers than biological fathers, the difference in ratio of abusers to non-abusers being 1 in 6 step-fathers compared with 1 in 40 biological fathers (Russell, 1983). These figures seem to present a very high rate of abuse, so the nature of the sample studied needs to be taken into account when considering the extent to which these findings can be generalised. With regard to the question of abuse by lone parents, Kempe and Kempe (1978) have reported the opposite finding, that lone mothers are less likely to physically abuse their children, perhaps because they know that they have sole responsibility for those children.

Expanding on the last point, when individual variables are considered in isolation from the whole circumstances of abusive incidents, undue importance may be attached to particular factors, such as the age of the mother and whether she has a partner or not. These factors are likely to be confounded with low income in many families, and many other aspects of personal and family functioning will be relevant.

Kempe and Kempe (1978) noted that abuse may occur across the range of the distribution of parenting abilities, and that inadequate parenting occurs in all socioeconomic groupings. There is frequently, but not necessarily, repetition of abuse, neglect and parental loss or deprivation from one generation to the next (this will be discussed further later). One factor that parents who physically abuse their children seem to have in common is a belief in the efficacy of physical punishment as a means of controlling their children. In general, Kempe and Kempe's findings have been substantiated over the years, with regard to physical and emotional abuse and neglect which commonly co-occur.

Kempe and Kempe (1978) described a number of characteristics of the parent(s) and the parents' circumstances which elevate the risk of physical abuse:

- low intelligence
- poor state of health
- personalities characterised by immaturity, impulsivity and lack of planning
- poor marital relationship in which they fail to support each other
- isolation from social support outside the family (see also Figure 3.1).

Models of abuse

As illustrated in Chapter 1, there is a relationship between theories, models and interventions. Theories provide an explanatory framework, linking together different variables involved in particular phenomena, such as child abuse, and make predictions about related events. Theory can be operationalised in the form of models to explain particular processes and specify more precise relationships between variables. Such understanding forms a basis for intervention. The following models demonstrate the complexity of the influences involved in an abusive situation. They place different emphasis on particular groups of factors, such as parental characteristics or features of the socioeconomic background, and are related to different developmental theories.

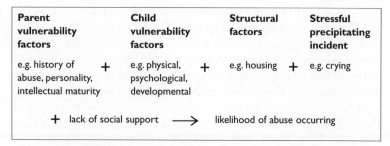

Figure 3.1 A model of Kempe and Kempe's (1978) findings on the contributing factors in child abuse

Kempe and Kempe's (1978) model

An incident of physical abuse typically occurs in the presence of risk factors in the parent and the child, but also when an environmental circumstance triggers the abuse. This crisis may be the result of a long period of build-up of tension and anxiety in the home, perhaps due to the baby crying for a sustained period, where the parent is not coping. Eventually, a trivial incident, such as difficulty in feeding or when the baby soils a clean nappy a number of times in quick succession, may be the last straw, and constitutes the provoking stimulus for the abuse.

Thus, a model which predicts the occurrence of abuse (see Figure 3.1) must be multifactorial and include risk factors in the family background, particularly the parent(s) life history, risk factors in the parent and the child and a circumstance which triggers the abuse. In addition, because the family is isolated there is nowhere to turn for help to prevent the abuse from happening; there is no available social support. This makes it likely that the abuse will remain hidden, particularly if the child is less than school-age.

Belsky's (1980) model

This model is similar to that of Kempe and Kempe but more extensive, building upon the different environmental systems in the ecological theory of Bronfenbrenner (1979) as well as the individual development of parent and child. Belsky describes the determinants of abuse in terms of risk and compensatory factors occurring at the ontogenetic level (which he sees as most important in determining parenting behaviour), as well as at the levels of the microsystem, the exosystem and the macrosystem (see Cicchetti and Carlson, 1989, p139 for a full description). Belsky (1993) develops these ideas further and these are presented later in this chapter.

Peterson and Brown's (1994) model

A more recent model for child injury is provided by Peterson and Brown (1994) and is shown in Table 3.1. The factors implicated as contributors to child injury by Peterson and Brown include aspects of the adult, the child and the environment, and thus represents a model similar to that of Belsky. The environmental factors are divided into background and immediate contributors and, as such, are similar to the earlier ideas of Kempe and Kempe. All these characterise components of sociocultural deprivation or risk.

Sociocultural risk was described by Garbarino et al. (1988) as 'the impoverishing of the child's world so that the child lacks the basic social and psychological necessities of life' (p32). The main sociocultural risk is poverty, with those with the lowest incomes being at highest risk of injuring their child(ren). When the high-

TABLE 3.1 FACTORS CONTRIBUTING TO CHILD INJURY (AFTER PETERSON AND BROWN, 1994)

	Sociocultural variables	Caregiver-based variables	Child-based variables

Background contributors	Poverty
	Chaos
	Crowding
	Change in residence
		Abused
		Emotional
		  disturbance
		Substance abuse
		Young, single
		Unrealistic
		  expectations
		Discipline patterns
			0–4 years old
			Non-rhythmic
			Distractable
			High activity

Immediate contributors	Stress Isolation Impulsiveness	Need for control Ineffective discipline	Non-compliance

risk environment is combined with a parental factor such as maternal depression and child behaviours of negativity and hyper-activity, the likelihood of abuse is particularly high. Indeed, maternal depression alone raises the risk four times when socio-economic status is controlled for. Emotional distress in caregivers is a feature of many or most situations of child abuse and accompa-nies many circumstances of family disturbance. The experience of distress is common to all parents and indicates the potential in all of us to be abusive. This should be emphasised rather than the differences between abusive and non-abusive caregivers.

Theories of child abuse

Psychiatric

Different explanations of how and why abuse of children comes about have placed differing emphasis on different components of the equation of abuse. The earliest theories focused on the perpe-trator as pathological, assuming that he had some form of mental illness. This was believed, despite the finding of Kempe and Kempe (1978) that only 10 per cent of perpetrators could be iden-tified as being seriously psychopathological. However, the likeli-hood of abuse is increased in families where one or both parents is an alcoholic or a drug addict. Overall though, the psychiatric approach draws attention away from the general population where most abuse occurs.

Social learning theory

Another prevailing early view emphasised the importance of the environment and the role of social learning (Bandura, 1977) in the genesis of physical abuse of children. Evidence that the tendency to solve problems with aggressive acts, and to respond to frustrations with aggressive behaviour, was learned in the family from an early age provided the basis of an explanation of the 'intergenerational transmission' of abuse. Parents who abused their children had a higher probability of having had a childhood of exposure to deprivation, harsh parenting and being abused themselves than parents who were non-abusive (Kempe et al., 1962). However, many adults who were abused as children do *not* go on to become abusive themselves. The work of Hunter and Kilstrom (1979) and Egeland and Jacobvitz (1984) demonstrated that at least two-thirds of parents who had themselves been abused were able to break out of the cycle of abuse. Belsky (1993) criticised Hunter and Kilstrom's conclusions as being based on inadequate evidence. Hunter and Kilstrom considered that the cycle of abuse was broken if the target child being studied had not been abused by the age of one year. There was no information as to what happened subsequently. Therefore it is critically important that the long-term experiences of children should be studied. The age at which abuse occurs and the duration of the maltreatment both influence the ways in which the effects of the abuse on the child are demonstrated.

Kaufman and Zigler (1987) criticised the evidence in support of the transmission model as unreliable, in that it was usually based on retrospective reports (which may involve under- or over-reporting) and involved biased samples, many of them clinical. Clarke and Clarke (2000) point out that those who sexually abuse were not necessarily abused themselves. Interviews with 53 abusers in prison revealed that only 41 per cent reported that they had been sexually abused themselves early in life. It could be that the abuse occurred too early in the child's life to be recalled, but it does support the evidence that there are other processes through which abuse is generated.

The importance of the longer term family history is also emphasised by Cicchetti and Rizley (1981). They argue that parental history is not unidimensional and many factors may intervene and interact to determine parenting outcome. Potentiating factors which may increase the likelihood of becoming abusive include difficulties in attachment, and not having had the opportunity to form a stable attachment at any subsequent stage in childhood, psychological immaturity, lack of forward planning and living in poor social conditions (Rutter, 1989a). Compensatory factors which exemplify non-abusive parents are having had good interpersonal relationships in adolescence, success in educational tasks at school, marriage to a non-deviant man (Quinton et al., 1984) and competence in understanding and adapting to the parent–child relationship (Newberger and

Cook, 1983). The relevance of the developmental maturity of the parents in the aetiology of abuse highlights the importance of the developmental dimension, not just of the child's developmental status but the changing functioning of family dynamics over time.

Attachment

Attachment history has been implicated in the development of abuse. George (1996) argues that the nature of parenting derives from the working model of the attachment relationship which develops in infancy, and this guides the way in which parents perceive, emotionally experience and interact with their own children. A number of different attachment patterns have been identified since the early work of Ainsworth (Ainsworth and Wittig, 1969; Ainsworth et al., 1971) which described differences between secure and insecure attachment relationships:

• secure attachment patterns were characterised by a self which was loved, autonomous and competent and saw others as available, cooperative and dependable
• insecure patterns were of two types:
    (i)   avoidant, in which the parent was rejecting
    (ii) ambivalent, in which the parent was neglecting and unreliable.

In both of these the child felt unloved and of low value. Later, Main and Solomon (1986) identified a fourth type of attachment. This was an insecure-disorganised pattern characterised by the child feeling negative and confused and the parent as frightening and unavailable (see also Chapter 1).

In the first three types of attachment relationship, the child organises his behaviour in adaptive response, which may involve defensive strategies to reduce anxiety and elicit caregiving, to the requirements of the relationship and to achieve some kind of proximity and 'felt security' from which to explore the world. In interactions with the child, the model of the attachment figures and the relationship between them will guide the reactions of the parent. Situations involving dispute or disagreement will involve heightened feelings which will trigger characteristic ways of regulating feelings, involving the defensive styles employed at times of stress. Some will be unable to cope with the emotional needs of the young child and will withdraw emotionally and become rejecting or dismissive (Main, 1995). The frustration of dealing with a child's negativity may lead to inappropriate attempts to control the child with heavy physical punishment; alternatively, emotion may be denied so the child is told to 'grow up' or 'be a big boy' (Crittenden, 1992).

It is estimated (Howe et al., 1999) that 80 per cent of maltreated infants are classified as disorganised or disorientated in attachment behaviour. Parents who abuse their children are unresponsive or respond unpredictably in negative or traumatic ways. This leads to the children perceiving themselves as unlovable, lacking confidence in their care, and the worse the care is, the more likely the child is to experience intense or chronic fear (Bowlby, 1980). Despite this, maltreated children do form selective attachments to caregivers (Ainsworth and Wittig, 1969), but these tend to be of the disorganised type and associated with defensive patterns of behaviour by the child as well as the parent. These include 'freezing' or psychological opting out, identifying with the source of the fear (seeing the self as bad) or becoming absorbed in self-feedback behaviours such as rocking or self-harm, which are at least under the child's own control. The more disorganised the attachment, the more aggressive are the children in later childhood. Thus, in many ways, the child behaviours mirror those of the parent and provide the foundations for difficult relationships with peers and subsequently with other adults. This is one mechanism whereby abusive relationships may develop out of earlier dysfunctional interpersonal behaviours. The parents' own attachment history as insecure and their experience of being parented, perhaps abusively, in their own childhood constitute risk factors for various kinds of insecure attachments with their own children, as well as being abusive towards them (Peterson and Brown, 1994).

Multifactorial theories

Recent explanations of why child maltreatment occurs have postulated the involvement of many factors operating at different levels in the social ecology, involving interactions or transactions between factors or groups of factors.

Garbarino (1982) explained abuse as being the result of interactions between societal and familial factors. Social stresses such as poor housing, unemployment and low income exert pressures on families and some families, with the characteristics described previously, are less able to cope with these stresses and one result is an outburst of aggression in the form of child abuse. When families are socially isolated, perhaps because they are dysfunctional, they will not have the social networks in place to mitigate the negative effects of stress. There is evidence to support Garbarino's views in the elevated incidence of abuse in families living in poverty, and in those families which are highly mobile as in the armed forces (James et al., 1984). Of course it could be the case that individuals with higher than average aggressive tendencies are more likely to join the forces.

Thus the identified risk factors for child abuse are organised into different contextual systems and the interactions between them. The influences stemming from the macrosystem are those that have been least integrated into the models of perpetrator and victim in a particular social milieu. Particularly important in the macrosystem is the cultural acceptance of violence and corporal punishment of children, the social learning of aggressive means of relating to others and the learning of maladaptive patterns of behaviour in distorted attachment relationships. The relationships between risk and compensatory factors are bidirectional. For example, early experience of relationships can influence the quality of the marital relationship and a good marital relationship may modify recollections or effects of adverse experiences in childhood.

Belsky (1993) updated his model of the aetiology of child maltreatment, which he now refers to as a 'developmental-ecological' analysis. This describes and discusses the various 'contexts of maltreatment'. One of Belsky's emphases is on the many pathways that are available to abuse and neglect, the importance of the balance of stressors to supports in determining the likelihood of abuse, and the many variables involved. Thus, studies which look for main effects are not examining the most important effects, which will be interactions between variables. Thus, as Bronfenbrenner put it, as long ago as 1979, the 'principal main effects are likely to be interactions'. Other methodological problems in studies of child abuse described by Belsky as being rarely attended to are the severity or chronicity of the abuse, and the comorbidity of different kinds of abuse, which Belsky states has been found to be as high as 100 per cent. Furthermore, most studies are cross-sectional and this methodology does not allow for the analysis of causative influences which longitudinal studies would permit.

The ecological-transactional (ET) approach

An approach which incorporates a longitudinal element as well as a number of ecological contexts, with varying degrees of proximity to the individual, and which interact and transact over time, has been used by Lynch and Cicchetti (1998) as a way of understanding the relationship between child maltreatment and the type of community the child grows up in. This analysis therefore integrates the transactional (Sameroff and Chandler, 1975) and the ecological (Bronfenbrenner, 1977) approaches.

A sample of 322 children in summer camp in two consecutive years was studied to test a number of different hypotheses generated from the ET model in relation to the child's developmental status (internalising and externalising behaviour problems, depression and self-esteem) and the contexts of the child's ecology (child maltreatment, level of community violence, witnessing violence) (Lynch and Cichetti, 1998). Evidence was found that different levels of the ecology influenced each other, for example the levels of community violence and physical abuse in families. Also, factors from different levels of the ecological context mutually shaped individual development. Both child maltreatment and exposure to community violence were related to a number of different measures of child adaptation, and they seemed to have an additive effect. The effects of the wider community were evident, even when more proximal contextual factors were controlled for, so may exert a direct effect on children's functioning.

Other hypotheses supported were of continuity between earlier and later measures of child functioning and contexts, although because correlations were only of moderate size, there was obviously change as well as continuity occurring. There were mutual influences between child and environment which helped to maintain continuity in the context and functioning of individuals, but change in either could introduce change into the system. Continuity was demonstrated by involvement in violence one year previously being associated with current functioning; a stronger relationship was found between earlier functioning in the form of externalising problem behaviours predicting later victimisation by, and witnessing of, violence in the community.

This ecological-transactional model of the relationship between community, child maltreatment and child functioning operationalises the factors which need to be taken into account when explaining the occurrence of child abuse. The relationship between 'potentiating' and 'compensatory' risk factors for the individual (Cicchetti and Rizley, 1981) at different levels of the ecology transact over time, influencing the likelihood of abuse and the developmental outcomes for the child (see next section). Such a model is securely based in theory, generates testable hypotheses, produces findings that can suggest interventions to minimise traumatic child experiences and outcomes, and, as such, is seen as the most useful way of conceptualising child abuse. It will be revisited in the final chapter of this text.

Summary

Many explanations of how and why child abuse happens have been offered by different researchers. These differ according to the level of explanation, from the sociocultural to the individual, and where interactions, or transactions, between influences are involved, there is variable emphasis on different factors. The early explanations tended to focus on the characteristics of the individual perpetrator as being abnormal in some way. But it became apparent that not all the children in a particular family are abused, and so characteristics of the individual child became important, and the quality of the relationship between adult and child. Thus, explanations involving concepts of attachment, social learning, such as modelling and imitation of aggression, and parental history and parenting style were developed. Abuse within families occurs within a sociocultural context, and the frequency of occurrence of some types of abuse varies between social groups.

So the current theories of the cause of child abuse are multifactorial, involving variables at all the different levels of the ecology as well as individual characteristics and family history.

Short- and long-term effects of abuse

As Johnson and Cohn (1990) comment, there are no psychological disorders which have not been associated with child maltreatment. Thus, the possible effects of child abuse are many and varied, with emotional consequences constituting a final common pathway of physical and sexual abuse and neglect. It should not be assumed, however, that children will necessarily experience negative after-effects of abuse. As Kagan (1983) points out, there are a number of variables which will influence the likelihood of negative effects. These are the child's age, prior interactions with parents, the child's interpretation of the abusive act and specific relationship with the perpetrator.

Methodological problems

It has been noted by a number of researchers that there are considerable methodological difficulties in estimating the effects of child abuse or maltreatment:

- the evidence differs depending upon the nature of the samples used (whether clinical, student or general population)
- there is a lack of standardised outcome measures
- usually no adequate comparison groups are used
- most studies only measure the effects of abuse at one point in time so may well find different effects, and are unable to look at the development and disappearance of effects longitudinally
- many studies are retrospective and open to the biases that long-term memory entails.

However, it is possible to identify some effects as being frequently associated with abuse, either in the short or long term. The most frequently occurring effects of physical and sexual abuse are emotional ones, that is, fear, anxiety, aggression, depression and anger.

In the longer term, these emotions become represented in poor interpersonal relationships, low self-esteem, self-destructive behaviour, problems with school work, substance abuse, post-traumatic stress disorder (PTSD), inappropriate sexual behaviour and feelings of isolation and stigma.

A number of characteristics of the abusive situation contribute to the likelihood of long-term effects. Longer-lasting experiences of abuse are more traumatic so that a series of incidents of abuse are associated with more long-term effects than an isolated incident. The use of threats or actual force accompanying the abuse has a more negative impact, as does abuse by adults rather than other children, by males rather than females and by fathers or stepfathers in particular. So those people who are normally expected to be carers, supporters and protectors of their children are those who are more frightening when they are abusive. Another set of circumstances associated with more trauma is when the child is not supported by other non-abusing adults and is removed from his home when knowledge of the abuse becomes public.

A stress model of the effects of abuse

A number of different researchers (see Johnson and Cohn, 1990; Hartman and Burgess, 1989) have argued that the experience of child abuse can be accounted for as a highly stressful circumstance, with the whole process of recovery being one of coping with a number of different stressors at different stages in the process.

Thus, as Johnson and Cohn describe:

- the actual abuse is stressful because of the threat of harm, or actual harm, inflicted by the perpetrator, who is himself lacking in stress management skills and this contributes to the likelihood of abuse taking place
- how 'stress-producing' a particular child is may also contribute to the likelihood of this specific child rather than others being abused (see Peterson and Brown, 1994)
- the chronically stressful circumstances in which the abusive family are frequently living – poverty, ill health, poor family

relationships – combined with the acute stress of a triggering incident – developmental, interpersonal or structural – all contribute to the likelihood of abuse occurring (see Kempe and Kempe, 1978)

- the consequences of the abuse constitute stress symptoms and the difficulties of coping with the damage, disability and even death which may follow the abuse
- disclosure of the abuse and the circumstances of treatment also involve stresses of different kinds.

Hartman and Burgess discuss the child's possible reactions to sexual abuse in terms of the symptoms of 'primary' and 'secondary response patterns'. The acute symptoms of the primary stress response are:

- physical (for example psychosomatic, vomiting, gynaecological and urinogenital)
- psychological (such as lack of concentration, day-dreaming, anxiety and depression)
- behavioural (such as sexual orientation, masturbation, decline in school performance).

Secondary stress response patterns develop if the abuse continues over a period of time and the child has adapted in defensive ways to the circumstances. These can be organised as:

- emotional reactions and self-perceptions (for instance fear, anxiety, isolation, stigma, self-abuse and suicide attempts)
- interpersonal relating and sexuality (for example difficulty in trusting others, anger against both sexes, sexual dysfunction, accompanied by flashbacks)
- social functioning (such as prostitution and substance abuse).

In the case of tertiary stress, the victim may not exhibit primary or secondary stress symptoms but instead identifies with the perpetrator and later may become a molester of children himself.

Thus, there is considerable consistency in the accounts of the stress-related possible consequences of child maltreatment. Accounts which utilise a stress framework can integrate causes and consequences within a unitary schema.

Developmental effects of child abuse

A developmental perspective on sexual abuse

Finkelhor (1995) considered the effects of sexual abuse in terms of the different forms of expression and different processes involved in children at different developmental stages. Post-traumatic stress disorder (PTSD) may result from the stress of sexual abuse and the symptoms are different in young children from those shown by older ones. Terr (1983, 1991) found that the younger victims had less psychic numbing and fewer visual flashbacks, but had additional problems. These were associated with a foreshortened view of the future and inability to look and plan ahead. The frequently reported sexualisation effects are overt in children aged two to six years, but there is sexual inhibition in older children and adolescents. Effects on development tend to be long term and pervasive because they reflect the distortion of the normal developmental processes, such as attachment or the development of autonomy, and restrict the achievement of normal developmental tasks or accomplishments.

With regard to cognitive development, appraisal of events may be affected in such a way as to show a negative bias and expectation of threat; in preschool children, fantasy abilities are developing and these too will be negatively influenced; dissociation, whereby the abusive events become compartmentalised into a particular unconscious part of the personality and experience, may be used as a mechanism of ego defence, with a resultant personality disorder (Putnam, 1991).

In young children, there may possibly be protection from some of the cognitive realisation as to what has happened in the way of abusive incidents through buffering by a non-abusive parent; the recognition of abuse may not occur because they lack the concepts, but realisation may occur later when older and create new disturbance.

In older children, physiological change such as the early onset of puberty can result from sexual abuse and be very alarming to the child (Putnam and Trickett, 1993), and increased cortisol production associated with stress is linked with behaviour problems.

Overall, then, the symptoms of child sexual abuse depend upon the child's cognitive and emotional developmental level, the available behaviours and the norms of behaviour at a particular age. Thus, a reaction to abuse in a preschool child may be disruptive behaviour which is replaced by self-blame and depression later on. Maladaptive means of coping such as substance abuse and self-harm are only shown by older children and adolescents.

The Minnesota Mother–Child Interaction Project

As argued previously, the developmental consequences of different kinds of abuse are best investigated by longitudinal studies, for example the Minnesota Project, because changes in behaviour with age and developmental status can be observed in the same children. The Minnesota Project examined the full range of qualitative aspects of caregiving but also focused on the question of whether specific patterns of maltreatment resulted in specific developmental outcomes. The four maltreatment groups identified were:

1. physically abused
2. verbally abused
3. neglected
4. children with psychologically unavailable mothers.

Although there was considerable co-occurrence of these different types, these were separated in the data analyses. A control group allowed the examination of other environmental influences such as poverty (Erickson et al., 1989).

The consequences for each maltreated group were varied and severe – functioning was worse in many aspects of social and emotional behaviour at each developmental stage compared with non-maltreated children from similar backgrounds:

- at 12 months, the physically abused children showed no effects
- at 18 months, they were more likely to show an anxious pattern of attachment (50 per cent compared with 29 per cent in the control group)
- at 24 months, the abused children were more angry and non-compliant when frustrated
- by 42 months, when faced with a task to do alone, the children in the abused group were more hyperactive and distractible, had less self-control and were more negative.

Overall, the physically abused children lacked persistence, enthusiasm for intellectual effort and creativity. These adjustment problems continued in later measures at four and five years of age.

The group subjected to hostile/verbal abuse showed behaviours similar to those in the physically abused group, which was not surprising in view of the considerable overlap between the groups. The neglected children also showed more attachment difficulties than the control group, in this case, anxious attachment. In the preschool children, they were also angry, negative and impulsive in their responses, lacking in positive behaviours and avoidant, yet reliant upon their mothers. Neglected children who were not also physically abused showed little difference from those subjected to both forms of maltreatment. So, neglect has an independent causative relationship with poor development.

The most striking findings came from the group of children whose mothers were psychologically unavailable, as expressed by a severe decline in competence during the early years. Security of attachment declined (44 per cent secure at 12 months but only 29 per cent at 18 months); negativity, non-compliance and lack of self-control became more severe. In the preschool years they were highly dependent on their teachers and showed many adjustment problems, both at home and at school. This latter pattern of child maltreatment was especially damaging to the child's development in the early years. This is important, as the emotional unavailability of parent(s) is the least likely form of maltreatment to be detected.

At six years, the neglected group of children showed the most severe and varied problems. Their cognitive development was much worse than other groups. Their classroom behaviours of inattention, anxiety, lack of comprehension and initiative and dependence upon the teacher impeded their success in educational tasks. It *may* be that the neglected children were particularly identifiable by their appearance, which led to negative expectations by teachers and a self-fulfilling prophesy with respect to school performance. The children of the psychologically unavailable mothers, although coping less well with academic tasks and social situations than the control group, were not as severely maladapted in their behaviour as in the earlier years. Perhaps emotional neglect then has greater effects in infancy. More detailed scrutiny of the families in this group showed that the children who were developing best had a loving relationship with another adult, a protective factor which modified the negative effects of the mother's unavailability.

When the participating families were studied at child ages of four to six years, an additional group was identified, that of sexually abused children. These children also showed a wide range of problems, which is not surprising considering the different circumstances of abuse. There were some general problems, though. The children tended to be impulsive and dependent, anxious and inattentive. Their social behaviour tended to be deviant, ranging from withdrawn to aggressive, and they had few friends. This social isolation from peers and dependency on adults constitute risk factors for further sexual abuse. The child's behaviour in physically abusive families may also be a stimulus for the continuation of physical harm – angry defiance and negativity leading to loss of temper and self-control in the adult.

The extent and severity of deviance in child development depend upon how chronic the abusive situation is and the age of the child when maltreatment occurs. Measures of intellectual development indicated worse scores for those children maltreated early in life, even if the abuse had since stopped, compared with children whose abuse started later in life. The early-abuse children also showed less confidence, assertiveness and initiative and were more sad and withdrawn. The currently abused children, irrespective of whether the abuse began early or later, had a greater need for closeness with, and dependency on, the teacher. Erickson et al. (1989) reported some suggestion from their data that if abuse occurred in the first two years, there were continuing adverse effects upon development which were very difficult to reverse even if the caregiving had improved.

Summary

The consequences of maltreatment for the development of the child are severe. They vary with the pattern and chronicity of the abuse, the nature of other relationships, and the age and developmental status of the child. The development of insecure attachments between the child and abusive parent may lay the foundations, through negative working models of individuals and relationships, for later social and emotional problems. The frequently occurring negativity, impulsivity and inattention shown by abused children are all behaviours which will hinder successful performance in educational tasks, and be associated with poor cognitive development. The ways in which the effects of abuse are expressed will depend upon the stage of emotional and cognitive development of the child. Abuse which occurs early in life may have continuing effects even after the abuse is no longer occurring. Some approaches to intervention to help families in which abuse is occurring are discussed in Chapter 6.

Conclusion

There are a number of different kinds of child abuse – physical, emotional and sexual abuse and neglect – which commonly co-occur. There are problems in defining and identifying each of these but emotional abuse and certain kinds of neglect are the most difficult to identify. There are many common risk factors for abuse in individuals and family circumstances but the processes whereby the abuse occurs will vary with different situations. Child maltreatment must be considered from developmental, psychological, relational and ecological perspectives in order to provide a meaningful account of the circumstances which are most likely to be associated with abuse. Theories of the aetiology of abuse must include factors interacting at many levels and a longitudinal analysis, that is, a multifactorial and ecological-transactional approach. Theories must also take into account the different kinds of maltreatment, in that different mechanisms may be important in the development of different kinds of abuse in families.

Discussion topics

1. Give your definition of child abuse.
2. Discuss the problems in providing an adequate definition of abuse.
3. What are the differences between physical abuse, emotional abuse, sexual abuse and neglect of children?
4. Discuss how different theories of child development relate to our understanding of child abuse.
5. To what extent are parental characteristics and background variables involved in different types of child abuse?

Recommended reading

Belsky, J. (1993) Etiology of child maltreatment: A developmental–ecological analysis. *Psychological Bulletin*, **114**, 413–34.

Corby, B. (2000) *Child Abuse. Towards a Knowledge Base* (2nd edn). Milton Keynes: Open University Press. An easy introduction to the topic of abuse and particularly good on definitions.

Finkelhor, D. (1995) The victimization of children: a developmental perspective. *American Journal of Orthopsychiatry*, **65**(2), 177–93.

Helfer, M.E., Kempe, R.S. and Krugman, R.D. (eds) (1997) *The Battered Child* (5th edn). Chicago: University of Chicago Press. A classic text which provides a comprehensive overview of the topic of child abuse.

Howe, D., Brandon, M., Hinings, D. and Schofield, G. (1999) *Attachment Theory, Child Maltreatment and Family Support*. Basingstoke: Macmillan – now Palgrave Macmillan. One of the few texts that is constructed around theory, in this case, attachment theory, and therefore of particular relevance to one of the themes in this book.

4

Emotional and Behavioural Difficulties

Janet Empson and David Hamilton

Introduction

This chapter examines the concepts of 'normality' and 'abnormality' or 'atypicality' in child development and considers whether it is feasible and useful to make such distinctions. The notion of 'the normal child' and how it provides a basis for distinguishing normality from abnormality such as emotional and behavioural difficulty in a child is discussed. Various definitions of abnormality are presented, specifically that of deviance from the norm, and the negative connotations of such usage. Criteria for child behaviour problems are discussed, which range from the concepts of age and gender appropriateness to considerations of quantitative and qualitative differences from the normal range of behaviours. The developmental psychopathological perspective is relevant to these considerations and this is described as a useful approach to understanding both normal and atypical forms of development. Perspectives on emotional and behavioural difficulties, which are sometimes in conflict, are the medical and the psychological. These are compared and evaluated; the approach adopted here is predominantly psychological. Both approaches have as their ultimate aim the recovery of the individual. A child's difficulties are presented as a function of the child's relationships, and particularly the relationship with her parent(s). So, the most important context for early child development, that of the family, is discussed in relation to possible influences upon the development of difficulty or disorder.

Classification, or taxonomy, of developmental disorders can be useful in communicating the nature of the problems between parents and professionals, and especially between different professionals who are involved in helping the child and her family. Some of the main types of disorder are discussed: 'externalising' disorders, such as attention deficit/hyperactivity disorder (ADHD) and conduct disorder (CD), and 'internalising' disorders, such as anxiety and depression. The factors which have been implicated in the development of these problems are highlighted, as they are particularly relevant to understanding these experiences and designing programmes of intervention.

Criteria of emotional and behavioural difficulties

The term 'emotional and behavioural difficulties' is used to refer mainly to behaviours which are deemed to violate social norms of acceptable behaviour and therefore are undesirable. This raises the question of whether the prevailing culture denies children a 'natural' expression of negativity which needs to be expressed to allow healthy development. Certainly, different parents, teachers and other individuals or groups have varying views on what constitutes acceptable or unacceptable behaviour in children (Woodhead, 1995).

The description of a behaviour as normal or problematic will of course depend on the context in which it occurs. The prevailing view nowadays is that the contexts or circumstances of children's lives are likely to elicit emotional or behavioural difficulties in the child (Rutter, 1990). Most problems in development constitute relationship difficulties, so it is particularly important to understand the relationships which a child has within the family and with peers. When it comes to some kind of intervention, perhaps by the school or referral to a professional, the reasons lie as often in the parents or the family as in the child. Rutter (1990) describes the case of Rachel, aged six, who was brought by her mother to his clinic. The problems with Rachel of which the mother complained turned out to be mainly expressions of behaviour which were common in that age group and the major problem was the mother's depression, heavy drinking and feelings of lack of control in her management of Rachel.

It is common for *observable behaviours* to be used as criteria of normality or atypicality, and assumptions are made that these reflect particular internal difficulties or conflicts. The description of these will differ depending on which perspective or theoretical viewpoint is preferred by the observer. There are two main guiding philosophies for describing and understanding developmental difficulties and these form the basis of the medical and the psychological models. Bancroft and Carr (1995) explained the differences between these approaches. The 'medical model' specifies physical cause(s) leading to 'symptoms' of an underlying condition or psychopathology which can be treated and cured. The 'psychological model', as described above, views children's developmental difficulties as being caused and sustained by problematic social relationships; the problem is not located in the child but in the systems of which the child is a part. Thus, Bronfenbrenner's ecological systems theory (introduced in Chapter 1) can be seen as a model for understanding the development and maintenance of emotional and behavioural difficulties. The approach adopted in this book is that of developmental psychology, which examines the risk factors for developing problems at a number of levels – physiological, psychological, interpersonal and sociocultural – all of which may interact in different ways in the development of difficulty.

The medical approach is likely to attach a label to the condition from which a child is suffering. Such labels are a useful device for communication between professionals and may reassure parents that their child belongs to a group with similar difficulties. But labels may lead to a lack of attention to individual need and create a gulf between those labelled and those seen as normal. Psychologists have made efforts to move away from labels. In the UK, for example, the process of 'statementing' by educational psychologists develops a profile of strengths and difficulties for each child so that her special needs can be attended to through the provision of an individualised educational programme.

What is agreed by both psychologists and psychiatrists is that the most appropriate model for conceptualising and helping those with developmental difficulty is a recovery model. All are working for the same outcome, which is to enable the child to cope in the circumstances of her life and have healthy interpersonal relationships with family and peers.

Most emotional and behavioural disturbances are quantitatively rather than qualitatively different from the norm. It can be seen from the criteria discussed below that most of them are in relation to behaviours which occur in most or all children but differ only in number, amount or degree, that is, quantitative differences. Qualitative differences are more difficult to identify and often amount to professional judgement or interpretation. Those conditions which have a biological cause are more likely to be identifiable as discrete categories and those which are interpersonal and psychological in origin are more likely to be represented on a continuum with 'normal' behaviours (Rutter, 1996).

Certain criteria need to be taken into account when considering whether behaviours are atypical or not (Gelfand et al., 1988), as described in Table 4.1.

TABLE 4.1 CRITERIA FOR ASSESSING ABNORMALITY

Normality is a statistical concept which takes into account the probability of occurrence of particular behaviours at particular developmental levels. For behaviours to be considered 'abnormal', the following criteria need to be taken into account.

1. Age (and gender) appropriateness of behaviour

2. Intensity and frequency of behaviours

3. Persistence over time of behaviours

4. Extent of disturbance: how many behaviours affected; whether they cover different areas of psychological functioning

5. Association with impairment: suffering, social restriction, interference with development, effect on others. Impairment must be seen in relative terms

6. Type of symptom, for example disturbed peer relationships are much more problematic than a tic or nail-biting

7. Situation specificity

8. Change in behaviour

9. Life circumstances of the child

10 Sociocultural setting of the family

Note: Criteria will change over time and vary in association with different environmental conditions.

Knowledge of which behaviours are typical of different *ages* leads to expectations of a certain range of behaviours by children of a particular chronological age. Judgements may then be made as to whether a particular child's reactions are appropriate to that specific age group. Many behaviours occur frequently and are normal at certain ages but not at others. For example, nail-biting is very frequent in early adolescence but highly unusual in one-year-olds; temper tantrums and negativity are common in two-year-olds but much less so in six-year-olds.

Quantitative differences between normal and atypical behaviours may be related to the *intensity* of behaviours, such as the extent of a particular child's reactions to frustration and aggressive behaviour. When children are prevented from doing something or having something they desire, they will react with different degrees of intensity, depending on a number of different aspects of the situation. These include:

- the personality or temperament and level of maturity of the child
- how important the need is that is being denied
- the way in which the child is prevented (usually by an adult) from achieving her goal.

Behaviours which are very intense and which bring about, or have the potential to cause, actual physical harm to self or others are relatively unusual in occurrence, unless the environment in which the child is growing up is very adverse and characterised by frequent violence and aggression.

The *persistence over time* of particular atypical behaviours is relevant in deciding on their importance. Children frequently grow out of behaviours thought to be undesirable and the duration of these behaviours is important in deciding whether something needs to be done. For behaviours to be viewed as truly problematic, they need to last at least six months (Webster-Stratton and Herbert, 1994); more transitory behaviours should just be viewed as part of the developmental process. Many short-term difficulties, such as school phobias, are common.

Also significant in the determination of emotional and behavioural difficulty are the *number and diversity* of the problematic behaviours shown, as well as the *severity* of their impact on the individual's well-being and concerned others. If particular undesirable behaviours are part of a constellation of disturbance, affecting different areas of psychological functioning, then it is more likely that they are something to pay attention to as a possible indication of serious underlying problems. If undesirable behaviours occur across the *range* of contexts in which the child lives, this is more problematic than if such behaviours just occur at home or at school. The more that particular behaviours are associated with impairment and suffering, restriction of social activities and relationships, and with hindering development, the more important it is that action should be taken to change the situation and behaviours.

It is also important to consider the *type* of problematic behaviour being shown. Those most indicative of underlying disturbance are disturbed relationships; minor manifestations like nail-biting are rarely indicative in their own right.

Change in behaviour is also indicative of the development of a problem. If a child has been 'difficult' (Thomas and Chess, 1977) from an early age, then any disturbance needs to be viewed in this context; if an 'easy' child suddenly becomes difficult, then this is more indicative of problems. *Life events* too can trigger temporary disturbance so the events in a child's life (for example the birth of a sibling) need to be known, particularly how the child herself interprets them. Many other risk factors have been implicated in the development of psychological problems (see Chapter 2). Their effects can combine in different ways in different individuals to facilitate the development of different disorders. Also, the same disorder in a number of children may result from different combinations of risks (Sroufe et al., 1996) (Figure 4.1).

Some behaviours are considered appropriate in some *sociocultural* contexts but not in others; similarly, some behaviours are considered appropriate for one sex, whereas other behaviours are more suited to the other. Expressions of aggression, for example, are considered by most to be more appropriate behaviours for boys than girls. It can be argued that many of the indications of, for example, 'conduct disorder' are more relevant to culturally prescribed male behaviours than female ones and this is one reason why more males than females are identified as conduct-disordered. Perhaps different criteria should be used in determining disorders in males and females. This issue is discussed further in the final chapter in relation to cultural norms and expectations.

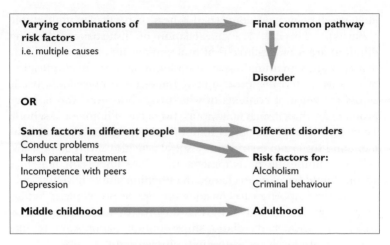

Figure 4.1   Risk factors and pathways to disorder
(adapted from Sroufe et al., 1996)

Criteria will *change over time*. The taking of drugs can now be seen as normative in adolescents, whereas a generation ago it was mainly restricted to the student population. On Saturday nights, thousands of typical young people across the country enliven their experience of 'clubbing' by taking a tablet or two of 'ecstasy' and claim that they experience no ill effects. This may not be seen as deviant behaviour. Many others, however, use class A drugs, such as 'crack' cocaine, which may begin as a way of avoiding difficulties in life and is accompanied by more serious problems. These include difficulties in relationships, in holding down a job or coping with educational demands. This type of drug-taking is likely to involve emotional and behavioural problems as both cause and consequence. Adolescent drug users are often 'impulsive, disruptive and sensation-seeking' (Berk, 2003) as young children, are often of low socioeconomic status, have parents with mental health problems or who take drugs themselves. The major consequences for the individual are adjustment problems, antisocial behaviour and depression (Luthar and Cushing, 1997).

Criteria will also *change with environmental conditions*. Recent immigrants to a country have changing cultural patterns and expectations as they adapt to the indigenous culture. This can be associated with more conflict between the generations than in indigenous families, particularly between parents and teenage children, each having different expectations for adolescent behaviours and goals in life. The parents' views are more likely to be based on those of the culture of origin and the young people's to derive from the current culture that they have adopted. On the other hand, cultural practices or patterns of behaviour brought from the country of origin may protect a child or family from experiencing problems. For example, Asian families who come to Britain may continue to live in extended families, as is the practice in their country of origin. In such families, children may receive more individual attention from adults resulting in fewer behavioural problems in the children (Erickson, 1998).

All these criteria need to be borne in mind when considering the different types of emotional and behavioural difficulties as described by the different classification systems of psychological disturbance.

Summary

There are many conditions which need to be taken into account when deciding if a child's development is abnormal or atypical. Abnormality is commonly thought of as significant deviance from the norm, and norms vary according to age, gender and sociocultural contexts. Deviations from normal development which are thought to be problematic may be quantitative or qualitative. Most indications of emotional and behavioural difficulties in children are expressions of quantitative differences in behaviours which occur in all children to a greater or lesser extent. Such differences in behaviour may be in terms of intensity, frequency, persistence, number or type. The most serious are disturbed relationships. It is assumed that emotional problems underlie disturbed behaviour. The range of contexts in which the problematic behaviours occur, the life circumstances of the child in her family, and the extent of impairment of development and social functioning as well as the distress experienced all need to be taken into account.

The main types of emotional and behavioural difficulty in children are presented in the next section.

Types of emotional and behavioural difficulty in children

The main types of emotional and behavioural difficulties in children are often described as 'externalising' or 'internalising' (Campbell, 1995). Externalising disorders are those in which the child's internal difficulties or conflicts are expressed in acting-out behaviours. The DSM IV (American Psychiatric Association, 1994) refers to externalising behaviour problems collectively as 'disruptive behaviour and attention-deficit disorders', constituting oppositional defiant disorder (ODD), attention deficit/hyperactivity disorder (ADHD) and conduct disorder (CD). Aggression, hyperactivity, inattention and defiant behaviours frequently occur in disorders such as CD and ADHD. In internalising disorders, the child's difficulties are expressed as disorders of mood, shown by emotional states like anxiety, depression and withdrawal. Different forms of anxiety state are the most frequently occurring. Specific fears and transient anxieties are shown by 90 per cent of children in their early years and therefore can be considered normally occurring behaviours (Valentine, 1956). First we describe the two main types of externalising disorder, ADHD and CD; and then we go on to discuss internalising disorders.

Attention deficit/hyperactivity disorder (ADHD)

ADHD affects three to five per cent of school-age children, with the vast majority being male. The ratio of boys to girls with ADHD is 4–9 to 1 (Erickson, 1998). It occurs more frequently in lower socioeconomic groups, which may be attributed to the more stressful living conditions for families in the poorer sections of society.

The primary 'symptoms' of this disorder are described in the DSM IV (American Psychiatric Association, 1994) as being developmentally inappropriate degrees of inattention, impulsivity and motor activity. The DSM IV presents two lists of symptoms, the first associated with inattention and the second with hyperactivity and impulsivity. The child must display at least six of these symptoms, and these must be:

- present before seven years of age
- present in two or more settings

- associated with impairment in social and/or academic functioning
- *not* better accounted for by another disorder (Erickson, 1998).

Referral to a professional may be in the preschool years when hyperactivity is the main problem or in the school years when problems with learning become apparent. It is significant to note that there are wide cultural variations in rates of referral, these being more frequent in the USA than the UK. The main source of evidence that the child has developmental difficulties is reports from parents and teachers. In continuous performance tasks, ADHD children show more errors of both commission and omission (Barkley, 1990).

Katz and Gottman (1991) account for the features of ADHD as being expressions of 'dysfunctional emotional regulation'. They defined 'emotional regulation' as:

> consisting of children's ability to (1) inhibit inappropriate behaviour related to strong negative or positive affect, (2) self-soothe any physiological arousal that strong affect has induced, (3) focus attention, and (4) organize themselves for coordinated action in the service of an external goal. (p130)

Difficulties in emotional regulation may be exaggerated by particular contexts which amplify the reactions of the child. So, for example, stress in the environment can act as a disrupter of a mother's discipline practices directly and indirectly by amplifying her antisocial behaviour and that of her child. Other influential situations include family disruptions, change of school and other transitions. A child with excessive emotional reactivity may place herself at risk of coercive or other maltreating behaviours by a parent or peers. In addition, emotional regulation is related to social cognition as demonstrated by Dodge (1991) in his model of social information processing. Children who have difficult interpersonal relationships may have a distorted interpretation of social communications from others, for example by attributing inappropriate hostile intent on the part of peers.

Poor emotional regulation can influence a child's learning and academic ability either directly by its effect on attention, concentration and application to educational tasks, or indirectly via relationship difficulties as described above. Cognitive deficits associated with ADHD have been described by Barkley (1998) as emanating mainly from poor central executive control (of information processing), typically manifested as impulsivity and lack of inhibition of responses, inadequate switching of attention as required for task performance and poor working memory capacity and use.

Problematic behaviours typical of children with ADHD are illustrated in the case of Joe, below.

Case 4.1 Joe

Joe, aged eight, is always on the go. His mother is exhausted, as Joe wakes at 5.30 every morning. He is out of bed and downstairs playing with one thing after another, making so much noise that his mother is obliged to get up to quieten him down so that he does not wake the rest of the family. She finds toys and games strewn all over the house. Usually something is broken or damaged. Joe has often poured himself a drink, spilling orange juice on the floor and forgetting to close the fridge door.

On the days that Joe is not at school, he requires constant attention. His older sister doesn't want to spend time with him and tries to ignore him. He has no friends coming round to play. As Joe is so impulsive that he cannot be trusted to cross a road safely, he is never allowed out on his own. If his mother takes him to the park to play with children there, he cannot even play football without alienating the other children, as he violates the rules, although he does play with vigour.

Most activities only hold Joe's attention for a short time, so he is always doing irritating things, such as opening and closing cupboard doors, or jumping on and off the furniture, to obtain attention. He is unable to take any responsibility, for example looking after a pet, and is careless of possessions and in using the toilet. He frequently breaks toys and takes his clothes off so violently at night that they rip. As Joe has been hyperactive, impulsive, lacking in self-control and attention-seeking from a very early age, his mother is at the end of her tether. She is a very orderly person, who likes to keep a nice home for her children and herself, but is constantly unable to. She is becoming increasingly anxious and depressed. Although she does not like the thought of giving Joe drugs, the idea of him taking Ritalin is becoming increasingly appealing, for her own survival.

Many children with ADHD experience severe interpersonal difficulties. It is estimated that peers reject half of children with ADHD, and problems in relationships also occur with siblings, teachers and parents (Nixon, 2001). The social behaviour of these children is particularly characterised by aggression and inappropriate processing of social information, such as facial expressions or gestures and communication. Problems in relationships are likely to contribute to the cognitive developmental difficulties linked with inattention, poor concentration and poor educational progress. Children with ADHD who have experienced a lack of acceptance by peers have also been found to have difficulties in adjustment in a number of different domains later in life. These mirror the findings for other socially rejected children (Barkley et al., 1991). So, the long-term outlook for many children with ADHD is poor.

Aetiology

There are a number of different possible causes of ADHD in different circumstances, and a number of risk factors may be causally related. Genetic factors are evident from family and twin studies; these factors are also relevant to the co-occurrence of ADHD and learning disability (Gillis et al., 1992). A link has also been found with maternal consumption of large quantities of alcohol during pregnancy and also with mothers who have a higher than usual rate of physical disorders in the first trimester of pregnancy (Erickson, 1998). Psychosocial factors are associated with the severity of symptoms rather than causality (Erickson, 1998). Continuing family disturbance may well contribute to the strong continuity of childhood ADHD into adolescence in 50–80 per cent of cases (Fischer et al., 1993). In addition, the prognosis for persistence of conduct disorder over time is worse for individuals with concurrent ADHD (Lahey and Loeber, 1991).

Interventions

Drug treatments are frequently used. The most common is methyl phenidate (Ritalin), a stimulant which improves attention and decreases activity and impulsivity. It also reduces non-compliance and aggression (Hinshaw et al., 1989). It does, however, have side effects which may be severe. The most characteristic are reduced appetite and lack of motivation. Cognitive-behavioural approaches are the most useful interventions for reducing impulsivity. (See also Kazdin, 1997, and Chapter 6 for a review of psychosocial treatments.)

Conduct disorder (CD)

Probably the most frequently occurring disorder, and the one with which parents have most difficulty in coping, is conduct disorder (CD). This is a broad label identifying a wide range of aversive and socially disruptive behaviours in children. For a child to be identified as having conduct-disordered behaviour, she must have disturbance lasting at least six months in at least three areas of functioning (Webster-Stratton and Herbert, 1994):

- having insufficient control over behaviour and so may be aggressive, bullying, destructive, have temper tantrums, steal and set fires. These behaviours are quantitatively different from normal, in terms of both intensity and frequency of occurrence
- going for immediate rewards, self-centred and showing little empathy and a disregard of the consequences of their actions on other people
- being impervious to the distress of others, showing no remorse, and, indeed, seeming to be unaware of the effects of their behaviours on other people's views of them, and their relationships with others, both adults and peers
- peer relationship problems including social isolation or being part of a particular group, the members of which are also likely to be deviant
- family relationships are also disrupted, much attention being focused on the behaviourally disturbed child so that other children in the family feel neglected. Parents feel out of control, embarrassed about their child's behaviour, as though they cannot participate in social activities with other families and so also become socially isolated
- problems in the community. If the child's behaviours are severely antisocial, the ramifications can be experienced by the child's school and people in the neighbourhood. Any interventions need to involve all those who are so affected.

An example of a child with CD is provided in the description of Garry below.

Case 4.2 A child with CD

Garry, aged eight, is becoming increasingly difficult to live with. He is constantly in trouble at school. At home his mother vacillates between ignoring Garry and letting him do what he wants, and feeling that things are going too far and reacting by smacking and shouting at him. Things weren't so bad when Garry's father lived with them, as he could be relied upon for heavy-handed disciplining of Garry. But father spent most of his time, and the family income, in the pub. When he had had a few drinks, he blamed his wife for Garry's bad behaviour and was heavy-handed with her too. Six months ago he announced that he had had enough, packed a bag and left.

The other children in the family, all girls, were cowed and intimidated by the marital strife, but Garry responded with negativity and violent and destructive behaviour. He was always picking quarrels with others, and beat up other children if they did not go along with what he wanted. His mother was frequently called into school to take Garry home, as he was so disruptive in his relationships with other children. None of them liked him and many feared him.

Garry is lagging further and further behind the rest of the class, partly because he was frequently excluded from school and partly because he would not do as the teacher told him. At home he reacts to any requests or instructions from his mother with defiance and hostility. He bullies his sisters and torments the cat. His favourite activities are playing violent computer games and it is only when playing on his computer that Garry seems happy.

Aetiology

As described by Erickson (1998), it is generally accepted that anti-social behaviour, as in conduct disorders, has many causes. Risk factors for CD operate at a number of different levels, ranging from genetic and physiological factors, through individual factors such as temperament and motivation, to family factors like child-rearing practices and discipline methods, marital discord and inappropriate parental models of behaviour, for example the use of aggression to control other people's behaviour.

As with ADHD, CD occurs much more frequently in boys than girls (Maughan, 2000). Rutter et al. (1998a) suggest that psychosocial processes may be implicated in boys' and girls' different risks for conduct problems in a number of ways. They may be differentially exposed to adverse environmental influences, differently susceptible to them and have different ways of expressing their reactions to these influences. There is some evidence that boys and girls experience different forms of socialisation from an early age, in which internalising modes of expression are particularly reinforced in girls, whereas boys are expected to be more active and intense in their behaviours (Keenan and Shaw, 1997). Boys appear to be more susceptible to environmental stressors, such as parental divorce and violence in the family (Rutter, 1982), although this does not seem to be the case for all domains (Deater-Deckard et al., 1998).

Like ADHD, there is a strong degree of continuity between CD in childhood and adolescence. There are two forms of CD – early onset and late onset. In early or childhood onset CD, there must be at least one problem occurring before ten years and lasting more than six months. In adolescent or late onset CD, there are no observable problems before ten years. Continuity is greater for early onset than later onset, which seems to emerge largely in association with peer pressure for particular kinds of behaviour. Early onset CD, which may be evident as early as three years of age, appears to have a different causation.

The connection between CD and family structure and adversity has been recognised for many years (Mallick and McCandless, 1966; Dumas and Gibson, 1990). These family features include family poverty, large family size, parental psychopathology, harsh parenting, conflictual relationships and family breakdown. All these are associated with personal and interpersonal stresses and poor relationships and parenting (Heath and Kosky, 1992). The emergence of disruptive and aggressive behaviours in young children happens in association with parenting which is inconsistent and negative, perhaps in interactions with a child temperament of the 'difficult' type (Thomas et al., 1968). Observational studies, such as those of Patterson (1982) and Patterson and Capaldi (1991) in Oregon, showed that such families have more negative interactions, more confrontations and less parental control in following through on instructions, together with little affection and few positive experiences. These kinds of interactions and relationships occur more frequently in families facing external stressors such as poverty and social disadvantage. In addition to such conditions of psychosocial disadvantage being associated with poor parenting, biological factors may also be implicated. There is evidence for a genetic component to antisocial personality disorder, as children who behave in antisocial ways have an increased likelihood of a parent also being antisocial and demonstrating poor parenting skills (Erickson, 1998).

As Maughan (2000) describes, the most proximal risks for the development of CD in children are harsh, coercive parenting behaviours to which the child is subjected on a continuing basis. In addition, the kinds of behaviours displayed by the child have been shown to evoke negative parenting behaviours. A 'reciprocal' dynamic evolves which in many circumstances can lead to a spiral of coercive behaviours. Initially behaviours such as nagging by the parent and defiance from the child have low levels of negativity. Later these escalate into more extreme levels characterised by aggression or even violence (Patterson, 1982).

Reciprocal influences can be investigated using longitudinal studies (where the same children are investigated at a number of different periods of time) and a statistical technique called cross-lagged correlation (where associations between variable(s) can be calculated over time to determine which variable influences which other one(s) later). Generally, the link between early maternal behaviour and later child behaviour problems, as shown by cross-lagged correlations, is stronger than the link showing the other direction of influence, that is, from child behaviour to parental control (Campbell et al., 1996). Cohen and Brook (1995) obtained similar findings, showing that punishment early in life is associated with later conduct problems, while child behaviour influences on parental punishment only held for the younger children into early adolescence, the effect having disappeared by later adolescence.

The suggestion is, then, that at least some of the effects of poor parenting are mediated by the following social processes: first, harsh, coercive, behaviour and the use of physical punishment by parents; second, hostile and critical relationships; and third, ineffective and inconsistent management, often involving poor monitoring and supervision. These aspects of parenting suggest obvious areas for ameliorative intervention. One of the most significant intervention programmes, based in part on the work of Patterson, has emphasised parental training (Webster-Stratton and Herbert,

1994). It should be noted, however, that all the best programmes, including this one, assess thoroughly the family dynamics in each individual family, as the effects of, for example, physical punishment will vary depending on the interpretation of the meaning of the punishment as well as its severity, and may well be moderated by the nature of the parent–child relationship (Deater-Deckard et al., 1996). In the context of a good relationship between parent and child, severe punishment tends to have less negative effects. In any family, each parent has different relationships with each of his or her children (Dunn, 1988) and this may well mediate the effects of punishment on the child. Individual differences in susceptibility to marked reactions to harsh punishment will render particular children more vulnerable than others sharing the same family environment.

Evidence has also been found for different influences upon the development of early and later onset conduct problems. Hostile, coercive parenting is especially implicated in early onset conduct problems, while later onset problems seem to be particularly associated with friendships with deviant peers (Moffitt, 1993a and b). The families of the latter group are more adequate than those of the former, in terms of important characteristics like income, social disadvantage, antisocial parents, number of family transitions, discipline practices and relationships between parents and children. Family stresses may contribute to a child developing an involvement with deviant peers through a lack of adequate supervision, or difficulties at home driving the child to escape to peer networks.

Extremely negative parenting, which can be described as maltreatment or abusive, is also associated with an increased risk of the development of conduct problems in the maltreated children. The risk is not just for antisocial outcomes, however. Outcomes of maltreatment have been found to be associated with a wide range of problems, including internalising characteristics such as low self-esteem, as well as externalising problematic behaviours (Cicchetti and Toth, 1995).

Conduct problems in children also show strong connections with discord between parents, the parents holding differing views of appropriate parenting, and family breakdown. Risks for externalising behaviours are approximately doubled for children from divorced families. Other undesirable outcomes – emotional distress, poor educational attainments and poor physical health – are more likely than in intact families (Rodgers and Pryor, 1998). The processes whereby marital problems and child behaviour difficulties are linked are several. Loss does not seem to be a central component, as similar negative effects do not follow parental loss through death. The discord and conflict that precedes parental separation looks likely to be a key component in the transmission of risk for the child, also the range of stressors for the child that follow parental divorce, such as moving house and losing friends, mother going out to work, reduced parenting, lowered financial status, possible loss of contact with grandparents and having to form new relationships with parent figures and step-siblings. There is considerable evidence as to the negative effects of parental conflict, and that repeated family transitions are associated with more child adjustment difficulties (Patterson and Capaldi, 1991).

The broad question as to whether it is better for children to live in an intact family with parents in conflict or in a family which has experienced divorce but is harmonious, as suggested by research funded by the Rowntree Foundation in England (Cockett and Tripp, 1994), is still an open one.

Internalising disorders

The term 'internalising disorders' refers to various types of anxiety and depression. Children who are fearful, anxious, shy, sad, have low self-esteem, habitually avoid difficult or unpleasant situations and whose feelings prevent them from functioning normally in everyday life might be thought to have an internalising disorder. DSM IV (American Psychiatric Association, 1994) does not use the term to indicate a single diagnostic category. Anxiety disorders listed in DSM, which commonly manifest during childhood and adolescence, include separation anxiety disorder, overanxious disorder and the phobic disorders. The DSM diagnoses of major depressive disorder and dysthymic disorder (chronically depressed mood without a major depressive episode) are also reported in children and adolescents.

There is substantial evidence that many children experience minor emotional difficulties as a part of typical development. This is most apparent in the development of specific fears, which for most children appear to be both transient and age- or stage-specific (King et al., 1988). For example, many preschool children are afraid of the dark, strangers or small animals, but these fears are generally mild and dissipate without treatment. Social fears, often associated with public embarrassment or negative evaluation by others, are more common in adolescence, but are less prevalent during early adulthood. Some children experience severe fears that might better be described as 'phobias'. Phobias are fears which are out of proportion to the demands of the situation, cannot be reasoned away, are beyond voluntary control, lead to avoidance of the feared situation, persist over an extended period of time and are neither adaptive nor age-specific (King et al., 1988). They are more durable than fears, and those that are acquired during early childhood can extend into adulthood.

It is conventional to distinguish between phobias and anxiety disorders on the basis of situation specificity. The phobic child will tend to avoid the feared stimulus or situation and will have an adverse reaction when coming into contact with specific environmental triggers. Anxiety, on the other hand, tends to be less situation-specific. It is characterised by aversive physiological arousal, sometimes accompanied by worrying thoughts, and may pervade most activities during the course of the day. Anxious children may find it difficult to identify specific triggers, and so behavioural avoidance of particular stimuli is less likely to be a feature of the problem. Nevertheless, children with separation anxiety, for example, will attempt to remain in their parents company whenever possible, and some children will feel a compulsion to perform rituals (such as checking or hand washing) in order to control their anxiety, and may avoid situations where this is not possible.

Children will occasionally experience intense sadness (such as following the death of a much-loved pet) but would not be diagnosed as depressed, even though their subjective experience is of intense trauma. A major depressive episode may be characterised by (American Psychiatric Association, 1994):

- depressed mood or loss of interest or pleasure
- significant weight loss or decrease or increase in appetite
- sleep disturbance
- motor slowness or agitation

- fatigue or loss of energy
- feelings of worthlessness or excessive or inappropriate guilt
- diminished ability to think or concentrate, or indecisiveness
- recurrent thoughts of death.

Not all depressed children exhibit all these symptoms, so they present as a heterogeneous group. Although the mood disorders do not manifest primarily as externalised problems, it is possible for major depression to be diagnosed on the basis of the observation of overt behaviour. This assists in diagnosing young children, or children and adolescents with developmental disabilities, who may have limited verbal skills.

If mild fears and occasional feelings of sadness are relatively common in young children, how common are anxiety and mood disorders? This is not an easy question to answer, as it is difficult to obtain accurate data on the prevalence of internalising disorders. We are reliant to some extent on self-reports, which may prove unreliable in some children. Kovacs and Devlin (1998) note that reported prevalence will vary according to variations in research methodology, and that it is only possible to determine general trends in prevalence rather than exact data.

Few reviewers have commented on the prevalence of internalising disorders, however, without reference to a series of articles that report on a longitudinal study conducted on a birth cohort of New Zealand children (Anderson et al., 1987; McGee et al., 1992; Feehan et al., 1993). These studies indicate that the prevalence of internalising disorders is likely to increase from late primary school into adulthood. The prevalence of both anxiety disorders and mood disorders is likely to double between the ages of approximately 11 and 18. The disorders are also durable; children who were diagnosed with anxiety or depression in their mid-teens were highly likely to carry these conditions beyond the age of 21.

It is very common for children and adolescents to suffer from more than one internalising disorder. Although internalising disorders can and do manifest independently, it is more usual for two or more to co-exist in the same person (Ollendick and King, 1994). While Achenbach and McConaughy (1992) suggest that four specific syndromes can be identified (anxious-depressed, schizoid, somatic complaints and social withdrawal), co-occurrence is so common that it has even been suggested that the internalising disorders might be variations in the expression of a single disorder (Maser and Cloninger, 1990). There is strong evidence suggesting that anxiety disorders frequently co-occur in children and adolescents (for example Last et al., 1992). While for any given anxiety disorder the most likely co-occurring disorder is another anxiety disorder (Kovacs and Devlin, 1998), there is substantial evidence supporting the proposition that anxiety and depression are closely associated.

The following case study illustrates the co-occurrence of separation anxiety and dysthymic disorder.

Case 4.3 Sarah

Sarah, aged ten, was an only child. At age eight, she began to miss many days of school after complaining of recurrent physical symptoms, such as headache, abdominal pain and nausea. Within 12 months she apparently experienced these symptoms at the weekend and during school holidays, but only when anticipating or experiencing separation from her parents. She refused to stay at her grandmother's house overnight, and missed a school camp. By age ten, she began to express excessive worry about loss of, or harm to, her parents. She frequently reported dreaming that her parents had been killed in a car crash, and would enter their bedroom during the night to ensure that they were unharmed. When not experiencing acute anxiety, Sarah appeared tired and lacking in energy. She frequently complained that she was poor at her school work, and that she did not have any friends. She was unable to respond when asked about her capabilities, likes and dislikes. Sarah found it difficult to make simple decisions about what to eat or wear. She had a poor appetite and found it difficult to go back to sleep once she had awoken during the night.

Findings on the natural history and co-occurrence of the internalising disorders have potential implications for how we might determine the factors that precipitate and maintain the disorders. Kovacs and Devlin (1998), for example, suggest that young children are predisposed to states of physiological hyperarousal under certain stress conditions, and may be developmentally predisposed to the development of anxiety disorders. While this might explain the commonly reported ages of onset, it does not explain the reasons that children do or do not develop anxiety disorders. Furthermore, Chorpita (2002) examined a sample of over 1500 children and adolescents and found that hyperarousal was related only to panic and not to the other anxiety disorders.

A substantial body of research has accumulated on family influences on the development and maintenance of childhood internalising disorders. This issue has been addressed from a variety of perspectives. First it has been suggested that children may be at risk if their parents suffer from anxiety or depression (Biederman et al. (2001), although McClure et al. (2001) found that maternal anxiety disorder, but not paternal anxiety disorder, predicted child anxiety disorder. Furthermore, mothers who were anxious and depressed placed their children at greatest risk, while the risk was substantially lower for children of mothers who were depressed but not anxious. A second body of research has examined the effect of interparental conflict and perceived family cohesion on internalising disorders, particularly with reference to adolescents. Johnson et al. (2001), for example, note that adolescents may experience loneliness, social anxiety and social avoidance when they perceive that their parents are in conflict, and when there is a lack of family cohesion.

A third body of research has focused on the effects of parenting style and parenting behaviour. Particular attention has been devoted to two dimensions of parenting behaviour: control versus autonomy, and rejection versus acceptance (for example Siqueland et al., 1996). Rapee (1997) suggests that there may be specific relationships between individual parenting styles and particular internalising problems. There are indications that parental rejection is associated with child depression, while parental control is associated with child anxiety. It can be argued that a transactional approach to this area of research might prove to be particularly fruitful. Greater attention must also be paid to the importance of validity in the assessment of key variables. McClure et al. (2001) failed to demonstrate that parental behaviour mediated anxiety in children of anxious parents. They suggest that anxious children may perceive their parents as controlling and intrusive when they are actually displaying normal parenting behaviour. This suggests that independent observations of parents may be required in order to validate the perceptions of the children.

In examining the occurrence of internalising disorders among members of the same family, it is important to consider genetic factors. While the focus of this book is the impact of the environment on child development, recent research in the field of behavioural genetics has produced some interesting and potentially important findings. Much of this research has been conducted using adult twins as participants and indicates strongly that internalising disorders in adults are influenced by genetic factors. Kendler and his colleagues have produced substantial evidence which is consistent with the hypothesis that vulnerability to anxiety and phobic disorders in adults is largely innate (Kendler et al., 1995; Kendler et al., 2002), although there is some evidence that family environment may play a more substantial role in the development of agoraphobia and social phobia in men (Kendler et al., 2001). A meta-analysis of studies on the genetic epidemiology of major depression in adults concluded that familial transmission is largely due to genetic factors rather than shared environmental factors (Sullivan et al., 2000), and that environmental factors specific to the individual are also important.

The smaller body of research with child participants has produced more equivocal findings. Thapar and McGuffin (1995), for example, found that estimates of the relative contributions of genetic and family environmental factors in the familial transmission of anxiety disorders depend on whether the data are obtained from the parents or the children. Similarly, Rice et al. (2002) note that while major depression in childhood is familial, estimates of heritability vary widely and seem to be influenced by methodological factors. They note that future research needs to take account of these factors. A more detailed discussion on genetic influences and atypical child development is presented in Chapter 7.

There has been recent interest in the role of peer relations in the development of internalising problems (Lavigne et al., 1998; Deater-Deckard, 2001). Mesman et al. (2001) suggest that internalising problems during school years can be predicted from early withdrawn and depressed behaviour in preschool years, at least in boys. They note that withdrawn children have difficulty making and keeping friends, and fitting in with a social group. Further internalising problems develop in these children, often associated with negative self-image and social withdrawal. According to Deater-Deckard (2001), children who avoid interaction with peers are most likely to develop internalising disorders.

Summary

Overall, the evidence suggests a strong environmental influence in developing and maintaining antisocial or conduct-disturbed behaviours in children; also that ADHD and CD frequently co-occur in individual children. There is also evidence for a genetic component to ADHD. Family processes have particularly been implicated and there is evidence that changing the social interactions within the family will result in the reduction of antisocial behaviour in the child (for example Patterson et al., 1993). The key components of parent–child interactions in conduct disorder are harsh, punitive and hostile parenting, coercive interactions and the reinforcement of child negative behaviours by the parent.

There is substantial evidence for the co-occurrence of internalising disorders in children and adolescents. Much research has been conducted on the influence of family dynamics and parenting behaviour on the development of anxiety and depression in children and adolescents. There are some indications that inter-parental conflict and lack of family cohesion may be significant influences. There is also research suggesting that unreasonable parental control may be associated with anxiety in children, while parental rejection may be associated with childhood depression.

The various contexts in which children live, and which have been identified as significant in the aetiology (causation) of internalising and externalising disorders, are discussed next.

Contexts of child behavioural disturbance

The main environments in which children live are home, neighbourhood and school. Behaviour which is considered desirable or acceptable in one context may well be completely inappropriate in another. Parents and teachers often have different conceptions of appropriateness and inappropriateness, and effective communication between adults lies at the heart of understanding developmental difficulty in children. Achenbach et al. (1987) reviewed studies of judgements of children's behaviour problems by parents and teachers, among others, and found only modest agreement between these groups. This issue is discussed further in Chapter 7.

The identification of child developmental disturbance is usually based on descriptions provided by parents to professionals, and these may be supplemented by information from other adults, such as teachers. But there are problems with such evidence. When children are said to have a serious disturbance, this is based not just on the actual manifest behaviour but also on the dissatisfaction felt by the parent(s) over these particular expressions of emotional difficulty. There is by no means a direct correlation between the degree of deviance and the amount of parental concern.

Case 4.4 Rachel

Rachel had been described earlier as a six-year-old who was popular with her peers and doing well at her lessons. However, she was reported by her mother as becoming increasingly difficult to manage. She was temperamental, overexcited, highly active and had sleep disturbance. When these reported difficulties were investigated, it was found that Rachel was simply showing the behaviours to be expected of a healthy, exuberant child and that her failure to sleep was due to being put to bed far too early, so that her anxious and depressed mother could have a break.

Case 4.5 Andrew

Andrew became a cause of concern to his teachers because he was falling behind his peers in educational achievement. He was in a world of his own in class, paying little attention to what was going on. If asked to work in a group, he was totally passive and silent. At playtimes too he seemed lacking in energy for playing, was solitary and had no friends to play with. He was the fourth in a family of five children and his mother had recently been deserted by his father, so she was depressed, preoccupied by her own emotional and financial problems and had little spare capacity for paying attention to changes in her individual children. Her view was that Andrew was a thoughtful boy.

The examples of Rachel and Andrew illustrate the two extremes of the spectrum. Rachel's case shows how parental misperceptions can lead to a child being inappropriately viewed as having developmental problems. This instance represents an overexaggeration of parental concern. On the other hand, the case of Andrew shows a child experiencing genuine difficulties which pass unnoticed by his mother. Thus, the context in which the child is growing up constitutes part of the problem.

One of the problems with classifying a child as having a particular developmental difficulty is that, having been given a label, the child is then viewed as having a permanent condition. In all cases, children who demonstrate disordered behaviour have behaviours that are similar to those which are widely distributed in the population and therefore present to a certain extent in many or even most children. But if particular traits are grouped with others, and if the persistence of behaviours is different from usual, then it is more likely that there are different causal processes involved.

Case 4.6 Peter

Peter is six-years-old. He lives with his mother and elder brother on an inner-city estate. Peter is very large for his age, not due to any disease but because his mother has always allowed him free access to junk food. Since he started school, he has been subjected to much jeering and has been called 'incredible hulk' or 'fatso' by the other children. Peter has recently taken to removing money from his mother's purse to give to his 'friends', so that now he is part of a group of children from his class who play together every day.

Case 4.7 Paul

Paul is four-years-old and lives with his mother and her partner on a large council estate. Neither is employed so the family is living on a low income in rather cramped accommodation. Paul has been difficult to deal with for a long time and his mother and partner are reaching the end of their tether. Paul has been expelled from nursery school for continually fighting with, and biting, other children. He is still unable to play with other children, as he is so aggressive and demanding. When efforts are made to get Paul to do things he doesn't want to do, he shouts, yells and physically attacks his mother. His grandfather sometimes looks after Paul and when he finds Paul defiant and negative, he beats Paul with his stick. Paul's mother finds it impossible to play with or show affection towards him, and her partner is afraid of losing his temper and hitting Paul hard.

The examples of Peter and Paul illustrate different causal mechanisms and a different likelihood of long-term problems. Peter's stealing behaviour has a clearly identifiable cause – he is trying to buy friendship and avoid bullying. If he did not have a weight problem so that his physical appearance was like that of the other boys, it is arguable as to whether he would still be picked on. Paul's behaviour, on the other hand, seems to be a function of his disturbed relationships with other family members. There would need to be long-term intervention and ideally a change in material circumstances to change these well-established patterns of behaviour.

The family context of child behavioural disturbance

A number of different family influences have been found to be associated with emotional and behavioural difficulty in children. 'Aggression' in children has been particularly shown to be associated with exposure to violence and aggression in their homes, as described previously for the families of children with CD. In these households, the parent(s) constituted models of aggressive behaviour and these behaviours become incorporated into the behavioural repertoire of the child (Bandura, 1965; Christopoulos et al., 1987).

'Emotional disturbances' in children are related to family characteristics such as marital discord, psychiatric disturbance in a parent, illness of other kinds, and parental absence following divorce, abandonment or death (Brown and Harris, 1978).

The strong link between ineffective parenting and problems in development is often associated with families living in 'stressful life circumstances'. Such stressors include poverty, large family size leaving little time for individual attention to each child, parents having ill health and who are themselves poorly educated (McGlaughlin and Empson, 1979).

However, it is important to note that there are many children growing up in highly disadvantaged circumstances who are doing well developmentally. What seems to be critical is to delineate what features of the child's home environment distinguish between those who are doing well and those who are experiencing developmental difficulty. In a study carried out in Hull in the 1970s (McGlaughlin and Empson, 1979), pairs of sisters were studied, each of whom had a child of approximately the same age. The transmission of parenting characteristics was examined by talking to grandmothers, interviewing their daughters and observing the interactions between the latter and their young children in a play situation. Empson and McGlaughlin (1979) found that, irrespective of the degree of sociostructural disadvantage experienced by the families, some parents had constructive plans and aspirations for their children and this was related to the mothers' use of language with their children and the facilitative and educational aspects of their play with their children. These mother–child pairs also had more fun in their play, and the children were developing well. Other children who were developing less well had mothers who were suffering a higher level of 'malaise' (stress and anxiety) and this was linked with a variety of interpersonal and structural stresses such as poor housing. These mothers played less effectively with their children and with less enjoyment. This study concerned families with children under the age of three years. As was described in Chapter 2, there are also characteristics of individual children which make them resilient to adversity, such as good self-esteem, intelligence and ego strength. These characteristics are particularly important in older children who have more autonomy and self-determination.

Many parents may feel inexperienced and uncertain of how to deal with issues of parenting which all parents have to face, such as establishing the boundaries of acceptable behaviour, and how much freedom of expression should be encouraged in their children. In today's cultural environment, there are different pressures on parents from those experienced by earlier generations. Parents today are more likely to live at a distance from other family members and to have had no experience of children before having their own. Parents and children are exposed to media examples of unsuitable role models and the relentless advertising of consumer goods. Many problems arise due to conflict between parental attitudes and demands placed on the child, and the child's developing personality.

There are many frequently occurring aspects of parenting which often lead to friction and conflict between the generations in a family (Illingworth, 1987):

- *Spoiling* or fear of spoiling can be linked with a lack of love and security in the child, lack of discipline or overprotection

- *Anxiety* in either parent can be associated with dependency and immaturity in the child
- *Rejection* of a child by the parent means lack of affection and positive attention to the child. This may lead to fears and anxieties, insecurity, bedwetting, jealousy and attention-seeking
- Parental *misjudgement of the child's developmental level*, either under or overexpectation, may lead to the child being unable to satisfy parental requirements
- *Lack of understanding of individual differences.* If, for instance, parents have a very intelligent and conscientious first-born child, they may have the same expectations of their second child which she may find impossible to fulfil, if she is very different in terms of personality, interests and intelligence
- *Inappropriate discipline.* Disciplining children needs to be consistent, fair and appropriate to the developmental level of the child and the kind of misdemeanour, so that the child can readily learn what the limits are and that all siblings are treated equivalently. Major difficulties for children occur if the two parents differ in their approach to child-rearing, for example if one is permissive and allows a whole range of behaviours which the other parent, being more strict and authoritarian, punishes in a severe way, such as hitting the child. This is a recipe for confusion, with all kinds of possible consequences
- The *parents' own problems*, for example the use of illicit substances, alcohol abuse and marital conflict, may cloud their perception and judgement, be associated with overreaction or apathy with regard to the children, inconsistent parenting and, if the parental problems are major, child neglect or abuse may occur.

In most households, parents have some insight into the effects of their own behaviour on their children, especially if they support each other. This may be demonstrated in discussions between the parents about how they are bringing up the children and establishing agreement as to how their children should be rewarded or disciplined. Here the problems are likely to be worked through and coped with, without outside intervention. In families which are conflictual and have little social support, the friction between adults and children can escalate and get out of control, leading to stress and suffering in everyone concerned. This is when intervention is necessary (see Chapter 6).

Thus, the personal and interpersonal processes which may act as mediators between parental conflict and child behaviour problems (Maughan, 2000) can be summarised as follows:

- observation of models of aggression and hostility may lead the child to adopt such behaviours
- continuously negative interpersonal interactions could give rise to distorted social information processing by the child, with concomitant effects on the child's relationships
- marital discord can have adverse effects on parenting, particularly on appropriate and consistent discipline, sensitivity to the child's needs, and the parents' ability to show love and affection to the child
- the 'spillover' effect (Engfer, 1988) suggests that negative parental relationships can directly affect the ways in which parents relate to their child, bringing hostility from one relationship into other relationships in the family
- emotional stress impairs the child's ability to regulate emotional responses and the development of coping strategies.

The socioeconomic circumstances of families in difficulties

The socioeconomic circumstances of families also are associated with greater or lesser risks for conduct problems in the children. This was introduced in Chapter 2, and the possible processes involved are discussed further here. Poverty and social disadvantage are associated with mental health problems in adults, poor interpersonal relations and a pervasive atmosphere of malaise and hopelessness. Of the risks to children associated with poverty, conduct disorder has the greatest risk of occurrence, at 36 per cent, but emotional disorders are not far behind at 32 per cent (Lipman et al., 1996). Deprived inner-city neighbourhoods have higher rates of conduct disorder than rural areas (Rutter et al., 1975; Wichstrom et al., 1996).

Poverty can exert effects through processes operating at a number of different levels. Antisocial activities in the neighbourhood, such as criminal and violent acts, may be witnessed by children, with negative consequences. Characteristics of the environment, for example lack of cohesion and support between neighbours, high mobility, poor housing and lack of amenities, are associated with stress on the family, affecting health and relationships and, in particular, parenting behaviours (McLoyd, 1990). Such features of the neighbourhood may also have direct effects on the children, shaping their outlook on life, consideration for others and motivation or lack of it.

Overall, it appears that the effects of living in a certain type of neighbourhood or community on the development of conduct problems in children are mediated mainly via the family, and to a lesser extent the school, and vary according to the developmental stage of the child. Young children experience an elevated risk of maltreatment within the home, while somewhat older children are also exposed to violence in the neighbourhood and can be more directly affected by what is happening outside the home. Schools attended by older children will vary between equally disadvantaged neighbourhoods and may offer a protective and enabling environment, or the opportunity to associate with aggressive and delinquent peers. Variations between schools appear to be associated with consistent differences in risk for behaviour problems (Maughan et al, 1990). Lynch and Cicchetti (1998) have found that there is not a strong relationship between exposure to neighbourhood violence and family relationships, so clearly there are protective and vulnerability factors operating at this level too. Families react in many different ways to similar environmental stresses.

There is also evidence that environmental influences interact with individual characteristics (Lytton, 2000) to influence the 'timing of onset' and 'severity' of children's conduct-disordered behaviour. The child's genotype has a small, indirect effect (Cloninger and Gottesman, 1987) mediated through interactional processes. Children's emotional disposition is also relevant to their susceptibility to environmental influences and the development of antisocial behaviour.

Individual differences therefore need to be taken into account. In particular, the co-occurrence of CD and ADHD is associated with greater disruption of family management practices and socialisation processes. Interventions with families in difficulties aim to change the contingent outcomes of negative behaviours, so that prosocial behaviours are rewarded. Increasing emotional self-regulation and consistent and effective management skills in the parent will have positive effects on the self-control and emotional regulation in the child. In this way, the dominant modes of interaction within the family can be changed in the direction of more positive feelings and greater harmony.

Conclusion

Children whose behavioural development deviates markedly from the typical are generally described as having emotional and behavioural difficulties (EBDs). This chapter has discussed some of the issues around the identification of children who show behaviours sufficiently different from the norm which are thought serious enough to require some kind of information. Criteria deemed appropriate by professionals may differ depending upon whether their orientation is psychological or psychiatric. EBDs are broadly classified in two main types – externalising and internalising disorders. The main features of the former are poor concentration, overactivity and relationship problems associated with negative behaviour. The most frequently occurring manifestations of the latter are anxiety, depression and poor social functioning. A child's behaviours are inextricably linked with context; the behaviours of other people frequently elicit problematic behaviour in the child. The most significant difficulties (as demonstrated by suffering and impairment of functioning) shown by children are problematic social relationships. As relationship problems are at the heart of developmental difficulty, understanding of the aetiology and maintenance of EBDs must focus on the families of children affected. Research has shown that the main features of the family implicated in EBDs in children are the mental health of the parents, the parents' developmental history, their parenting behaviours, especially harsh, punitive and excessive control, and the degree of warmth and acceptance in the parent–child relationship. The contextual resources of the family, especially socio-economic are also important. The contexts of disturbed behaviour in children are explored further in Chapter 7.

Children function not only within the family environment but increasingly, as they grow up, in the contexts of school, neighbourhood and the wider world. The reciprocal interactions between the child and others in these different contexts will influence and be influenced by the developmental status of the child. This exemplifies the ecological model in action. Thus, any interventions must assess the child's functioning in these different situations and work on any difficulties, wherever they may arise, involving, for example, parents and teachers in any intervention programme. Different approaches to intervention and their relative effectiveness in different situations will be discussed in Chapter 6.

Discussion topics

1. What are the similarities and differences between medical and psychological approaches to child atypicality?
2. What are the contextual factors which influence our views on whether a child's behaviour is within normal limits?
3. How might parental conflict and family instability influence the development of externalising behaviours?
4. How strong is the evidence that parenting style may be associated with child anxiety and depression?
5. Why are there difficulties in obtaining reliable assessments of children's emotional and behavioural difficulties?
6. How might children be affected by the family's socioeconomic circumstances?

Recommended reading

Barnes, P. and Bancroft, D. (1995). Issues and applications. In D. Bancroft and R. Carr (eds), *Influencing Children's Development*. Milton Keynes: Open University. Provides a discussion of psychological and medical models, labelling and assessment.

Empson, J.M. (2001) Problematising Development: Concepts and Conceptions of Normality. In K. Dunn (ed.) *Child Development and Education. Different Experiences, New Voices*, pp. 26–44). Sheffield: Philip Armstrong Publications.

Erickson, M.T. (1998) *Behaviour Disorders of Children and Adolescents: Assessment, Etiology and Intervention* (3rd edn). Upper Saddle River, NJ: Prentice Hall. A clear description of the classification of disorders of childhood and the different categories of disorder. Rather clinical in approach.

Mash, E.J. and Wolfe, D.A. (1999) *Abnormal Child Psychology.* Belmont, CA: Brooks/Cole. A general text on developmental problems, it traces the developmental course of each disorder and discusses the interaction of biological, psychological, sociocultural and environmental factors.

Silverman, W.K. and Treffers, P.D.A. (eds) (2000) *Anxiety Disorders in Children and Adolescents: Research, Assessment and Intervention.* New York: Cambridge University Press. A comprehensive review of recent theoretical and empirical developments in the field and covers cognitive, biological and social influences on children's anxiety disorders.

Woodhead, M. (1995) Disturbing behaviour in young children. In P. Barnes (ed.), *Personal, Social and Emotional Development of Children.* Milton Keynes: Open University. A useful introduction to issues of normality, epidemiology and the role of the family and child in disturbing behaviour in children.

5

Learning Disability in Context

Dabie Nabuzoka

Introduction

Children with learning disabilities have been variously regarded as having generalised intellectual disabilities and/or having problems in the academic domain. In this chapter we shall discuss these two types of problems as associated with children in this category of atypical development. That such problems may be covered by an umbrella term of 'learning disabilities' or that they are entirely different conditions is really a matter of emphasis. It is generally recognised however that the social context plays a significant role in defining developmental problems. This chapter aims to demonstrate how a social-ecological approach may be useful in understanding the psychological and social implications of learning disabilities. In discussing each type of problem therefore, the need to consider the context within which they occur is emphasised. First, general issues related to the definition of learning disabilities are discussed. Then different perspectives along a person–environment continuum are presented, together with their implications for intervention. Finally, various aspects of the social context are discussed in relation to the manifestation of disability, assessment and the planning of activities aimed at addressing the presenting problems.

Defining learning disabilities

The term 'learning disabilities' has acquired slightly different meanings in different parts of the world, notably as used in North

America compared with the UK. In the UK, 'people with learning disabilities' refers to the broader category of people with intellectual difficulties, including those who in the USA and elsewhere may be referred to as 'mentally retarded'. The latter term is not generally in common usage in the UK except in the context of some clinical discourse and journals. Thus, in one context, the term 'learning disability' may be used to include those individuals with generalised intellectual disabilities characterised by a low intelligence quotient (IQ). In other contexts it is only used to refer to those who have difficulties in the academic domain (that is, reading, writing, mathematics). In the USA, the term 'mental retardation' is generally used in the former case, while 'learning disability' generally refers to the latter case.

In theory, a distinction can be made between learning disability and what has traditionally been referred to as mental retardation. However, some have argued that there are areas of overlap that can only be meaningful if the former were considered as secondary to the latter (Polloway et al., 1997). In later sections, we will examine how a distinction between the two aspects of atypical development may be better understood with reference to the context within which a child is functioning.

In developmental terms, debates regarding the nature of problems faced by children with learning disability have focused on whether they are essentially different in terms of attainment of milestones in the cognitive domain or simply developing more slowly. According to maturation theory, there is a sequential progression in the maturation of cognitive skills, and a child's ability in a specific cognitive area will depend on his maturational status (Piaget, 1970; Lerner, 1993). Children with learning disability have been described as being characterised by a maturation lag, reflecting slowness in certain aspects of neurological development. In this case such children are seen as not being qualitatively different from normally developing peers but rather just developing more slowly (Bender, 1957; Koppitz, 1973; Lerner, 1993). The other view is that processes different from those of typically developing children underlie the development of children with intellectual disabilities. This view, as we will see in a later section, seems to be supported in the specific case of children with Down's syndrome.

In summary, descriptions of learning disability have focused on the range and scope of problems characteristic of affected children: whether they are generalised across domains or limited to specific domains such as academic functioning. Theoretical perspectives have focused on the nature and progression of problems faced by these children. Developmental theories have tended to consider these problems in terms of maturation lag in specific domains accounting for differences in functioning. Others consider that different processes underlie the development of children with learning disabilities. In the sections that follow we will consider the nature of problems characteristic of each of these considerations.

Generalised intellectual disabilities

The general usage of the term 'learning disabilities' includes what has sometimes been referred to as 'mental retardation'. It describes an overall intellectual deficit and associated difficulties. The wide spectrum of problems represented by these terms has often also been referred to as 'intellectual disability'. This term will generally be used in this section, although the other terms will be retained and used interchangeably to reflect the contexts in which they have been applied.

Intellectual disability, especially when severe, is a condition that tends to interfere with the normal course of human development in various domains. Thus, difficulties in a single area of functioning such as academic tasks in school may be related to problems in both the cognitive and social domains. This often leads to serious and chronic difficulties of adaptation for the developing child and also for his immediate family. One condition that falls into this category of generalised intellectual disability is Down's syndrome, and another is autism. We will briefly discuss each of these in turn in the sections that follow.

Children with Down's syndrome

In recent years, the delay/difference question, first posed for people with intellectual disabilities in general, has been specifically applied to Down's syndrome. The question is whether the development of such children is quantitatively or qualitatively different from that of typically developing children. Does the child with Down's syndrome follow the same pattern of development as the typically developing child but just go through each stage more slowly, or do different processes underlie the development of such children? Another interesting question is what role the environment plays in the development of such children.

In the area of early cognitive development, there are some indications that children with Down's syndrome develop differently from other children. For example, babies with Down's syndrome take longer to process visual information than other babies (MacTurk et al., 1985). They also process tactile information differently (Brandt, 1996). In addition, there is some evidence which suggests that different processes underlie language acquisition in children with and without Down's syndrome (Kasari et al., 1995). It has been argued that a delay model of development cannot explain these findings.

Children with autism

Kanner originally defined autism in 1943. The outstanding feature of children with this condition is their inability to relate to, and form relationships with, other people. Other areas of development also tend to be severely delayed including language acquisition, verbal communication skills, pretend play and symbolic development. The majority of children with autism are also likely to have some degree of intellectual impairment. Thus, autism is generally associated with a variety of cognitive deficits as well as with social, emotional and behavioural disturbances. There is often great variation in the nature and severity of autistic features and in the degree of associated intellectual impairment. This has led many to consider autism as reflecting a continuum of impairment rather than a syndrome (Waterhouse et al., 1989).

Consensus on the nature of functional limitations

Studies of intellectual disability often focus on identifying and documenting causes, the special needs created by the disability for the individual child and his family, and the implications for intervention. An initial practical concern is with the assessment methods employed to identify the target children and their specific needs. However, objectivity in the assessment procedures used can be difficult to demonstrate. This is particularly the case in determining overall intellectual functioning. Assessment which has a specific focus on academic, sensory, or motor functioning tends to be relatively straightforward. One concern, with implications for assessment, is the extent to which intellectual disability is amenable to a universal definition and is a specific condition identifiable in various contexts or cultures. There are some indications that such agreement is possible at a general level, demonstrated in the use of the term 'mental retardation'.

The first indication has been in identification. This has mostly been from epidemiological studies. In medicine, such studies are concerned with the incidence and distribution of diseases and other factors related to health. For 'mental retardation', it has been generally accepted that the condition represents intellectual functioning that is significantly below average. One's score on an intelligence test often establishes such functioning. Epidemiological studies on siblings of children with IQs below 75, and also of various social class backgrounds, have been conducted to document the distribution patterns of intelligence test scores. Such studies appear to suggest that the most severe impairments of intellectual functioning reflect a distinct pattern of causation that is probably of an organic nature (WHO, 1985). In addition, Piagetian research that has a bearing on the universality of intellectual functioning has shown developmental patterns of the sensory–motor stage to be more closely followed in various cultures than patterns of later stages. Serpell (1988), for example, observed that at the earlier stages of development (that is, the sensory–motor stage), major environmental demands on a child's cognitive functioning show a higher level of generalisability across cultures than the more subtle demands that feature at later stages. This probably has a lot to do with the earlier functions having more of a biological basis than the later functions, which may have greater influences of social experience and learning.

The second general agreement has been in definitions put forward by international bodies such as the World Health Organization, the international Association for the Scientific Study of Mental Deficiency and the International League of Societies for Persons with Mental Handicap. Such definitions include 'marked impairment in the ability of the individual to adapt to the daily demands of the social environment' (WHO, 1985, p8; see also

WHO, 1993). This inclusion places the criterion of intellectual disability within the social context, especially the cultural context of the child's society. Thus, it allows for variations reflecting the values and expectations of the child's local culture. At the same time, adaptability in context is a key element in a definition of intellectual disability applicable to most cultures.

Universal domains of functioning

Serpell and his colleagues (1988) concluded, on the basis of the above observations, that a child designated as having severe intellectual disability

> may turn out to have certain common features irrespective of the definition of intelligence prevailing in his or her home's culture: organic impairment, significantly delayed attainment of certain transculturally early milestones of child development and a locally recognised failure to adapt to the local norms of social behaviour. (p120)

The question then is what emphasis is put by assessors on the largely common features of functioning relative to more culturally variable criteria. Serpell and his colleagues addressed this question in a study of the criteria used by professional review teams to determine severe intellectual disability in nine Third World countries. Their findings indicated some general consensus on five domains of functioning (Serpell, 1988):

1. Social habits and skills
2. Self-help/self-maintenance habits and skills
3. Rate of learning/understanding new tasks
4. Communication habits and skills
5. Physical coordination.

These domains represent aspects of functioning that have also been areas of focus in Western assessment procedures (Luckasson et al., 1992). Because they represent features of every society, they were deemed to constitute 'cross-culturally universal domains for the psychological assessment of severe intellectual handicap' (Serpell, 1983):

1. *Social habits and skills* – every society has certain forms of interaction which a child of a particular age is expected to follow. It is

therefore possible to specify objectively which behaviours are socially deviant and displayed by children with severe intellectual disability.

2. *Self-help/self-maintenance habits and skills* – every society expects children of a given age range to perform a number of routine functions for themselves in respect of such things as hygiene, feeding and dressing. Inability to perform such functions may thus signal some difficulty.

3. *Rate of learning/understanding new tasks* – it is also common for societies to expect children to begin to learn some more specialised skills that may ultimately be linked to economic activities. This therefore is another function that may signal the presence or absence of intellectual difficulty.

4. *Communication habits and skills* – these are psychological functions that play an important role in determining a child's adaptation to the demands of social interaction and learning new tasks. Assessment of this domain generally focuses on the extent to which a child has mastered language, in speech or comprehension.

5. *Physical coordination* – a rather broad psychological and physiological function especially often impaired in children with severe intellectual disability.

While there might be some consensus on each of these domains, the particular form and specific behaviours involved differ from one culture to another. Because the manifestation of intellectual disability within a domain may differ from one context to another, this has implications for assessment and the planning and execution of activities aimed at reducing the impact of disability. Issues related to this point will be discussed further in a later section on learning disabilities in context.

Summary

Intellectual disabilities represent a wide spectrum of learning disabilities including what has been referred to as 'mental retardation'. The need to identify the target children has led to concerns with assessment methods, and especially with the extent to which learning disabilities may be amenable to universal definition. Areas of general consensus across contexts and cultures include intellectual functioning significantly below average and patterns that may have a biological basis. There is also a general consensus in placing the criterion of intellectual disability within the socio-cultural context of the developing child. A key element in such a criterion is adaptability within context. Serpell (1983) identified five 'universal' domains in which such adaptability may be examined. These include social habits and skills, self-help (maintenance) habits and skills, rate of learning/understanding new tasks, communication habits and skills, and physical coordination.

Problems in the academic domain

Difficulties in the rate of learning and/or understanding new tasks can be identified in the academic context of the educational setting. Learning disability, as a category of special education, is of relatively recent origin. Early work on children with developmental disabilities identified a subpopulation which did not fit the traditional description of overall intellectual deficits (Werner, 1957). Such children were found generally to lag behind their cohort group in achievement in types of school-related tasks. In the USA, the use of the term 'learning disabilities' to describe these children can be traced to Samuel Kirk (1962, 1963). Kirk proposed that the term should be used to denote the difficulties some children have in school-related basic skill areas (for example speech and language, reading, spelling, writing, mathematics). This group also included children of normal intelligence experiencing similar cognitive deficiencies but whose difficulties in adapting seemed specific to a relatively narrow range of problem types.

Kirk suggested that there was a need to dwell less on speculating about the causes of learning failure and more on specifically identifying and treating the learning problems. There then followed a number of alternative definitions of learning disabilities to reflect an increasing awareness of the plight of 'disabled learners' and the need to identify and treat their problems (Hallahan and Kauffman, 1976). However, the tendency within the education profession has been to retain a broader definition of learning disabilities. As suggested by Hallahan and Kauffman (1977), a child with a learning disability was simply one who was not achieving his full potential. Such a child may have any intelligence level, may have a learning problem for any number of reasons (some cognitive and some not), and may or may not have emotional problems.

One of the key components in the definitions currently in use is the discrepancy between a child's ability and his achievement. Underachievement has tended to be the main basis of classification to learning disability status by educational or school committees (MacMillan et al., 1998). Some of these children may be without any other apparent physical, sensory or emotional problems that could have a significant impact on their social functioning. For such children, their impairment is not such that education out of the mainstream is considered necessary. Because they tend to be integrated into mainstream schools, their academic attainments may have a significant impact on their social experiences and resultant social adjustment. For other children, difficulties in the academic domain may occur concomitantly with other handicapping conditions such as sensory impairment, intellectual disability, serious emotional disturbance or cultural differences. However, the learning disabilities of such children are not considered to result from those conditions or influences (see National Joint Committee on Learning Disabilities, 1994).

General and specific classifications

In the UK, the Warnock Report of 1978 influenced the current definition and classification of children experiencing difficulties in the academic domain. Until then, such children were classified into various separate categories that included physical, emotional and intellectual difficulties (Pritchard, 1963). The Warnock Report recommended that the term 'children with learning difficulties' be used for *all children requiring special educational provision*, and that such learning difficulties might be described as 'mild', 'moderate' or 'severe'. Children with particular difficulties only, such as reading, may be described as having a 'specific learning difficulty'. This classification represented a move away from using several *labels*, towards statements of educational *needs* based on a detailed profile following an individual assessment. This process is discussed further in a later section.

These, then, are functional classifications based essentially on curricular requirements. They place more emphasis on what the child may require and less on the presenting limitations of the child. However, identification of an appropriate curriculum for the child requires an understanding of the nature of the child's problems. In this respect, an understanding of the child's cognitive abilities is also necessary when considering learning difficulties (Dockrell and McShane, 1993). One argument is that categorisation solely on the basis of educational needs as suggested by the Warnock Report tends to be too inclusive of children whose difficulties might be sensory, physical, emotional, or due to general intellectual disability. These difficulties represent different social experiences for the children affected and, in instances where the concern is mainly with social functioning, such differences may not be reflected in a classification of special educational needs (Nabuzoka, 2000).

Summary

Children with problems in the academic domain include a subpopulation which does not fit the description of overall intellectual deficits. Such children generally lag behind their peers in achievement on types of school-related tasks. Some may be of normal intelligence but with difficulties in adaptation specific to a narrow range of areas. A key component in identifying a learning disability in such cases is the discrepancy between a child's ability and his achievement. Other children in this category may or may not have other handicapping conditions. In the UK, the term 'learning difficulties' is generally used to describe academic problems faced by all such children within a context of special educational needs. Such a description is based more on curriculum requirements and less on the presenting functional limitations of the children. Understanding of the latter is nonetheless important in guiding intervention approaches.

Conclusion

Descriptions of learning disabilities have focused on the range and scope of atypical development characteristics of affected children: whether it is generalised across domains or limited to specific domains such as academic functioning. Thus, in one context the term 'learning disability' may be used to include those individuals with generalised intellectual disabilities characterised by a low IQ. In other contexts it is only used to refer to those who have difficulties in school-related tasks such as reading, writing and mathematics. Lerner (1993) outlines some common elements in descriptions of learning disabilities of the latter type:

- *Neurological dysfunction:* The view that learning disability is related to atypical brain function is suggested by a consideration that all learning originates within the brain. Thus, a disorder in learning could be caused by dysfunction in the nervous system.

- *Uneven development:* As mental ability, or intellect, is not a single capacity but is composed of several underlying mental abilities, these component abilities or subabilities do not develop in an even or normal way for children with learning disabilities.

- *Difficulty in academic and learning tasks:* Individuals with learning disabilities present different types of problem. Some may have problems in the acquisition of speech and oral language, others in reading, arithmetic, writing, motor skills, thinking or psychosocial skills. The affected learning tasks are wide-ranging, but difficulty in academic learning is often included as a key component of learning disability.

- *Underachievement:* Discrepancy between potential (what the child is capable of learning) and achievement (what the child has learned or achieved) is a common element of descriptions of learning disabilities. This criterion emphasises under-achievement while minimising other aspects such as disorders in basic psychological processes.

- *Excluding other causes:* Some descriptions of learning disability focused on the academic domain do not consider other causes as primary. Accordingly, children with learning disability may not have general intellectual disability, emotional disturbance, visual handicap or hearing impairment, and are not considered to be culturally, socially, or economically disadvantaged. In practice, however, children with learning disabilities tend to have some other problems in one or more of these areas. In this respect the general term 'learning difficulties' is generally used in the UK to include those who, in the USA, are referred to as having 'learning disabilities'.

Overall, descriptions of learning disability reflect some assumptions about development, which can be identified in various models of typical and/or atypical development. Such models have various implications for intervention and some of these are described in the next section.

Theoretical models relevant to learning disabilities

Development, whether typical or atypical, has generally been attributed to person variables (for example the inherited genetic make-up of the individual, or such things as brain injury), environmental variables (rich versus deprived environments), or a combination of both. Hagen et al. (1982) identified the following theoretical approaches to learning disabilities: deficit or neurophysiological models; behavioural models; developmental lag models; and deficiency models. These models can be placed along a person–environment continuum. Thus, theoretical perspectives taken by researchers and clinicians may not always be confined to one of these positions. For example, most proponents of a neurological deficit position, which emphasises the person, would not wholly disregard the constraints of various environments encountered by a child with learning disability. Similarly, those who focus on behavioural factors do not ignore certain physiological features often associated with learning disabilities. For conceptual clarity, however, each of these models will be discussed separately here.

Deficit models

Neurophysiological models attribute learning disabilities to pathological conditions of the child. In this regard, different types of learning problems are linked to abnormalities, dysfunction or damage to the central nervous system, nutritional deficiencies during the foetal period and infancy, genetic-constitutional factors, or abnormalities and integrative deficits of the sensory modalities. One particular approach has an underlying assumption that perceptual–motor developments precede, and are necessary for, cognitive and conceptual development. In this regard, academic performance of a child with difficulties in the academic domain may only improve when perceptual–motor deficits are remedied. In the social domain, it is argued that problems faced by such children may be primarily a result of neural dysfunction (Rourke and Del Dotto, 1992; Spafford and Grosser, 1993). In this respect, it is suggested that abnormalities of the nervous system, for example, trigger deficient language processing, which in turn may lead to unsatisfactory social interactions.

Some descriptions of characteristics associated with problems faced by children with learning disability have identified subtypes of disabilities. For example, Rourke (1989) suggested two primary types: the 'non-verbal learning disability syndrome' and the 'verbal (phonological) learning disability syndrome'. Those with the non-verbal type are said to have poor overall social adaptation (due to social problem-solving deficits and difficulties identifying non-verbal communications), whereas those with the verbal type may not. Some studies have documented the social perceptual difficulties of children with learning disabilities as a group (Holder and Kirkpatrick, 1991; Nabuzoka and Smith, 1995). In all, the approach emphasises the need for neurological assessments and intervention, sometimes in conjunction with training behavioural interventions that focus on addressing those deficits manifested by the children.

Behavioural models

Unlike the neurophysiological models, the behavioural approach assumes that learning disabilities are associated with deficiencies in learning behaviours. Learning problems are considered to reside in the environment rather than the child. It is suggested that knowledge of causative factors may not be very relevant to the actual process of intervention. Instead, behavioural and environmental deficiencies are regarded as contributing significantly to the learning difficulties of these children. For example, in the case of children with problems in the academic domain, it is considered that some instructional underpinnings that cause setbacks need to be examined more carefully rather than focusing on hypothesised processes present in the learner (Weisberg, 1992).

Weisberg (1992) suggested three kinds of children who may have maladaptive school problems.

1. One type has the necessary conceptual and rule-governed strategies for identifying and completing tasks but fails to attend for some reason. This child is likely to have *low motivation*. For such children, modifications of ineffectual circumstances or conditions within the school and home setting have been applied with great success. Behavioural modification principles are seen as effective in raising and sustaining a child's attention and motivational behaviour.

2. Another kind is the child who has the desire to perform tasks but *lacks the skills* or does not have the *conceptual understanding* to master or complete the tasks. Such a problem may arise from poor or insufficient instruction and, in this case, reinforcement or special contingencies alone may not rectify the problem. An added difficulty is that such a child may also take on many 'don't care' behaviours and attitudes.

3. The child who lacks *both the ability and motivation* to perform tasks constitutes the third category of children with maladaptive problems. Difficulties in diagnosis and remediation may arise for this kind of child, if the basis for problems is thought to be motivational when it is only part of a larger problem stemming from failure, followed by the development of a non-caring attitude. According to the behavioural model, norm-referenced tests may help to isolate difficulties of children who cannot perform the necessary tasks. In order to facilitate learning, remembering and generalising, principles of effective programming and delivery systems are considered to be essential.

Developmental lag models

Some developmental theorists hold the view that the development of children with disabilities, irrespective of the nature of the disability, proceeds in the same sequence as children who do not have any disabilities. As indicated earlier, this position is reflected in maturation theory. This holds that there is a sequential progression in the maturation of cognitive skills, and a child's ability in a specific cognitive area will depend on his maturation status (Piaget, 1970; Lerner, 1993). Children with learning disabilities have been described as being characterised by a 'maturation lag', reflecting slowness in certain aspects of neurological development. Because their rate of development is significantly slower, such children may frequently function at an immature stage for their age and consequently fail to attain the same final level of competence.

The 'developmental lag' model mainly attributes the origin of a learning disability to the child. In this sense the model is similar to the deficit approach but, unlike the latter, retarding factors in the environment are at times also taken into account. The concept of immaturity also implies that the child continues to develop in the area of relative weakness and may eventually reach an adequate level of competence in certain tasks. In this sense, the developmental lag model may imply a more passive approach to intervention than the behavioural model. It could be argued, for example, that if children develop at different rates, it would be easier to wait until an individual child has achieved readiness for the task at hand. Provision of a stimulating and enriched environment may be important; but the major responsibility for developmental progression rests with the child.

Deficiency models

The deficiency approach, to be distinguished from the deficit approach, is largely derived from research on information processing (Atkinson and Shiffrin, 1968) and cognitive developmental psychology (Piaget, 1952; Newman and Hagen, 1981). The basic hypothesis is that children of normal intelligence who have learning disabilities are developmentally immature. Similar to younger children, such children have great difficulty in using specific strategies or problem-solving skills that are basic to successful performance in academic and social environments. As a result, these children have difficulty acquiring and integrating new information and are less proficient than average learners in using their general knowledge base. This approach is thus similar to the developmental lag model, but focuses more on the information-processing abilities of the children.

A number of studies aimed at identifying the deficient processes in children with learning disabilities have focused on memory development. This is largely because of the general importance of memory processes in structured academic situations and in unstructured learning and social situations. Such studies have produced some evidence supporting the deficiency position (Newman and Hagen, 1981; see also review by Nabuzoka, 2000, on social information processing). In such studies, children with learning disabilities have been found to perform more poorly on standard memory or social information tasks than children without disabilities matched on intelligence.

Transactional models

A more generally accepted position regarding the various influences on child development (introduced in Chapter 1) is the transactional model of Sameroff and Chandler (1975; Sameroff, 1987). This model recognises the continual interaction of child attributes and environmental variables at various points of development. Such interactions further influence and determine the nature of successive interactions, accounting for a child's level of functioning at any given point. Because such functioning occurs in a particular context (physical and/or social), the nature and significance of a particular condition such as a learning disability is by definition only relevant with reference to the context within which it occurs. This point is considered in more detail in the next section.

Conclusion

Theoretical perspectives relevant to learning disability have generally attributed atypical development to person variables, environmental variables or a combination of both. Relevant models of such development include the deficit or neurophysiological models; behavioural models; developmental lag models; and deficiency models. These models fall on various points along a person–environment continuum. Thus, theoretical positions taken by researchers and clinicians may not always be confined to one of these categories. For example, most proponents of a neurological deficit position would not wholly disregard the constraints of various environments encountered by a child with learning disability. Similarly, those who focus on behavioural factors do not ignore certain physiological features often associated with learning disabilities. However, it is the relative significance put on either of these influences that defines a particular theoretical position. The transactional model of development focuses on the way learning disability can be influenced by factors intrinsic to a child and contextual factors in continual interaction across time.

Learning disability in social context

Consideration of the role of contextual factors in both the aetiology and manifestation of learning disability owes much to Bronfenbrenner's (1979) ecological model for studying human development. According to the model, the socialisation and functioning of a child occurs at various levels, each of which has certain implications for the development of an individual (see Chapter 1). At the macro-level, the child with learning disability is situated in a given society and culture. The presenting disability is defined within the context of that culture, as are the responses of others including the opportunities that may exist for amelioration of the condition. At the micro-level are the personal contacts and relationships that exist, largely in the context of the family or immediate neighbourhood, but may also include relationships in other contexts such as the school. In this section we will consider separately the sociocultural context and the situational contexts, as they might each have a separate bearing on the functioning of children with learning disabilities.

The sociocultural context

As we saw earlier, widely accepted definitions of intellectual disability include a criterion of impaired adaptation relative to social expectations. This is in recognition of sociocultural factors in human functioning. Other widely acknowledged criteria include below-average intellectual functioning and manifestation during the period of child development. Serpell et al. (1993) point out that, of these criteria, only statistical distribution (that is, related to below-average functioning) is difficult to convey to persons without technical training in Western science. The dimensions of 'intelligence' and 'development', as well as 'organic impairment' and 'social participation' are easily related to concepts in non-Western cultures, such as those in rural African communities. However, associations or relations among these broad concepts seem to differ in significant respects in such cultures from the ways in which they are conceptualised in psychological theories and professional practices of modern Western societies (Serpell et al., 1993). Thus, as regards the construct of intellectual disability (referred to as mental retardation), they point out:

> While the contemporary scientific construct ... has emerged from a unique process of interaction among Western popular culture, socio-political history, professional concerns, and scientific research, some of its most important ingredients are intelligible to indigenous African audiences. ... however, ... the concept ... only has social validity in rural African subsistence economies when the degree ... is sufficiently severe to become conspicuous against a background of loosely defined biological consequences. (p5)

In this sense, the form taken and impact of the same level of disability is likely to vary in the African context from that of the West. Serpell and his colleagues go on to point out, as an example, that individual differences in developmental rate are easily tolerated in rural African societies. It is suggested that this is because multi-age groups are the norm both in play and work settings, and socially distributed cognitive work is a highly valued pattern of social activity. In this respect, while the perception of the presenting disability may be similar, the impact of the condition on both the individual and community is likely to vary in different cultures. Similarly, the criteria for judging the adequacy of a child's intellectual functioning are likely to differ in some African contexts from Western ones. In the former, this is intimately tied to aspects of social integration, while in the latter emphasis may be on children's ability to perform tasks on their own.

The sociocultural context can therefore have a bearing on how disability is perceived. This in turn can provide indicators as to the relevance of specific intervention strategies. For example, a focus on the development of 'individualised' skills alone may not be useful to a child in a culture that emphasises social integration. Similarly, intervention strategies that emphasise a reliance on community participation may have limited effects in an individual-istic context.

Social context and situations

While sociocultural factors are very important in the definition of disability and intervention, contextual factors related to the particular situations in which children with learning disabilities find themselves also play an important role. This may be particularly so in terms of the ways in which difficulties may present themselves. Some situations obviously present more difficulties for children with disabilities than others. For example, research on social cognition suggests that children with learning disabilities may function more adequately in situations with cues that are easy to interpret than where such cues are unclear (Nabuzoka, 2000). Thus, such children may misunderstand some social situations and consequently behave inappropriately in those contexts, but not in others. For example, rough and tumble play in the school playground could be interpreted by the child with learning disability as aggressive (Nabuzoka and Smith, 1999), and thus elicit an aggressive response. This may in turn contribute to their lack of popularity. The same child may behave appropriately in the more controlled classroom situation.

Thus, problems in interpreting social situations may lead to such children not being able to understand when to perform certain behaviours (Perlmutter, 1986), but such difficulties may not be as easily identifiable in the classroom as in the playground. In the classroom social roles are clearly defined, whereas in the playground they are much more subtle and implicit (Nabuzoka and Smith, 1993). Similarly, difficulties in academic tasks are much more classroom-specific. Even though this may have a bearing on a child's overall social behaviour, some children may show more competent behaviours outside such contexts. Assessment of social understanding in one situation may therefore predict behaviour in that situation, but not necessarily also in a different situation. Such variations in abilities across situations can make the task of identifying factors associated with adjustment of children with learning disabilities difficult.

Two levels of a social situation can be identified. At one level are the contextual features of the setting in which the child is functioning. At another level is the content of the situation itself. Contextual features may include the home setting, the school setting, the classroom, the playground or the laboratory. The content of the situation may include such things as conflict versus no-conflict situations, peer group entry or initiation of friendships. The content of the situation has to do with the child's task at hand, while the context sets the scene for the task. Both the content and contextual features of the situation can have a strong effect on the general functioning of a child.

A focus on social cognitive abilities of children with learning disability, and how this may be associated with their social adjustment, is largely based on the assumption that disordered behaviour arises from factors within the individual. Accordingly, such children are seen as characterised by some dysfunction that accounts for their behavioural orientation. The context in this respect is only seen as offering opportunities for demonstrating the child's abilities or limitations. However, it can also be argued that the context plays a more active role. An example is in the social domain where context is considered important in the stimulation of social skills. For example, peer relations in the context of the school setting, especially the integrated school setting, are seen as important in the development of such skills. Some studies have documented some specific social skills that may be promoted depending on the context of the school. For example, children with disabilities have been reported to show improvements in patterns of social interaction in inclusive compared to separated special school settings (Guralnick and Groom, 1988; Jenkins et al., 1989). Similarly, it has been suggested that certain contexts can perpetuate maladjustment (Nabuzoka, 2000). However, the particular ways in which this may be the case are not well documented.

Nonetheless, there are a number of reasons to expect some difficulties faced by children with learning disabilities to be a consequence of the contexts they find themselves in. For example, it is generally accepted in behaviourism that many inappropriate social behaviours are maintained by the environmental consequences. Thus, in certain situations, children's deviant behaviour may be reinforced. However, academic difficulties faced by children with learning disabilities may sometimes also be associated with expectations of such children being socially deficient. Such expectations can lead others to treat children with learning difficulties in ways that reinforce negative behaviours. Therefore, while it may be the case that some children with learning disabilities show maladaptive behaviours as a result of lacking the necessary social skills, others may not. It is equally possible that for some children with learning disabilities such behaviour may be reinforced by expectations of deviant behaviour.

In all, the social-emotional development of children with learning disabilities may significantly be affected by the social ecology of the setting in which they are being assessed. The social ecology in this sense includes settings and opportunities for social interactions between children with learning disabilities and others around them and also between them and the general environment in which they are situated. The social-ecological basis of children's functioning is perhaps exemplified more clearly when we compare the developmental outcomes of the home in comparison to the school setting.

The home environment and school setting

The potential of the home environment to stimulate a child's cognitive development has in the past been contrasted with that of the school setting. The focus on the home setting leads to consideration of parents as agents for such stimulation. In one study, Tizard and Hughes (1984) examined the relative impact of young children's interactions with adults at home compared to that in the preschool setting. Children's conversations with their mothers at home were compared to that with teachers at school. Tizard and Hughes found that the conversations with mothers were richer and had more depth and variety than those with teachers. Other studies also found more, and more varied, interchanges in conversation between parents and their children than the same children experienced at school (Clarke-Stewart and Fein, 1983). On the other hand, teachers have been found to differ from parents by using language that is often more complex, asking questions and providing more direct teaching (Tizard, 1985). In all, studies suggest that the home setting may provide a much more realistic stimulation of the children's language abilities (Rutter, 1985b).

There are some indications that socioeconomic status may also be important. For example, more varied conversations between parents and children were observed in upper-working-class homes (Clarke-Stewart and Fein, 1983). In addition, working-class children seemed inhibited at school in their language usage

(Clarke-Stewart and Fein, 1983), but were freer in their use of language at home, which was also reflected in conversations that explored the development of ideas (Tizard and Hughes, 1984).

Such findings have a number of implications for children with learning disabilities. For example, they suggest that assessments made solely in the school context may underestimate the capabilities of children categorised as being at risk for developmental delays. It would appear that some skills possessed by children might be inhibited at school but not in the home. In addition, these findings indicate that the home setting may be a much more effective context for intervention than it has been credited for. Related to this is the recognition of parents as agents for ameliorative programmes and the significance of socioeconomic factors.

The role played by parents in the development and education of children has long been recognised. In the 1960s, empirical studies focused on developing effective strategies for parents to utilise in educating and managing their children. Notable in the USA was the Portage approach, developed in 1969 in Portage, Wisconsin as an education service for preschool children with disabilities and their families. The approach was introduced into the UK in 1976 (HM Inspectorate, 1990). The model is based on a home visiting system with emphasis on parents as teachers of their own children (Boyd and Bluma, 1977). The parents are in turn helped by professionals to develop their own teaching skills (Boyd et al., 1977).

In all, Portage projects have been positively evaluated both in the US and UK sites where they were implemented (Boyd et al., 1977; HM Inspectorate, 1990). Such positive outcomes emphasise the importance of intervention and functioning in context for children at risk for developmental or learning disabilities. One reason may be that the home context provides meaningful situations for the exercise and application of relevant skills for the children. However, for such programmes to succeed, assessment of both the children's functional limitations and the resource requirements of the various settings are necessary.

Issues in assessment and intervention strategies

Professional intervention on behalf of children with developmental or learning disabilities requires an assessment of the child's level of functioning. This includes his emotional, social, moral and intellectual skills, dispositions and needs. Intervention can then include the design of an environment to respond to those needs. In the case of children experiencing difficulties in school in the UK and until recently (Fisher, 2000), assessment of levels of functioning occurred in the context of 'statementing'. This is a process by which an educational psychologist, a medical doctor and other professionals make an assessment of the functioning and special needs of a child. On the basis of this, a profile of the strengths and needs of the child is drawn up, together with a recommendation as to the best form of educational placement for the child. This may be a mainstream school with resources to cater for the special needs (integrated setting), or a separate school with more specialised resources (special school). Below is an example of a summarised 'statement' for James aged eight years.

Case 5.1 James

James was diagnosed as having moderate learning difficulties. He has significant delay in cognitive development, with significant specific delays in expressive and receptive language (comprehension and vocabulary is at five-year level).

In his 'statement' of needs he is described as requiring an individualised approach for basic education skills, and specifically needs overlearning at each stage. He also needs development of attention skills and self-confidence, speech therapy and an individual programme to develop language skills. He is described as mildly clumsy and that he would benefit from attention to the development of fine and gross motor skills.

In the social domain, James is considered to be 'friendly and willing' and seems to benefit socially from access to a range of peers. However, although sociable, social skills are immature and need development. He socially seeks out younger children but appears to benefit from the company of mainstream pupils who serve as models of behaviour. Healthwise, James has asthma, but is symptom free on medication.

The outcome of the statementing process was that James would benefit from a modified curriculum and close home–school liaison. It was therefore recommended that he be placed in a mainstream school with integrated resource facilities to meet special needs.

The statement thus provides an educational and social profile of a child with great emphasis on what he may require. The recommendation for and eventual placement would be in an educational environment deemed to best meet those needs identified in the assessment. In the case of James, for example, accessibility to a speech therapist and a range of mainstream peers were seen as some of the key factors for recommending an integrated mainstream school with a resource facility. The choice of a particular school to host the child would depend on the availability of the resources and support systems to meet the stated needs. In addition, links between the school and home setting were seen as important for James.

Statementing also implies that an assessment is made, in some way, of the suitability of a given setting to cater for the child's needs. Assessment in this sense should involve several aspects aimed at informing professional interventions in response to the presenting disability. The need for *multidimensional assessment* is consistent with the ecological perspective on human development (Bronfenbrenner, 1979; see Chapter 1 of this volume). This does not focus on a static categorisation of the child's current level of functioning, or on a predictive estimate of his potential to benefit from a fixed type of service. Rather an appraisal is required of the child's behavioural skills in relation to the developmental potential of various systems in which he operates. These include caregiver–child microsystems, family, and friendship networks, instructional programmes and so on.

A profile of the child's skills, dispositions and needs must therefore be tied in to a continuum of support representing the various contexts within which he functions. In the case of James, referred to above, it may therefore not be enough to identify a need for home–school liaison: it would be more appropriate also to analyse the home care unit as an integrated microsystem that includes the child and his immediate caregivers. For example, addressing the presence of language problems may not be helped by a situation where the language used at school (English for example) is not frequently used in the home.

The links between social-ecological factors and learning difficulties have been recognised for some time. Such recognition led to a series of major government-led projects in the 1970s, in particular Project Headstart in the USA (Weisberg, 1992) and the

Educational Priority Area projects in the UK. Strong links have specifically been shown to exist between social disadvantage and various types of learning and behavioural difficulties in school. For example, Maxwell (1994) found a strong correlation between social disadvantage and disabilities in the intellectual/cognitive, physical and sensory domains for pupils in various secondary schools of a British city. Studies such as this suggest the need to examine individual, familial and community factors in the assessment of needs for children with learning disabilities (see Lynn et al., 1983; Rutter, 1989b). Intervention strategies would then be informed of the strengths and risk factors at various levels of a given child's environmental systems.

Conclusion

In this chapter the term 'learning disability' has been used both in the sense of specific difficulties in the academic domain and also to include children who may have difficulties arising from general intellectual disability. Such children manifest conditions that tend to interfere with the normal course of development and often lead to difficulties of adaptation. Two fundamental views regarding the presenting condition include a biological or neurophysiological model that focuses on deficits within the child, and a largely behavioural approach, which examines task and situational variables. Nevertheless, most approaches fall along a person–environment continuum. In the particular case of generalised intellectual disability, a generally accepted view emphasises both the individual's level of functioning and adaptation relative to demands of the social environment. Thus, the social context is considered to be as important as the individual's level of functioning in determining the presence or absence of disability.

Various aspects of the social context can be identified. These include the society in which the child lives, including the local culture's values and expectations. Within this lie different levels of contexts or subsystems that are connected and coordinated in their functions. The latter may include the home or school context or, within the school, the classroom or playground. Each of these contexts presents different tasks for a child, the performance of which may indicate the presence or absence of difficulties. On the other hand, different contexts also offer different opportunities for addressing the needs arising from learning disability. The validity of an assessment as to the presence or significance of a disability is a function of both the task at hand and the social expectations regarding its importance. The link between social-ecological factors and the incidence and prevalence of different forms of learning difficulties indicate the importance of multidimensional assessment to inform professional interventions.

Discussion topics

1. Outline some areas of consensus in the definition of intellectual disabilities.
2. What are the five domains of functioning on which assessment of intellectual disability may be based?
3. What are the common elements in the description of learning disabilities?
4. How may the different theoretical models of learning disability be placed on a person–environment continuum?
5. Discuss the role of sociocultural context in the aetiology and manifestation of learning disability.
6. What considerations might you make in the assessment and design of intervention strategies for children with learning disabilities?

Recommended reading

Dockrell, J. and McShane, J. (1993) *Children's Learning Difficulties: A Cognitive Approach*. Oxford: Blackwell. Provides a good overview and discussion of the cognitive development of children with learning difficulties.

Lerner, J.W. (1993) *Learning Disabilities: Theories, Diagnosis, and Teaching Strategies*. Boston: Houghton Mifflin. Provides an introduction and discussion of theoretical and practical issues relating to intervention for children with learning difficulties.

Lewis, V. (2003) *Development and Disability*, (2nd edn). Oxford: Blackwell Chapters 5 and 6 are particularly relevant, focusing on the development of children with Down's syndrome and autism.

Nabuzoka, D. (2000) *Children with Learning Disabilities: Social Functioning and Adjustment.* Leicester: BPS Blackwell. Examines the relationship between social cognitive development and the behavioural and socioemotional adjustment of children with learning difficulties.

Serpell, R. (1988) Childhood disability in sociocultural context: Assessment and information needs for effective services. In P.R. Dasen, J.W. Berry and N. Sartorius (eds), *Health and Cross-cultural Psychology: Towards Applications.* Newbury Park, CA: Sage, pp. 256–80. Provides a good discussion of some of the cross-cultural issues relevant to addressing the needs of children with disability.

6

Intervention Approaches

David Hamilton

Introduction

In this chapter we will examine empirically validated approaches to intervention with children displaying atypical patterns of development. The chapter begins with an introduction to two general approaches to intervention; behavioural, child-centred intervention based on social learning theory (Bandura, 1977), and systems-based, family-focused and school intervention (see Dowling and Osborne, 1994). While these types of intervention can be used in isolation, it is now common practice to employ multi-modal approaches which recognise the need, not only to equip the child with adaptive skills and coping mechanisms, but also to modify key aspects of the environment which place the child's well-being at risk. The particular ways in which intervention strategies are applied to specific developmental problems are discussed. The chapter concludes with a discussion of issues which are of interest to both researchers and practitioners. These issues concern the need to demonstrate the effectiveness of interventions before recommending their use, and to determine the acceptability of treatment goals and methods and the social significance of treatment outcomes.

Approaches to intervention

What is intervention?

A broad array of approaches to intervention for children has been reported in the literature and is in use in clinical practice. Intervention approaches can be classified in terms of the timing of intervention, the methods of intervention and the person or persons toward whom the intervention is directed.

With regard to the timing of the intervention, Mash and Wolfe (1999) suggest that the intervention spectrum for childhood disorders includes prevention, treatment and maintenance. 'Prevention' refers to interventions which aim to reduce the likelihood of future problems. Such interventions may be provided to all children or families in a population (through universal service provision or modification of service systems), small groups of children or particular identified individuals. Preschool education, for example, might be made available to all children in order to promote social competence and prevent social dysfunction in later childhood. Children living in poverty might be selected for intervention in order to build resilience to socioeconomic factors thought to affect the development of academic skills. A young child displaying non-compliant behaviour might be provided with early intervention if she is seen as being at risk of developing a conduct disorder. In this book, we have emphasised an ecological systems theory approach to the examination of developmental problems in children and adolescents. As noted in Chapter 1, the ecological perspective associated with Bronfenbrenner (1979) has implications for our understanding of atypical development. This approach is particularly important in the identification of potential targets for preventive intervention, and may assist in identifying possible systemic effects.

'Treatment' refers to interventions which aim to ameliorate or reduce the negative impact of problems which have already occurred. Parents who are traumatised following the birth of a baby with a severe physical disability might receive counselling. Chris, a boy with a diagnosis of attention deficit/hyperactivity disorder (ADHD), could be prescribed medication and managed using a structured behaviour intervention programme. Joanne, who has autism, could receive training in functional communication skills in order to reduce self-injurious behaviour. Treatment may be provided to targeted groups, individual children or families.

'Maintenance' refers to interventions which aim to ensure that positive changes in the child's or family's functioning continue into the future and that treated problems do not return. We not only want Joanne to acquire communication skills, we also want her to continue to use them so that her self-injurious behaviour is less likely to return. It would be unusual for us to set a goal for intervention which was only important in the short term. Consequently, maintenance of intervention effects will almost always be important.

Most of the discussion in this chapter will be on the methods that have been used to assist children with developmental problems. The main focus will be on empirically validated methods (King and Ollendick, 1998). In professional psychology, and indeed in other professional disciplines, there is increasing emphasis on the importance of 'evidence-based practice'. It is standard practice in the training of educational and clinical psychologists to adopt a 'scientist-practitioner model' (Hayes et al., 1999). The scientist-practitioner collects relevant data on the problem at hand, selects empirically validated interventions on the basis of analyses of the data, and evaluates interventions using the appropriate methodology, thereby contributing to the knowledge base on intervention effectiveness.

While the term 'intervention' is in common use, some readers may find it controversial. In using the term, we do not mean to imply that the individual child should necessarily be regarded as displaying pathological adjustment to an optimal environment. Nor do we suggest that the child should always be the target of change while the circumstances remain constant. Interventions can equally be applied, at various levels, to the social systems that affect individuals. Positive parenting programmes, for example, have been used in order to help prevent child problems. Alternatively, interventions may need to focus on making school curricula developmentally appropriate, or on improving the quality of communication between home and school. It should be noted, though, that empirically validated methods have disproportionately taken a child-centred focus. Likely explanations for this include key methodological considerations, including ease of implementation and the need for some researchers to demonstrate immediate effects which can be shown to result directly from the intervention. Multi-system, population-targeted methods of assisting children with special needs, while highly desirable, are seldom favoured by researchers or professionals because they are expensive, difficult to tailor to individual needs and tend to produce long-term, rather than short-term, effects.

We will also examine the theoretical basis from which specific intervention methods are derived. Consider Peter, who has a mild learning disability and has developed a fear of attending his primary school. A 'psychodynamic approach' might suggest that Peter's problems are due to unconscious factors about which he is unaware. Treatment would involve bringing these factors to light and helping Peter to resolve them. A 'behavioural approach' would be based on the assumption that Peter's problems are learned and that his school refusal is somehow maintained by the consequences of his behaviour, such as being allowed to stay at home. Behavioural intervention could include a reward system for attending school, ensuring that he is not allowed to stay at home, and skills training to enable Peter to deal more effectively with aspects of school which he finds difficult. 'Cognitive' treatment would be based on the assumption that Peter's fears are largely due to faulty or distorted perceptions of the school situation, and perhaps false beliefs. He may imagine that peers are teasing him when they are not, or that he is incapable of completing class-room tasks. Cognitive intervention might involve challenging Peter's assumptions and attempting to demonstrate to him that they are inaccurate. A 'family-centred approach' might be based on an assumption that Peter's difficulties result from problems in the family system or, perhaps more broadly, that school factors interact with problems in family functioning to produce an undesirable outcome for Peter. Therapy might involve the whole family, and could focus on relationships and communication among family members. It might also address possible communication problems between Peter's parents and his teacher, if this is relevant.

Who should be the target of intervention?

Interventions for developmental problems in children can be conceptualised in terms of whether it is the child or significant others in the child's life who should be the target of intervention. Historically, there has been an emphasis on child-centred interventions. Children with social-emotional difficulties might receive individual psychotherapy in a hospital setting, or children with learning difficulties could be given structured educational programming at school. It is now more common, however, to include parents and other caregivers in the intervention system.

There are many arguments in favour of parental involvement. First, parents are a valuable resource. Under the instruction of professionals, they can provide continuity and add intensity to the intervention. Second, they can assist in extending the application of the intervention across settings. Intervention by professionals alone can prove to be inadequate if the effects are situation-specific. Third, it is acknowledged in the field of applied behaviour analysis that programmes that are effective in improving a child's functioning in one setting can actually result in a deterioration in settings where the intervention is not applied; a phenomenon known as 'behavioural contrast' (Sulzer-Azaroff and Mayer, 1991). Fourth, many professionals consider that parents have a right to be involved in the delivery of interventions if they so wish.

So far we have discussed only the rationale for parent involvement in the delivery of child-centred intervention. There are also arguments for including parents as targets of the intervention. This is clearly appropriate when the parents are contributing to the problem. The most obvious example is in cases of child abuse and neglect. The child might benefit from individual therapy, but it would be foolhardy and unethical to assist the child to deal with the effects of parental abuse while allowing abuse to continue. Less obvious, although just as pertinent, might be the case of a child who has acquired a simple phobia through parental modelling. Attempts to treat the child may be compromised if the parent does not receive treatment.

The extent to which child- and family-focused approaches to intervention are used in combination will depend on the nature of the problem and the individual characteristics and life circumstances of the child and family. There is growing evidence that, in general, intervention will be optimised through the adoption of a combined approach based on:

1. a clear description of the nature of the problem
2. a thorough assessment of the problem at the individual and contextual level
3. a rationale for assisting the child who is experiencing difficulty in the current context
4. determination of how best to minimise such difficulty
5. a plan for the evaluation of attempts to minimise difficulty.

Much of the literature on assisting children who display atypical development consists of group studies which fail to provide specific programmes for individual participants. Similarly, preventive programmes are usually provided for populations of children who may or not be at risk of developmental difficulties.

Application to specific problems

Child abuse and neglect

Child abuse and neglect are unusual in that they refer to the cause of atypical development rather than describing the nature of the condition. Of all the problems discussed here, one might imagine that child abuse and neglect are preventable, as they are socially rather than biologically determined and the perpetrators are known (at least to the child). Child abuse is also unusual, though, in that it is both hidden and illegal. This makes prevention and treatment potentially more difficult than it is for other problems of child development.

Reppucci et al. (1997) note that although many preventive parent education programmes have been attempted, there is little evidence to suggest that they are effective in actually preventing child maltreatment. They offer as an explanation the observation that many factors contribute to the onset of abuse and neglect. These include socioeconomic factors, family history, social support and social isolation and family and community values. Consequently, multi-component and comprehensive programmes may be needed which target individual children, families and communities, as well as addressing problems at a societal and cultural level.

Attempts to involve at-risk families in prevention or treatment programmes are often compromised by the identification of target families and provision of assistance programmes by organisations responsible for child protection. Families most in need are unlikely to seek help (Mash and Wolfe, 1999). Parents may be coerced by the legal system into involvement in treatment programmes under threat of removal of the child from the family (Melton et al., 1995). Professionals involved in the delivery of therapeutic interventions may be associated, at least in the minds of the parents, with child protection workers. It is difficult for parents to establish trusting relationships with therapists under these circumstances, if they feel that their parenting behaviour is being monitored (with possible reporting to child protection services). It may also be impossible for professionals to determine the effectiveness of intervention programmes when involved parents are likely to be reactive to perceived monitoring. Even when there is a clear organisational separation between child protection and family intervention and support services, the therapeutic relationship may be threatened if reporting of child abuse is mandated in legislation.

Despite potential difficulties with the delivery of therapeutic services, there is some evidence of effective intervention. Interventions have targeted children, parents or the social system within which abuse occurs (Edgeworth and Carr, 2000). Child-centred treatments need to address child resilience in the face of unfavourable social circumstances or the treatment of developmental problems occurring as a result of abuse. Cicchetti and Rogosh (1997) suggest that children are better able to withstand the effects of abuse if they have been exposed to supportive individuals such as teachers, other relatives or foster parents. Edgeworth and Carr note that residential treatment, therapeutic daycare and resilient peer therapy may be effective in promoting positive adjustment in abused children.

Child-centred interventions are less common than family-focused interventions, because in cases of child maltreatment it is the behaviour of adults that is of primary concern. Clear evidence of effectiveness, therefore, is far from substantial. Elmer (1986) reports on the effects of a residential treatment programme for infants who had been abused or were at risk of abuse. One group of children received residential treatment, consisting largely of developmentally appropriate activities, while a second group of children received the usual community-based services. Parents visited the children in care and were provided with coaching on infant care skills. The residential children functioned better at the end of treatment but there was no difference between the groups at follow-up. Note, however, that the design of this study did not allow for the determination of the relative importance of child therapy and parent training.

Family therapy is a common approach to child abuse and neglect, and may be particularly important in cases of sexual abuse. The goals of treatment will depend on whether the objective is to reunite the offending person with the remainder of the family, or whether the family needs to adapt to the exclusion of the offender. Where there is an attempt to maintain the family unit, therapy will focus on relapse prevention, the avoidance of risk situations and the establishment of rules regarding the safety and privacy of the children (Swenson and Hanson, 1998). Although therapy is typically conducted with single families, a recent study has found that multifamily group therapy is potentially more effective in treating child abuse and neglect (Meezan and O'Keefe, 1998). Families receiving therapy within a multifamily context evinced lower child abuse potential and higher levels of social support than families receiving therapy in isolation.

Day treatment programmes for abused children have also been evaluated (Culp et al., 1987, 1991). In each study, young children were provided with a service characterised by low child to adult ratios and multidisciplinary therapeutic input which focused on language, cognitive and social-emotional functioning. Both studies reported superior effects when participating children were compared with a control group of no-treatment children. In each case, however, the effective programme included an element of parent training and counselling, and was not a true test of the efficacy of child-centred intervention alone.

While most child-centred interventions have used adults as therapists, Fantuzzo et al. (1996) report on the use of peer-mediated strategies to improve social functioning in young abused children. Socially withdrawn children who had been abused or were at risk of abuse were given the opportunity to interact with typical peers who were skilled in initiating and maintaining peer social interactions. Following 15 hours of treatment over two months, treatment group children evinced higher levels of peer-related social skills and fewer behaviour problems than children in a no-treatment group. This study built on previous research by Fantuzzo and colleagues which demonstrates the efficacy of employing competent typical peers in the therapeutic process (Fantuzzo and Holland, 1992).

Far more research effort has been devoted to evaluating parent-focused methods. It is commonly reported that abusive parents have unreasonable expectations of children and place too much emphasis on control and discipline. They may also try to avoid contact with their children and appear not to know how to enjoy the child's company (Mash and Wolfe, 1999). Abusive parents, therefore, may focus on negative rather than positive child behaviour, and may lack the skill or motivation to employ positive parenting strategies. This unfortunate combination of characteristics suggests the need for cognitive-behavioural interventions, with dual emphasis on adjusting parenting expectations and modifying parenting behaviour. Kolko (1996), for example, found that adult-focused cognitive-behavioural therapy (CBT) resulted in improvements in parenting stress, child behaviour problems and family conflict and cohesion. Effective CBT programmes are likely to contain most of the following elements:

- Training in effective, positive parenting skills, such as the use of positive reinforcement of appropriate child behaviour
- Refocusing adult attention to positive rather than negative child characteristics
- Relaxation and anger management training
- Positive problem-solving strategies
- Challenging false assumptions and expectations about child behaviour
- Learning ways to promote child development through developmentally appropriate daily activities.

It has already been noted that attempts to change the cognitions and behaviours of abusing parents may falter if related risk factors are not addressed as part of the treatment programme. Just as the development of children is determined by environmental factors, so is the behaviour of parents. Lutzker et al. (1998) and Lutzker and Campbell (1994) have spent the last two decades developing and evaluating an ecobehavioural model of intervention for child abuse. Intervention is provided in the family home, and in community and educational settings. It is 'behavioural' in that intervention methods are based on the principles of behaviour (learning theory). It is also 'ecological' in that individual family characteristics, circumstances and needs are acknowledged in designing and implementing interventions. Lutzker et al. (1998) suggest a comprehensive intervention model which incorporates 12 types of service:

1. Parent–child relationship training
2. Stress reduction training for parents
3. Basic skill training for the children

4. Money management training
5. Provision and recruitment of social support
6. Home safety training
7. Behaviour management training across settings
8. Health and nutrition instruction
9. Training in problem solving
10. Marital counselling
11. Alcohol abuse referral
12. Services for single mothers.

This model is particularly appropriate for families in which the abused child has a learning disability, as it addresses concerns about the child's developmental progress and seeks to reduce the social isolation experienced by many parents of children with disabilities. It is also suitable for parents who have an intellectual disability. There is evidence that such parents have identified their need for training and advice on child development, activities for children and non-punitive, child management strategies (McConnell et al., 1997; Llewellyn et al., 1998, 1999).

Conduct problems

In this section we consider the evidence for the effective treatment of conduct problems in children, including oppositional defiant disorder (ODD) and early onset conduct disorder (CD). Over the last decade, the work of Webster-Stratton and her colleagues (Spitzer et al., 1991; Webster-Stratton, 1993; Webster-Stratton and Herbert, 1994) has been prolific and extremely important. Typically, interventions have attempted to help children with conduct problems to acquire social and problem-solving skills, or to strengthen parenting competencies. These approaches have also been used in combination. It can be argued, though, that even this combined approach is limited in scope and potentially problematic with regard to the maintenance of intervention effects. As Webster-Stratton (1998) notes:

> Research suggests that certain family characteristics put children at particular risk for developing conduct problems – namely, low income, low education, teenage pregnancy, isolation, high levels of stress, single parenthood, parental psychiatric illness, parental criminal history or substance abuse, and high levels of marital discord and depression. (p715)

Webster-Stratton (1997) argues that successful interventions should include attempts to provide social support for parents of conduct-disordered children in order to increase their involvement in the school and broader community. This may be beyond the scope of any individual professional involved with a family, and suggests the need for collaborative relationships among all services involved with the family.

Child-centred interventions have addressed the common finding that deficits in key skill areas present a significant risk for the development of conduct problems. Webster-Stratton et al. (2001) provided a social skills and problem-solving programme to children aged four to eight years with early onset conduct problems. The participants did not have physical or intellectual disabilities or psychosis, nor were they receiving any other form of psychological treatment. Children were accepted into the programme if they had engaged in misconduct for at least six months. As the training programme provided an excellent model curriculum for young children with conduct disorders, it is presented here in detail. It contained the following key features:

- A teaching curriculum which addressed interpersonal difficulties such as social skill and conflict resolution skill deficits, loneliness and negative attributions, lack of empathy, limited ability to express feelings and inadequate problem-solving skills
- Videotaped modelling of positive social skills and coping strategies in stressful situations
- Discussion of vignettes and opportunities to practise skills in a variety of situations
- Collaboration in finding new solutions to typical problems and discussion of feelings that arise from them
- Strategies to improve attention to task, strengthen motivation to participate and retention of newly acquired social skills
- Homework assignments signed off by parents when completed
- Strategies to involve parents and teachers in attempts to generalise skill use from the training setting to home and school.

At the end of the training programme, participating children evinced significant reductions in conduct problems, whereas the waiting list control group children evinced significant increases in conduct problems. Treatment group children also made significant improvements in a test of social problem solving, whereas the control group children did not change between pre- and post-test. Interestingly, neither family stress nor hyperactivity risk predicted the rate of improvement in the treated group. Negative parenting, however, was a significant predictor of improvement in conduct problems at post-test. Fewer children whose mothers had one or more parenting risk factors improved at post-test. This suggests that the training programme for children may need to be combined with a parent training programme in order for clinically significant improvements to be obtained in such cases. Webster-Stratton et al. also found that all treatment gains were maintained at one-year follow-up. In addition, the study produced the remarkable finding that 80 per cent of treated children classified as having ADHD at pre-test no longer met the criteria for the diagnosis at follow-up.

Several reviews of the parent training literature suggest that this approach can have beneficial effects on conduct problems (Serketich and Dumas, 1996; Kazdin, 1998; Behan and Carr, 2000). Typically, parents are trained to observe and record occurrences of problematic behaviour, use reinforcement strategies to strengthen positive child behaviours and deal with undesirable child behaviour in a consistent, firm and non-punitive manner. This training not only provides parents with the means to act as effective change agents for their child's behaviour, but also allows the therapist to address problematic parenting behaviours, some of which might indeed put the child at risk.

Collaboration between parents and professionals is an important factor in supporting children who have conduct disorders. In a recent preventive study, Webster-Stratton (1998) taught positive discipline strategies and effective parenting skills to mothers of children involved in the Head Start programme. Small-group sessions were conducted and both parents and family service workers were trained to act as group leaders. Teachers and teacher aids received two-day workshops in which they were familiarised with the parent training content and presented with ways in which they could support the efforts of the parents. Home observations conducted post-intervention revealed that mothers in the intervention group were more positive and competent in their parenting than control group mothers, and they used fewer negative tactics and less harsh discipline. At post-test and one-year follow-up, the intervention group children evinced fewer conduct problems, less non-compliance, less negative affect, and more positive affect, than the control children.

Webster-Stratton (1997) notes that her training programmes have evolved, initially taking a relatively narrow focus on skill-based training programmes for children and parents, but more recently expanding to include community-building components. She suggests that parent support is essential and can be derived from a number of sources:

- support from a one-to-one relationship with a therapist
- promotion of within-family support, by involving fathers and grandparents in the training process
- a collaborative, partnership-based method of service provision (see also the section on learning disability)
- group work as a form of support and the first stage of community building
- assisting parents to communicate with professionals in order to build cooperative links between home and school
- training components which assist teachers to understand and empathise with parents' fears and concerns.

We conclude this section with this succinct summary statement from Webster-Stratton (1997):

> Parenting interventions must be broad focused and delivered within the communities where the families live. They must be designed not only to help parents adopt parenting strategies that promote their children's social competence and reduce behaviour problems but also to give them the support they need to become engaged citizens collaborating with teachers, involved in their schools and communities, and supporting one another as parents. If we are successful in promoting social support and community involvement we will reduce the risk of parents maltreating children and strengthen communities for all our children in the long run. (p169)

Internalising disorders

Anxiety disorders present the practitioner with the challenge of determining whether or not intervention is warranted. Everyone experiences fears and anxieties at some time in their lives. There are many situations in which fear is expected, and is adaptive for the individual. Children who experience fear in life-threatening situations are more likely to survive than children who are fearless. Furthermore, certain fears are age- or stage-specific and their appearance might be regarded as part of normal development (King et al., 1988; Morris and Kratochwill, 1991). Typical infants, for example, learn to discriminate between familiar and non-familiar people and become distressed on separation from their parents. Failure to develop this fear reaction could be regarded with some concern. Reluctance to separate in later childhood, however, can result in severely dysfunctional behaviour, such as school refusal. Fears of small animals in preschoolers are quite common, but many adults who are animal phobic report initially developing the fear in early childhood.

Fearful and anxious children often fail to receive treatment, as many children grow out of their fears and are less likely to disrupt others than are children with externalising problems (Mash and Wolfe, 1999). Children who experience fears and anxieties which are out of proportion to the demands of the feared situation should be referred for professional assessment. Children with anxiety disorders tend to share common characteristics (Moore and Carr, 2000). They may perceive environmental stimuli as threatening and tend to be vigilant in anticipating or attending to threatening stimuli. They also tend to believe that contact with the feared situation will be harmful, embarrassing or catastrophic, and experience intense feelings of fear, dread, foreboding, a lack of control and physiological hyperarousal when exposed to the feared situation. These children will also avoid or attempt to escape from feared stimuli or situations, and this may result in deteriorating personal adjustment, characterised by poor peer relations and social isolation.

Currently there are no reported preventive interventions. Mash and Wolfe (1999) suggest a model for the development of anxiety disorders involving transactions among child and parental characteristics. The children may have an inborn predisposition to be anxious or fearful, fail to develop secure attachments with the parent and live in a state of psychological vulnerability. The parent may also have insecure attachments, and an overcontrolling and overprotective parenting style. While suggesting some potential targets for preventive intervention, these relationships are somewhat speculative, and the utility of the model as a basis for intervention remains to be determined.

There is overwhelming evidence that the most effective interventions for children with phobias and anxiety-related problems include exposure to the anxiety-eliciting situation (King et al., 1988; Silverman and Kurtines, 1996). Gradual (graded) exposure is generally preferred, as sudden and intense exposure (referred to as 'flooding') can be traumatic for children. In graded exposure, a hierarchy of fear-eliciting situations is compiled by the child and therapist. The child is then exposed to each situation in the hierarchy in step-wise fashion, moving from least to most fear eliciting. Progression through the hierarchy is dependent on the child becoming comfortable and more or less anxiety-free at each step.

If graded exposure is combined with teaching the child to relax, it is called 'systematic desensitisation'. This is a three-step procedure (Mash and Wolfe, 1999):

1. teaching the child to relax on cue, usually through deep muscle relaxation
2. constructing an anxiety hierarchy
3. presenting the items in the hierarchy while the child stays relaxed.

The hierarchy can be presented in a live situation or by asking the child to imagine the situation. The live situation is preferable, as one cannot be sure that the child is able or willing to imagine traumatic scenes accurately. Participant modelling has also been employed successfully to enhance the effects of live exposure.

Systematic desensitisation addresses the avoidance and arousal components of anxiety directly. If cognitive and affective elements of the anxiety undergo change through this process, then its effect is indirect. Cognitive-behavioural therapy, however, attempts to change cognitive aspects by direct manipulation. As exposure to the feared situation is thought to be an essential element of effective treatment, cognitive therapy is usually combined with exposure. Case 6.1 illustrates the use of graded exposure and cognitive therapy to treat a simple phobia.

Case 6.1 Jim

Jim is dog phobic. After being bitten by a dog two years prior to treatment, he assumed that all dogs would bite him. He felt powerless whenever confronted by a dog, as he believed that he could do nothing to stop the dog from biting him. He would avoid walking down certain streets where he was likely to see dogs, and on two occasions ran across busy roads when he saw a dog coming towards him. Jim was given cognitive therapy, which consisted of challenging this belief. He was given information about the diversity of dogs, which highlighted the fact that the minority of dogs are actually dangerous. It was pointed out to him that he had only ever been bitten once. He was also asked to recall times before the biting incident when he was able to interact with a dog without incident. Jim was also given live exposure to a number of dogs of different sizes. Exposure focused on modelling dog-handling skills. Following treatment, Jim was able to remain in close proximity to dogs without feeling frightened, could distinguish between dogs that were likely to bite and those that were not, and had begun to believe that he had the skills to deal with any difficulties with dogs that might arise.

Cognitive therapy can also be used successfully to treat social phobia (Barrett et al., 1996; Flannery-Schroeder and Kendall, 1996; Kendall and Treadwell, 1996). Kendall and his colleagues have proposed a model of therapy which is both well-developed and carefully evaluated (see Mash and Wolfe, 1999). Flannery-Schroeder and Kendall (1996) present the FEAR plan which addresses both cognitive and behavioural aspects of anxiety. The four-step process is described as follows:

1. ask yourself whether you are feeling frightened
2. ask yourself what you are expecting to happen and what you are saying to yourself in this situation
3. ask yourself what else you might say to yourself and what alternative actions you might take
4. monitor your performance and decide whether or not you deserve a reward.

There is an obvious self-management component in this treatment plan. The child is provided with skills to monitor, change and evaluate her actions, and if successful should be independent of the therapist in maintaining the effects of the treatment. This treatment approach is combined with skills training and exposure, and attempts to teach the child to monitor her own thought processes.

A recent development is the inclusion of family-focused elements within treatment packages for anxious children. Barrett et al. (1996), for example, included a treatment group which received both child-centred CBT and a family anxiety management package. The family package included:

- contingency management of the child's anxious behaviour
- reinforcement procedures to encourage courageous behaviour
- personal anxiety training based on the child-centred CBT model
- problem solving, conflict management and communication skills.

In this study, the addition of the family package enhanced treatment outcomes. Ollendick and King (1998) suggest that CBT, with and without family treatment components, is the only approach to anxiety disorders that has been empirically validated. However, they add that few studies have addressed the treatment of clinic-referred children and more research is required to examine:

> the pathological processes involved in the onset and maintenance of phobic and anxiety disorders as well as the change processes used to treat these disorders. (p156)

Similar conclusions may be drawn regarding the efficacy of psychosocial treatments for depressed children and adolescents. Kaslow and Thompson (1998) note that the majority of reported effective treatments are based on a cognitive-behavioural model, applied at individual, group or family levels. There has been recent interest in the use of CBT programmes to prevent depression in children and adolescents. Shochet et al. (2001), for example, ran a universal school-based programme for groups of adolescents, which consisted of 11 weekly sessions, run during class time. Three parent group sessions were also run, at three-week intervals. Participants in the programme reported lower levels of depression and feelings of hopelessness post-treatment and at follow-up than did waiting list control participants.

A systems analysis of factors that influence childhood depression suggests that multi-component interventions are required

(Eamon, 2001). Comprehensive interventions may need to address a broad range of factors including:

1. child characteristics, such as temperament and cognitive style
2. parental psychological distress and coping strategies
3. unsupportive school environments and maladaptive peer relations
4. adverse socioeconomic factors.

Learning disability

The focus in this section is on learning disability (also known as intellectual disability) as a global developmental disability affecting both intellectual functioning and adaptive behaviour. Learning disability has a major life-long impact on both the child and the child's family. Interventions have addressed both skill deficits, which are manifest in all children with learning disabilities, and the severe behaviour problems displayed by some children. Parent training has also been widely used as a means of influencing child behaviour. Recently, these child-centred approaches to intervention have been supplemented by family-centred approaches, through which the needs of all family members are addressed. At a community level, the last decade has seen the emergence of an approach to education that seeks to include all children, regardless of the severity of their disability.

Of all children, those with learning disabilities may have received most benefit from developments in the field of applied behaviour analysis. The principles of behaviour have been used to develop structured teaching programmes that have consistently produced meaningful increases in cognitive skills and adaptive functioning. Simple reinforcement procedures, and more complex procedures such as shaping and chaining, have produced reliable and lasting increases in attentional skills, discrimination learning, self-care, language and communication, functional academic, community living and social skills (see Snell (1993) for excellent coverage of contemporary approaches to skill development in children with learning disabilities).

While there is good evidence that children with learning disabilities can acquire important life skills through structured teaching, concerns remain about the ability of such children to function independently in the selection and use of these skills. Some children remain dependent on adults to prompt skill use, while others fail to generalise skill use outside the teaching situation. There has been recent interest in the value of cognitive-behavioural training to address these problems. Whitman et al. (1991) suggest that children with learning disabilities can be engaged in meta-cognitive training in which they are taught to select, apply, evaluate and review strategy use in a wide range of situations. This is an extension of self-management training, an important form of empowerment and an essential element of independent functioning in adult life (Browder and Snell, 1993).

Behavioural approaches have also been used to great effect in the management of challenging behaviour. Challenging behaviour has been defined as:

> Culturally abnormal behaviour(s) of such intensity, frequency or duration that the physical safety of the person or others is likely to be placed in serious jeopardy, or behaviour which is likely to seriously limit use of, or result in the person being denied access to, ordinary community facilities. (Emerson, 2001)

It has become standard practice to develop behaviour support plans based on hypotheses about the functions of the challenging behaviour. A functional analysis is conducted which results in a clear definition of the problem, identification of the circumstances under which the behaviour is most, and least, likely to occur and identification of the consequences which appear most likely to be maintaining the behaviour (Iwata et al., 1990). A treatment programme is then devised and implemented, based on the assumption that the challenging behaviour can be replaced by a more appropriate behaviour which can serve the same purpose, or produce the same outcome, as the challenging behaviour. An example of a functionally based treatment programme for challenging behaviour is provided in the following case study.

Case 6.2 Bill

Bill was 10 years old and had a severe learning disability. He injured himself by slapping his face with an open hand. This produced severe reddening of the skin, was distressing to his parents and made him very conspicuous when in the community. A functional assessment indicated that Bill tended to slap himself during the hour before meals, but rarely after meals. He also slapped himself when given difficult tasks, but not when given easy or enjoyable tasks. It was hypothesised that Bill might slap in order to obtain food, or as a means of escaping from high-demand situations. He was taught to produce manual signs to indicate that he was hungry and to request help. His parents were taught to prompt him to use the appropriate sign, and were instructed how to ensure that slapping did not result in Bill being provided with food or escaping from activities. After three months, Bill's use of signs increased and he was free of self-injury. Treatment gains were maintained during a 12-month follow-up period.

O'Neill et al. (1990) suggest that challenging behaviour may be maintained by the person gaining or avoiding social attention, increasing or reducing sensory stimulation, obtaining objects or other tangibles, or avoiding or escaping from unwanted events, activities or situations. Durand (1993) notes that many challenging behaviours serve a communicative function. In such instances, functional communication training would be the appropriate treatment option (Carr et al., 1994). Children are taught to use a communicative response that serves the same function as the challenging behaviour. This might include speech or another form of symbolic communication, depending on the child's current repertoire of skills or ability to acquire new skills.

In the last decade, simple, functionally based interventions have been expanded to include ecological support procedures (Horner et al., 1993). Rather than simply attempting to change the child's behaviour, the child's life circumstances, as they relate to the challenging behaviour, are also taken into account and modified. Various changes at the microsystem level (Bronfenbrenner, 1979) are possible. For example, the support plan might require changes in physical settings, the provision of increased health or medical support, changes in activity patterns or schedules, curriculum changes in school settings and changes in the behaviour of significant others such as teachers and caregivers. Note that all these treatment components are based on the identification of contextual elements which require improvement in order to put the child at best advantage.

For example, a comprehensive support plan would be required for Joe who attends a special school. Joe is most likely to engage in loud screaming when he is feeling tired, confused, the noise level in his classroom is high and staff are busy and do not notice his appropriate attempts to gain their attention. The principle underlying the use of ecological support plans is that it makes little sense to attempt to change the child's behaviour when aspects of the child's physical and social environment, and perhaps the child's physical state, predispose him to engagement in challenging behaviour. There will be occasions when the child's behaviour may be viewed as a reasonable response to undesirable environmental circumstances. Attempts to eliminate challenging behaviour may also be futile when the environment does not support more appropriate behaviours. Ecological support plans have more chance of success, and are more ethically justifiable, than treatments that attempt to eliminate behaviour without addressing the needs of the child.

The traditional approach to service provision in the field of learning disability has been child-centred. It is only in the last few decades that professionals have accepted that children with learning disabilities are best served within the context of their natural families and communities. It was common practice in Western countries, even during the 1970s, for parents to be advised to institutionalise their disabled children. With increased emphasis on community living, service providers are now attempting to address the life-long support needs of people with learning disabilities and their families (Berry and Hardman, 1998). Parents are now more likely to be seen as key players in the service system rather than passive recipients of services (Lutzker and Campbell, 1994).

The last three decades have seen the rapid development of early intervention services for young children and their families. Early in this period of service development, service provision in general, and intervention services in particular, were child-centred and provided in specialist settings. These services were concerned with prevention, treatment and maintenance, but with particular regard to enhancing the developmental level of the child or minimising behaviour problems. Typically, children were provided with therapy, while family members provided 'back-up' by implementing treatment programmes at home. The needs of the parents and siblings of the child with a disability may not have been addressed or, at best, were addressed incidentally and for the

TABLE 6.1 COMPARISON BETWEEN TRADITIONAL AND FAMILY-CENTRED PARENT INVOLVEMENT

Traditional	Family-centred
Parents are involved, in that they receive an array of supports	Parents are included as decision makers and programme designers
Parents are involved as back-up to the efforts of professionals	Parents are involved so professionals know that the child and family are receiving appropriate services
Parents are assessed on their capacity and willingness to comply with the directions of professionals	Families choose their own level of involvement and are not judged or penalised
Source: Adapted from Duwa et al. (1993)	

purpose of facilitating child-centred aspects of the intervention. Duwa et al. (1993) describe the key differences between traditional and family-centred services, which are summarised in Table 6.1.

More recently, the emphasis of service provision has moved from child- to family-centred intervention. Beckman et al. (1994) outline the following principles underlying family-centred intervention:

- children are dependent on their families for survival, growth and development
- diversity of family patterns and structures must be acknowledged
- each family has its own structure, roles, values, beliefs and coping styles
- intervention strategies must honour racial, ethnic, cultural and socioeconomic diversity in families
- families must be able to choose the level and nature of early intervention
- family–professional collaboration and partnerships are keys to successful intervention
- services and programmes should be flexible, accessible and responsive to family needs
- services should promote normalisation and the integration of the child and family within the community
- no one agency or discipline can meet all the needs of any one child or family.

A recurring theme in these principles is that children with learning disabilities are best served within the context of families that are functioning effectively and service provision should be individualised, with decision making and service implementation shared between parents and professionals (Dechillo et al., 1994; Roberts et al., 1998; Turnbull et al., 1999). Duwa et al. (1993) suggest that family-centredness can be examined with regard to a range of variables, including the nature of parental involvement, responsibilities for the design of the service system and the determination of concerns, priorities and resources, the appropriateness of assessment procedures, the design of support plans and service coordination.

Despite the sound theoretical and philosophical basis for the provision of family-centred services, it appears that many families do not have the opportunity to experience family-centred intervention. Bruder (2000) notes that family support plans often emphasise child rather than family outcomes, some services struggle to include family members as active participants, and researchers and practitioners have failed to deal with the potential conflict arising from the inclusion of professionally directed parent training programmes as a component of family-centred service provision. She notes that these difficulties arise as a result of an inability to employ evidence-based practices consistently within a value-driven service model.

A logical extension of the family-centred model is that the extent to which parents become involved in service planning and decision making should be a matter of individual choice. There are periods during which some parents may operate independently, seeking only occasional advice from a professional. On the other hand, some parents experience periods of emotional difficulty when they may require substantial emotional and practical support. It is a common misconception that concerns about having a child with a learning disability are resolved when the child is young. Many parents experience periodic and recurring difficulties in coping, and require life-long support (Berry and Hardman, 1998). Mash and Wolfe (1999) note that infancy and toddlerhood, school entry periods and entry into young adulthood can present particular challenges to parents of children with a learning disability. During these key periods, parents are reintroduced to the need to adjust their expectations about the typical life course of their daughter. Delays in reaching developmental milestones, the need for specialist educational services and continuing dependence on parents during adulthood are reminders of the child's disability status. Although there is increasing recognition of the need for lifespan family support services, support for parents of adolescents and adults with an intellectual disability is often inadequate (Baker, 1996).

We noted in Chapter 1 that it is important to identify developmental risk factors within the social-ecological context, and that opportunities for addressing problems may be found at the micro-level, in terms of existing personal contacts and relationships within the family or immediate neighbourhood, or in other contexts, such as the school. The ecological systems approach to meeting the needs of children and adolescents with learning disabilities is best illustrated by recent efforts to provide inclusive education. Inclusive education is thought to benefit (Stainback and Stainback, 1990):

- *children with learning disabilities*, in that it provides a more diverse and stimulating learning environment and the opportunity to make friends in the neighbourhood
- *typical peers*, because they have the opportunity to learn about diversity
- *classroom teachers*, because they acquire skills in meeting the particular needs of individual children
- *society*, as inclusion supports the concept of individuals having social value and equal rights.

Effective inclusive education is also purported to encourage a *community approach* to service provision, because the parents of the child with special needs, teachers, school support staff, the child's peers and their parents need to collaborate. While inclusive education has been criticised for its lack of empirical support (Fuchs and Fuchs, 1994), recent research has demonstrated some promising outcomes for both included children and their peers. Inclusive primary school education has been shown to produce increases in self-perception of cognitive skills for both children with and without disabilities, and improved social skills in children with disabilities (Tapasak and Walther-Thomas, 1999). Questions remain unanswered, however, about some key aspects of inclusion, such as how best to ensure that individualised instruction is provided and how to enable the student to feel part of the education process (see Wilson, 1999, for a review of key issues).

Autism

Autism is a pervasive developmental disorder characterised by significant deficits in social and communication skills and the presence of ritualistic, rigid or repetitive behaviours (Howlin, 1998). Much of the information provided on children with learning disabilities in this chapter also applies to children with autism and their families. It is generally acknowledged that the majority of children with autism also have a learning disability. Children with autism, however, present particular additional challenges to parents and service providers. This section considers intervention and support issues particular to autistic children, and the important area of parental stress.

Several comprehensive reviews of educational approaches to children with autism have concluded that there is no universal panacea (Howlin, 1998; Jordan et al., 1998; Dempsey and Foreman, 2001). Most researchers and professionals, however, acknowledge the need for early and intensive educational intervention, the use of structured teaching environments and substantial family support services. Dawson and Osterling (1997) suggest that early intervention programmes for children with autism need to focus on teaching core or keystone cognitive skills (for example joint attention and imitation), emphasise language, communication and social interaction training and use intensive and structured teaching at home in centre-based programmes. Furthermore, they suggest that parental training and support, multidisciplinary input in the design and implementation of interventions and a functional approach to the management of challenging behaviour will also be required.

While children with autism and children with an intellectual disability have many service needs in common, the provision of intensive, structured teaching appears to be essential for children with autism. A large number of studies have documented the effectiveness of an approach to structured teaching referred to by its proponents as 'applied behaviour analysis' (ABA) (Smith et al.,

2000). Originally developed by Lovaas at UCLA (Lovaas, 1987), ABA has been shown to produce significant improvements in intellectual functioning, language skills, socialisation and self-care skills (Birnbrauer and Leach, 1993; McEachin et al., 1993; Smith and Lovaas, 1998; Luiselli et al., 2000).

Typically, children with autism enter an ABA programme on receiving the diagnosis (before the age of three years) and receive up to 40 hours per week of training. Teaching generally consists of one-to-one sessions directed by the adult, with teacher prompts and planned reinforcement and correction procedures being the predominant teaching strategies (note, however, that Anderson and Romanczyk (1999) suggest that there is a continuum of behavioural intervention, and that less intensive or small-group applications may be appropriate). Significant skill increases and high levels of parent satisfaction have been reported (for example Smith et al., 2000), yet ABA has attracted controversy. High levels of intensity of programming are required, inevitably involving parents, relatives and hired help. Augmentative communication systems are excluded so as to avoid interference with speech acquisition. Perhaps unfairly, Lovaas's system also has a reputation for its inclusion of aversive procedures (for example loud verbal reprimands and thigh slaps). Lovaas (1987) has also claimed that a substantial proportion of children graduate from his programme with levels of functioning in the normal range and that the children are virtually indistinguishable from typical peers. Critics of the ABA approach, such as Mesibov and his colleagues (for example Schopler and Mesibov, 1995) suggest that autistic children benefit from the use of picture symbol communication systems, need programmes which build on their strengths in visual information processing and learn best through techniques which eliminate error, thus minimising the need for correction procedures.

While the debate continues about how best to deliver child-centred programmes to autistic children, there is general agreement that parent training and support are essential. Dunn et al. (2001) suggest that parents of children with autism are more likely to experience stress than either parents of typical children or parents of children with other disabilities. Typical sources of stress include loss of confidence in parenting competence, marital disharmony and stresses related to the child's behaviour and difficulty in establishing reciprocal social relationships. This can result in a variety of negative outcomes for the parent, including depression and social isolation.

Parents of autistic children may experience stress from very early in the child's life. One source of early stress is the process of diagnosis. While the diagnosis of autism can be unreliable before the child reaches 24 months, parents report that the average age of diagnosis is around six years (Howlin and Moore, 1997). Although recently there have been some promising advances in the early diagnosis of autism, there is still a real risk of errors occurring if diagnosis is attempted before 18 months. It is to be hoped that as the diagnostic process becomes more exact, receiving information and acquiring skills earlier will assist parents, thereby minimising this source of stress. Furthermore, practical help subsequent to diagnosis is often very limited. Autism-specific services are less readily available than services for children with learning disabilities alone, and relatively few professionals, even in the disability field, have autism-specific knowledge. Parents need a wide range of supports including:

- information about autism spectrum disorders
- practical suggestions on how to develop the child's language and social skills
- management strategies for challenging behaviour, with particular emphasis on dealing with obsessions, rituals and the child's need to preserve sameness.

Parents of autistic children may be subject to further stress when they find that health and education professionals have only a rudimentary knowledge of autism. This is often most problematic in the school system as adults other than the parents are responsible for the care of the child during the day. Many high-functioning children with autism spectrum disorders are entering the general education system where it is unusual for teachers to have a thorough knowledge and understanding of autism. Even in the special education system, the majority of children in the UK, for example, attend schools with a mixed special needs population (Jordan et al., 1998), and the particular requirements of autistic children may not be fully understood. In these situations, parents may find themselves cast into the role of expert. They may also have to act as an advocate on occasions when the specific needs of the child are unmet. It is essential that parents and professionals establish open, honest and cooperative working relationships, each acknowledging the skills of the other and working together to identify and address the needs of the child.

Special issues

In the final section in this chapter, we discuss some important contemporary issues in the provision of interventions for children with developmental problems. Methodological problems that compromise the quality of outcome research are addressed first. This is followed by a discussion on some current controversies in the provision of therapeutic intervention. The section concludes with a discussion on the social validation of interventions for children with atypical development.

Methodological issues

It was noted earlier in this chapter that it is useful to focus on interventions that are empirically validated. In order to do this, one needs to be able to make judgements about the quality of evidence available on the effectiveness of interventions. Independence in this task requires a solid background in research design and analysis. While it is not the purpose of this book to provide this background, there are some basic rules for the conduct of good intervention research. Carr (2000a) and his colleagues have recently conducted a meta-analysis of psychological interventions for children. A set of criteria was developed in order to include for consideration only intervention studies that were methodologically sound. The criteria stated that included studies should have:

- a comparative group design rather than a single case design
- participants that were diagnostically homogeneous
- participants randomly assigned to treatment and waiting list or control groups
- at least five participants included in each group
- pre- and post-intervention assessments.

This is not to suggest that intervention research which fails to meet these criteria should be ignored. The key issue is that one should make judgements about the quality of research evidence before coming to conclusions about the efficacy of a proposed intervention. The application of these criteria at least gives the practitioner an indication of the possible limitations of research and how much weight to give to claims of treatment effectiveness. It is incumbent on the scientist-practitioner to avoid treatment strategies that have been shown to be ineffective.

Controversial practices

An important issue closely related to that of treatment effectiveness is the adoption of practices which may be considered controversial (Silver, 1995; McWilliam, 1999). McWilliam (1999) suggests that a therapeutic practice may be controversial if:

1. it is claimed that the practice will produce a cure for a developmental disability
2. trained professionals are required to undergo further specialist training before being permitted to utilise the practice
3. the quality of efficacy research is questionable
4. the practice requires intense application of treatment programmes (for example 40 hours of therapy per week)
5. the practice is associated with litigation.

This has become an important issue due to the proliferation of treatments for children with disabilities which might be regarded as controversial. A thorough examination of these treatments is beyond the scope of the book, but the reader should be aware of the key issues of concern and is encouraged to be alert to questionable treatments. Here it will suffice to illustrate the point with some well-known examples.

The Doman-Delacato patterning approach to the treatment of cerebral palsy became controversial in the 1980s (American Academy of Pediatrics, 1982). The treatment involved parents and volunteers spending many hours per week assisting the child to engage in passive gross motor movements. It was claimed that this would assist the child to establish cerebral dominance and discard primitive reflexes, and was even said to improve reading ability in children with specific learning difficulties. The practice was controversial because of the intensity and cost of the treatment required, the theoretical basis of the treatment was said to be unsound and it was in widespread use without adequate evaluation of effectiveness.

More recently, the facilitated communication approach has been suggested for people with communication disorders, and has been used most frequently with people with autism (Biklen, 1990; Crossley and Remington-Gurney, 1992). In this procedure, a facilitator assists the child to use an augmentative communication system, usually a keyboard, by making physical contact with the child. The point of contact may be the hand, arm, shoulder or back of the child. The purpose of this contact is to provide support, not guidance. Using this method, many people with disabilities, often thought to be incapable of communication, have apparently produced quite complex messages, indicative of a person with above-average intelligence. Concern was raised about the validity of this technique after many adults with disabilities apparently made claims of abuse by caregivers. Many attempts have been made to establish the validity of the communications, that is, to establish that it is indeed the person with the disability who is producing the message. In almost every independent assessment of the technique, it has been shown that it is the facilitators, not the person with a disability, who is producing the communication (Hudson et al., 1993; Green and Shane, 1994; Kezuka, 1997). The practice is controversial, not only because its effectiveness is in serious doubt, but also because it has offered false hope to some caregivers, while others have been falsely accused of committing criminal offences. Smith (1996) advises that practitioners who continue to use facilitated communication should be avoided.

Some controversial practices are more benign. Auditory integration training (AIT) has been suggested as a useful treatment for sound sensitivity in children with autism (Bettison, 1996). Anecdotal reports of sound sensitivity are common, with autistic children frequently displaying apparently aversive reactions to certain sounds. Autobiographical accounts indicate that some people with autism experience aversive distortions of auditory perception (Grandin, 1992). In AIT, the child is desensitised to certain sounds through a particular process of exposure. The practice is controversial because many thousands of children have been provided with AIT when there is scant evidence of its effectiveness (Green, 1996; Gillberg et al., 1997; McWilliam, 1999). Consequently, these children and their parents may have spent time and effort with no benefit, and on some occasions will have suffered resultant financial loss.

Current controversies in treatment approaches for children with atypical development are useful, in that they remind us of the need to approach the selection of treatments from a scientist-practitioner perspective. McWilliam (1999) suggests that unproven practices continue to be adopted because of their ease of implementation, professionals may rely on the word of colleagues and fail to read the literature, the treatments have a rationale based on values concurrent with those of the professional, or the treatments offer hope to people faced with what may appear to be insurmountable problems. It is the responsibility of professionals to ensure that children with developmental problems have access to validated interventions that are likely to provide real benefits.

Social validation

'Social validation' is an important concept, which might assist us to address some of the controversies surrounding current practice. The term was used by Wolf (1978) with reference to applied behaviour analysis. Social validation can be regarded as an approach to the evaluation of interventions. It does not examine the effectiveness of an intervention (Schwartz, 1999), but it does address the acceptability of the goals, methods and outcomes of the intervention. The details of these three components can best be expressed as a series of questions provided in Table 6.2.

Social validity is now regarded as an important concept in clinical and educational psychology (Finn and Sladeczek, 2001). An examination of the factors that make adoption of empirically validated treatments more likely should extend beyond the evidence on effectiveness. Parents and professionals will not adopt effective support methods if they disapprove of them, or if the goals of treatment are not meaningful and relevant. We need to understand more about the process by which parents form views on the acceptability of intervention strategies.

TABLE 6.2 SOCIAL VALIDATION QUESTIONS

Questions that relate to the acceptability of intervention goals:

- Are the intervention goals important and meaningful?

- Are the programme goals clearly stated?

- Are the goals important to me and my child/student/client?

- Do the goals seem achievable?

- Would goal achievement make a difference to the family and their child?

Questions that relate to the acceptability of intervention methods:

- Are the procedures acceptable in terms of time, cost and appearance?

- Are the methods acceptable to me and would I be happy to use them?

- Am I happy for others to use these methods with my child/student/client?

- Given the stated goals of the intervention, do the methods seem to make sense?

Questions that relate to the acceptability of intervention outcomes:

- Are the achieved outcomes acceptable, meaningful, important and lasting?

- Have data been collected on intervention effects?

- Have 'independent' evaluations been conducted?

- How convincing are the data?

- Are the effects meaningful (large enough to make a real difference)?

- Is the intervention effective for all children or just some?

- Are the effects long-lasting?

- Given the effort required in implementation, does the intervention seem cost-effective?

Future research

In this chapter we have provided a brief overview of the intervention literature on quite a broad range of developmental problems. We have provided some examples of outcome research and introduced some important contemporary issues in service provision.

The discussion sections on specific developmental problems are intended to be illustrative and indicative rather than comprehensive. There are many questions about how best to deliver intervention services for children at risk, which remain unanswered. In the discussion that follows, we provide some examples of outstanding research questions. Again, these are intended to be indicative, and further reading in the individual problems areas will reveal the full scope of gaps in our current knowledge.

Increasing numbers of people with a learning disability are having children. There is some indication that these children may be at risk of being abused, neglected or at least provided with an understimulating environment in infancy and early childhood. Most of the child abuse intervention research has been conducted with parents who, while they may be poor and undereducated, do not have a learning disability. There is a need for further research on the effectiveness of support services provided to parents with learning disabilities as a means of preventing child abuse and neglect.

As we noted in the section on children with conduct problems, there is considerable evidence for the success of programmes which combine child-centred training in social skills and problem solving with parent-focused behaviour management training. An important issue which complicates the picture is that many children with conduct problems have co-occurring problems such as specific learning difficulties. We know little about how these additional difficulties affect treatment outcome. Further research is required on how co-occurrence patterns should affect treatment selection.

Most of the information we have about treatment of anxiety disorders in children relates to simple and social phobia, obsessive-compulsive disorder and, to some extent, generalised anxiety disorder. We know little about the treatment of post-traumatic stress disorder and panic disorder in children. Controlled intervention studies are required with children who have these types of anxiety disorder. Supports for children with depression have tended to be child-centred, downward extensions of adult cognitive-behavioural treatments (Kaslow and Thompson, 1998). We need to know more about how these treatments can be adapted to acknowledge children's cognitive and social functioning at various developmental levels, and to incorporate modification of influential factors within family and school systems. There are promising signs that school-based universal programmes may be effective in preventing depression. This also needs further investigation.

Hauser-Cram et al. (2001) note that both mothers and fathers of children with disabilities report increasing levels of child-related stress as the child moves from early to middle childhood. Consequently, parenting stress increases at a point in the family's life course when service provision is disproportionately child-centred. Further research is required on how best to prevent this stress and reduce stress that is already manifest.

Many questions remain unanswered about the efficacy and social validity of intervention for children with autism and their families. We need to know more about the combinations of child characteristics and intervention strategies that lead to success. To what extent, for example, can we assume that interventions that are successful with high-functioning autistic children are likely to be successful with children who also have a learning disability? We also have little understanding of personal characteristics that lead parents to choose one kind of intervention over another. It would be particularly important to determine which parents are attracted to interventions which require great effort or sacrifice, and why.

Finally, Carr (2000b) notes that for children and adolescents with all types of psychological problems, the best available treatment does not work for up to one-third of cases, and that further research is required to determine which children do or do not respond to intervention. We suggest that this failure may be accounted for, in part, by a preponderance of child-focused psychological treatments. The challenge is to conduct research that addresses contextual and system issues without compromising methodological rigour.

Conclusion

In this chapter we have provided an overview of some of the key issues and concerns regarding intervention for developmental problems in childhood. We have suggested that it is useful to examine the intervention literature from the perspective of the scientist-practitioner, and to appreciate the importance of a focus on empirically validated treatments. We have also highlighted the fact that intervention can be delivered before developmental problems are apparent, in order to correct atypical development already manifest or maintain the effects of preventive or treatment programmes.

The question of 'Which approach works best and for whom?' is difficult to answer. Just as there are many possible factors which put a child at risk of having developmental problems, there are many factors which contribute to intervention success or failure:

- child factors, such as age, ability level and cognitive style
- the nature of the problem and its severity, chronicity and associated co-occurring difficulties
- situational factors at home and school
- intervention factors, such as duration, intensity and the setting in which it is provided.

There is substantial evidence to suggest that cognitive-behavioural interventions for children, and behavioural family interventions, are applicable for a wide range of developmental problems. Further systematic research is required in order to determine why some children and families do not respond to intervention. For some families, there may be a greater need to focus on their life circumstances, their involvement in the community and the cultural values which guide their modes of operating than is generally the case in traditional psychosocial intervention. It may also be necessary to examine the respective roles of the client and the professional, and the dynamics of the client–professional relationship, in order to optimise intervention efforts.

Discussion topics

1. What is empirical validation and why is it important?
2. What are the basic elements of the scientist-practitioner model?
3. What are cognitive-behavioural and family systems interventions and how have they contributed to the treatment of developmental problems in children?
4. Why are some interventions regarded as controversial?

5. How might an examination of the social validity of intervention help to address controversial issues in treatment?
6. What are some remaining research questions about intervention for children with atypical development?

Recommended reading

Clements, J. and Zarkowska, E. (2000). *Behavioural Concerns and Autism Spectrum Disorders: Explanations and Strategies for Change.* London: Jessica Kingsley. A useful manual for practitioners written from the perspective of two British trained clinical psychologists with extensive experience in the field of developmental disabilities.

Hill, J. and Maughan, B. (eds) (2001) *Conduct Disorders in Childhood and Adolescence.* New York: Cambridge University Press. An extensive text that deals with causation, treatment and prevention.

Lucyshyn, J.M., Dunlap, G. and Albin, R.W. (eds) (2002) *Families and Positive Behavior Support: Addressing Problem Behavior in Family Contexts.* Baltimore, MD: Paul H. Brookes. A comprehensive text written from a North American perspective with an emphasis on building family–school partnerships to assist children with developmental disabilities.

7

Understanding Atypical Development in Context

Janet Empson and Dabie Nabuzoka

Introduction

This chapter looks more closely at how atypical development may be better understood by examining the context within which a child functions. There is an overview of the main explanations of atypical development introduced in earlier chapters. Such explanations often represent different theoretical approaches to particular problems in the development of children. One of these is the perspective focusing on development as the unfolding of innate capacities of the child. This perspective largely views biological factors as playing a significant role in the causation of atypical development. A specific example is the condition of Down's syndrome, which is characterised by chromosomal abnormalities. Another explanation is the ecological perspective, which emphasises the role of the social and physical context of development. This perspective is a main focus of this chapter.

The role of cultural, family and sociostructural factors in atypical development is specifically discussed. Particular issues related to the impact of child-rearing perspectives and practices on the incidence, prevalence and manifestation of developmental problems are discussed. This section links together literature from cross-cultural research to illustrate the lives of the participants in the research process.

We then discuss the transactional explanation of atypical development. The role of context in atypical development is particularly emphasised, although not at the expense of ignoring individual or biological factors. There are two main areas of focus for this discussion, health problems in children and parenting.

Next we revisit an integration of the ecological and transactional (ET) perspectives following the work of Lynch and Cicchetti (1998). They used this theoretical framework in explaining the relationship between violence and aggression in neighbourhoods in relation to child maltreatment. This section also discusses how the ET approach may be applied to the development of aggression in individual children, and in behaviour associated with nutrition of children.

Research and practical implications of considering atypical development in context, particularly the ET approach, are then discussed. Some general areas for research questions are identified, aiming to refocus our attention in ways that can further enhance our understanding of atypical development. Some implications for the practices of professionals working with children and their parents are then identified. Finally, it is concluded that individual child variables and environmental ones, including social-ecological factors, may not in themselves be sufficient in determining the course of individual development. The ways in which they interact and mutually influence each other over time need to be incorporated into efforts aimed at the amelioration of atypical child development.

Explanations of development

As we saw in Chapter 1, the study of development is essentially concerned with change and growth over time. While growth usually follows a fixed programme and is characterised by orderly progression, change can be continuous or discontinuous. This change occurs in all domains (biological, cognitive and social-emotional) as children acquire new competencies and skills.

Most research into child development has focused on describing changes in behaviours and competencies with age. However, in order to understand and explain developmental change, the fundamental question must be: what are the underlying causes of change – how and why does development occur? In attempting to answer these questions, we can also address the issue of how atypical development may arise. Over the years, theoretical explanations of development have varied in the emphasis they place on contributions made by the characteristics of the individual and characteristics of the environment. This debate has traditionally focused on the relative contribution to development of nature and nurture, or biological and environmental factors. In studying atypical development, certain conditions clearly illustrate the contribution of one or the other of these groups of factors, while others are not so straightforward. We discuss these two groups of factors first, and then elaborate on the role of sociocultural and physical aspects of the environment. Sociocultural factors represent the main focus of the discussions in this chapter.

Biological factors in atypical development

The traditional perspective focusing on biological characteristics of the individual viewed development as the unfolding of innate capacities of the child (maturation). This perspective saw biological factors such as genes and chromosomes playing a significant role in the causation or aetiology of atypical development. Genetic and chromosomal abnormalities can disturb the normal maturational process. Atypical development in this view resulted from a failure in the realisation of largely innate capacities due to some aberration in functioning or biological structure. A specific example is the condition of Down's syndrome, which is *caused* by chromosomal abnormalities. Down's syndrome also illustrates how a condition with a clearly identifiable biological origin manifests in different ways depending upon the environment in which the person with Down's syndrome is growing up.

As described in Chapter 2, children with Down's syndrome are characterised by specific atypical facial features, short stature and learning disabilities. The extent of the child's intellectual difficulties depends upon the environment in which the child is growing up. The study of Harris et al. (1996) demonstrated the relationship between efforts by the parents to stimulate the child and developmental outcome. Many years previously, with the encouragement of his parents, a young man with Down's syndrome wrote his autobiography, which gave a unique insight into what is possible for someone with this condition, and the nature of his experience (Hunt, 1967).

There is evidence that the child's genetic make-up (genotype) is implicated in a wide range of conditions and circumstances of atypical development in interaction with the environment. Lytton (2000) discusses how environmental influences interact with individual biological characteristics to influence the *timing of onset* and *severity* of children's conduct-disordered behaviour. The child's genotype has a small, indirect effect (Cloninger and Gottesman, 1987) mediated through interactional processes. The child's emotional disposition is also relevant to his susceptibility to environmental influences and the development of antisocial behaviour.

Temperament (the biological substrate/component of personality) in infants and young children has long been implicated in the development of disturbed behaviour in children since the seminal work of Thomas and Chess in the 1960s and 70s, referred to in Chapter 2. A child's temperament, particularly if he can be described as 'difficult', has also been implicated as a risk factor for child abuse (initially by Kempe and Kempe, 1978).

Currently, one of the most significant and rapidly progressing areas of research in the study of both typical and atypical development is that of behaviour genetics. Rutter et al. (1990a and b) reviewed the current state of knowledge in the area of genetics and psychopathology and this can be referred to for further information. Overall, Rutter et al. have shown that there are important advances in the understanding of the contribution of genes to the major disorders of childhood. The two conditions which appear to be most hereditable are autism and attention deficit/hyperactivity disorder (ADHD). The evidence comes from twin studies, which began in 1977 with the first systematic study by Folstein and Rutter. The concordance rates for identical and fraternal twins of 35 per cent and 0 per cent increased to 82 per cent and 10 per cent when the diagnosis was broadened to include the other disorders in the autistic spectrum. Studies that implicate particular chromosomes highlight autism as resulting from the action of many genes, which contributes to the way in which it may manifest in different degrees of severity (see Chapter 6 for further information on autism). ADHD was considered in some detail in Chapter 4 where the influence of genes in its causation was described. A number of different twin studies have shown similar findings, whether hyperactivity is considered as a category or a continuum (Levy et al., 1997). Thapar et al. (1999) estimate heritability to be at least 70 per cent which 'implies that the genetic component is stronger for this disorder than for most other types of psychopathology in childhood, other than autism' (Plomin et al., 2001, p228). Studies of adopted children also provide some support for the importance of genetic influence in ADHD (Plomin et al., 2001). This significant genetic component in the occurrence of these two major disorders of childhood has implications for the management of these conditions.

Another important area of focus for behavioural genetics is the consideration of siblings growing up in the same family environment. Traditionally, it has been thought that a shared environment makes brothers and sisters psychologically similar, for example they are subjected to the same parenting styles, have access to similar levels of resources and so on. Now it is realised that it is genetics that makes for similarity, the shared component of heredity from parent to child, whereas the environment creates differences between siblings. One of the reasons is that much of the experience that siblings have is non-shared rather than shared. Parents treat their children differently and the children often have different resources allocated to them. In relation to general cognitive ability in childhood, it is estimated that about a quarter of the variability is due to shared and a quarter to non-shared environment (this refers to variance not explained by heredity or shared family environment) so both are equally important. It is also the case that a shared environment does not necessarily lead to similarity in characteristics, abilities and behaviour, as shown in studies of adopted children in a shared family environment who are found *not* to resemble each other on many traits (Plomin et al., 2001). The family environment has also been shown to have a strong influence in the occurrence of conduct disorders (see also Chapter 4), particularly in the context of parental negativity and ways of disciplining their children.

The influence of genetics also extends to the genes influencing the environment in which a child is developing. Genetic influences on parenting have been demonstrated in observational studies of mother–infant interaction (Dunn and Plomin, 1986) and genetic differences between children can lead them to select different environments in which they feel comfortable, or utilise the opportunities of different contexts in different ways, for example making use of books in the home in relation to their intelligence (Plomin et al., 2001).

In current thinking about the relative contributions of heredity and shared and non-shared aspects of the environment, another established notion has been overturned. Until the recent work in behavioural genetics, it was assumed that the importance of genetic influence upon development decreased as the individual grew older. It seemed obvious that as experience and the products of learning and the use of the intellect accumulated, then these would become more influential, the genes having done their work at conception and in early development. However, as the shared component of the environment reduces through the course of childhood and into adolescence, there is an increase in the genetic influence. So, for example, the heritability of general cognitive ability increases throughout the lifespan, changing from 40 per cent in childhood to reach a peak of 80 per cent in later life (Plomin et al., 2001). The changing importance of heredity to human functioning at different ages does not mean that the environment is unimportant. What is particularly significant is that genetic influence can operate in different life stages, and interact with other characteristics of the individual and the environment in different ways at different stages.

Sociocultural factors in atypical development

There are many respects in which children's developmental problems can be seen as context-embedded. Aspects of context include the society in which the child lives, including the local culture's values and expectations. Within this lie different levels of contexts or subsystems that are connected and coordinated in their functions. The latter may include the home, neighbourhood and school context. Each of these contexts presents different tasks for a child, the performance of which may indicate the presence or absence of difficulties. On the other hand, different contexts also offer different opportunities for addressing the needs of the child. Other factors such as socioeconomic status can operate at any level and further define the social ecology of the child's development.

The validity of an assessment as to the presence or significance of a problem would therefore depend on both a child's behavioural repertoire and the social expectations regarding its importance.

These can be mediated by other factors such as socioeconomic status, which could be associated with the onset and either exacerbate or help to limit the impact of developmental difficulties. The link between social-ecological factors and the incidence and prevalence of different forms of atypical development indicates the importance of a multidimensional assessment to inform professional interventions. In all, sociocultural factors may be implicated in the causation, definition, manifestation and perception of developmental difficulties. We shall examine each of these in turn and elaborate on the specific role of environmental and cultural factors.

Risk factors

It is generally difficult to determine environmental causes of developmental problems on their own, as these may also be inextricably linked to biological factors. However, research has consistently demonstrated that factors such as social disadvantage significantly predict a variety of developmental problems in childhood, which tend to lead to a higher risk of psychological and psychiatric problems in adulthood (Rutter and Madge, 1976). A study by Maxwell (1994) suggests that extreme levels of special educational needs are significantly determined by the level of social disadvantage associated with the areas in which children live. In that study, a strong link was also established between main groups of special needs including learning difficulties of an intellectual/cognitive, physical or sensory nature and learning difficulties of a social, emotional or behavioural nature.

The possible pathways linking developmental problems with social and environmental factors are of necessity complex. It is often held, for example, that there is a relationship between adversity of environmental stimulation and disability. Where health, social, psychological and education processes are below a fundamentally acceptable level, poor development is expected. It is believed that such adversity will result in poor physical and psychological development. For example, brain structure may not develop adequately in terms of the growth of dendritic connections, resulting in psychological and neurological damage. This could account for intellectual disability.

However, the same social and psychological factors and also a range of physical (including nutritional) factors can have variable effects on different children. For example, a high level of psychological stimulation may produce positive effects in some children and negative effects in others. Such variability has implications for the definition of what may constitute atypical development.

Definition, manifestation and perceptions

Parental characteristics have been implicated in the causation, manifestation and maintenance of developmental difficulties in children. Such characteristics may be individual, social or cultural. Schaffer (1996) described parenting in terms of three dimensions: universal practices; culture-specific practices; and individual practices. Some of the universal practices are feeding, bathing, playing, educating, disciplining and loving (for example Erikson, 1963; Whiting and Edwards, 1988). These practices contribute to the satisfaction of psychosocial needs in children in their cultural context. Practices may differ between cultures because of particular contextual demands. Migration of people from one country to another may constitute an entry point for difficulties between the family and the new culture. This has implications for what may be construed as developmental difficulties.

The role of sociocultural factors in the definition of atypical development can be illustrated in the particular case of emotional and behavioural difficulties. Standards of behaviour expected by parents of children vary, especially in different cultural settings. Different rules, rituals and regulations may obtain and these may also be related to the age of the child. Such variations can account for different expectations of children's behaviour, the tolerance of 'difficulties' and the effectiveness of approaches to address them. A cross-cultural study by Weisz et al. (1993) illustrates this very well. They used a standardised behaviour checklist to compare parents' perception of problems in 11–15-year-olds in Kenya, Thailand and the USA. In that study, white American parents often reported their children as disobedient and argumentative, while Kenyan (Embu) parents' concerns mostly centred on their children's fears and anxieties. Such variations could reflect some combination of variation in child behaviours and parental expectations between the two cultures. A point noted in the study was that while American children were growing up in a relatively more permissive and child-centred atmosphere, Kenyan child-rearing practices were much more strict and controlling. Thus, behaviour that is adapted to one social or cultural context may be maladjusted in another.

In terms of the manifestation of developmental problems, different contexts offer different opportunities and place different demands on children. These contexts can be in terms of physical setting, social groups, activities and routines. As a result a child may cope in one situation but not necessarily in another. Similarly, children may behave differently in different contexts, such as home and school. The relationship between behaviour and the social context has been reflected in some differences in the way various parental and professional groups judge children's behavioural problems. For example, an analysis of over 100 studies by Achenbach et al. (1987) only showed modest agreement between such groups, including parents and teachers. Such problems can be exacerbated where differences in social contexts also mirror cultural differences, as in the case of ethnic minority children. In one study, African-Caribbean parents were reported to have disagreed with teachers as to the existence of problems with their child (Peagam, 1994). Such discrepancies in perceptions have been explained as possibly arising from a number of factors including children behaving differently at home and at school, the same behaviours being perceived differently at home and at school, or different cultural perceptions of appropriate discipline (Department of Education and Science, 1989; Peagam, 1994).

Also relevant is the wide variation between parents in terms of their parenting styles, which are usually described as resulting from combinations of dimensions of parenting – permissiveness/restrictiveness and warmth/hostility. Four patterns of parenting emerge, which can be labelled 'democratic', 'neglecting', 'overprotective' and 'authoritarian'. It is the styles, rather than the isolated dimensions, that are associated with child behaviour (Schaffer, 1996). Associated with the different styles are different parental beliefs and values which will influence parental judgements of what is appropriate or otherwise in their child's behaviour.

Developmental niche: physical settings, customs, beliefs and practices

As has been emphasised throughout this book, the most useful approach to understanding atypical development in context is to consider developmental problems as essentially systemic (Bronfenbrenner, 1979; Brown, 1991; Bronfenbrenner and Morris, 1998). A related perspective is the concept of the 'developmental niche' introduced by Super and Harkness (1986). This was presented as 'a framework for examining the cultural structuring of child development' (p545). The developmental niche is said to have three components:

1. the physical and social settings in which the child lives
2. the customs of childcare and child-rearing
3. the psychology of the caregivers.

These components or subsystems operate together as a larger system; each subsystem also operates conditionally with other features of the culture. They share the common function of mediating the individual's developmental experience within the larger culture. Thus, the developmental niche forms a cultural context for child development. Recognition of any condition of atypical development as being systemic entails some appreciation of the constituents of each component and how they might contribute to the condition. Let us look at each one in turn.

Physical settings can include contexts such as the home environment, the neighbourhood and school within which are the resources available to stimulate development. Other aspects of the physical setting can shape the growing child's experience by altering the processes of biological growth (for example the existence of infectious pathogens and parasites or availability of adequate nutrients). The people who frequent the physical environment provide the social settings. Such people include parents and other relatives, neighbours, teachers, peers and so on. These are seen as especially formative of social behaviours because they determine the kind of interactions children have the opportunity and need to practise. The provision of settings for daily life is considered to be a powerful way in which culture influences child development.

Physical aspects of the setting are mediated by cultural adaptations in childcare practices. Parents and other caregivers adapt the customs of childcare to the ecological and cultural settings in which they live, according to the human and technological resources available. Such adaptations or ways of coping with developmental issues tend to be regarded by members of a culture as the 'reasonable' or 'natural' thing to do. Super and Harkness (1986) go on to point out that although most child-rearing customs are accepted without critical examination, they tend to be accompanied by specific beliefs as to their significance. Such beliefs and values, as regulated by the culture and in turn regulating the development of the child, are referred to as the 'psychology of the caregivers'.

How might this all be relevant to understanding conditions of atypical development? First, the concept of the developmental niche can highlight the interactive nature of the causation, manifestation and impact of many, if not all, conditions of atypical development. For example, Brown (1991) suggests the concepts of 'primary' (or precipitating) and 'secondary causation' where the secondary causation may be more damaging than the original condition. Let us take an example of a child for whom an onset of an infectious disease (an aspect of the physical environment) in early childhood led to disability. In a developing country, the remoteness of the child's rural environment from educational facilities (Nabuzoka, 1993) could make it impossible for the child to receive early educational intervention. Alternatively, the attitudes of the parents to disability (beliefs), if negative and leading to fewer interactions with the child, could also make it less likely for the child to get the necessary stimulation in the home (Silwamba, 1990).

Beliefs and customs of childcare can have different implications for a child with developmental problems, depending on the condition and cultural setting. Thus, a child with delayed language development may not get the needed intensity of linguistic stimulation where caregivers do not naturally teach speech to young children, but believe that children pick up language as they develop. On the other hand, certain practices may account for some conditions being 'self-correcting'. For example, carrying an infant on the back tied with a shawl or piece of cloth has been a customary method of infant care in many societies. A number of positive consequences that could be of particular significance for a child with developmental difficulties have been identified. These include the pattern of visual experience, social interaction and physical exercise through bodily adjustments to the caregiver's movement (Super, 1981; Super and Harkness, 1986). The functional level of the child at any point in time is therefore likely to be a result of various aspects of the child's developmental niche.

A transactional view

The main perspectives that have informed our understanding of atypical child development are the transactional and the ecological. As discussed in Chapter 1, the transactional approach was particularly significant because it stressed, in the 1970s, the longitudinal component to development, which was at that time relatively ignored by the ecological approach. This omission is now recognised. In Bronfenbrenner's more recent ecological model,` this component is called the 'chronosystem' (Bronfenbrenner and Morris, 1998). The transactional and ecological approaches both emphasise the dynamic nature of development, but the ecological approach elaborates better the role of 'systems' in development (see Figure 7.1 later in this chapter).

The ecological perspective does not focus on a static categorisation of the child's current level of functioning; nor does it provide a predictive estimate of his potential to benefit from a particular kind of intervention or service provision. Instead, a systemic approach requires a holistic appraisal of the child's competencies and skills in relation to the developmental potential of the various systems in which he lives (Bronfenbrenner and Morris, 1998; also Chapter 1). These systems include caregiver–child microsystems, family and friendship networks, educational programmes and so on. According to this view, a profile of a child's skills, dispositions and needs must be tied in to a continuum of support representing the various contexts within which the child functions. Any intervention to help families and communities in difficulty must take all these factors into account. An example of such an approach is the community-based approach promoted by the World Health Organization in the 1980s (WHO, 1983). This approach is illustrated in the case of community-based programmes promoted for children with disabilities in some rural Zambian communities (Nabuzoka, 1993).

The case of a community-based service in rural Zambia

A community-based rehabilitation (CBR) approach was implemented in a rural district of the eastern province of Zambia to cater for the needs of children who had various forms of disabilities. The rationale for the approach was based on a recognition that most children would grow up to live in a low-income environment, in many cases rural. An ideal setting for learning the skills with which to master such an environment is the home into which they were born, provided that the child can command sufficient attention from his impoverished and overworked family. What was considered of equal importance here was the reciprocal value of getting the family and the community used to having a child with disability among them, accepting them as a person with rights and obligations, and making certain allowances for them, as they do for special personalities, moods and so on of their more able members. Another consideration was the scarcity of highly trained professionals available to work with children who have disabilities. The strategy of CBR was to try and pass on from the professionals to the children's families and community the skills required for addressing the needs of such children within their homes (Serpell and Nabuzoka, 1985).

Intervention on behalf of the children with developmental disabilities required on the one hand an assessment of the child's emotional, social, moral and intellectual skills, dispositions and needs, and on the other the design of an environment to respond to those needs. The latter required enlisting the participation of one or more suitably motivated and skilled members of the child's regular effective environment as agents of intervention. This entailed an analysis of the care unit as an integrated microsystem including the child and his immediate caregivers. Such analysis would include the identification of the strengths and weaknesses of the agents' existing pattern of response to the child's needs, and providing them with appropriate support (Serpell and Nabuzoka, 1989).

Intervention programmes were applied at four levels:

1. hands-on work involving parents, relatives, friends and so on as agents to teach or stimulate the child with disability to acquire and develop useful skills and abilities.
2. local supervision provided by responsible people in the community such as local teachers, health workers, leaders and so on to support the agents in implementing the programmes.
3. an itinerant district-level rehabilitation team (DRT) who would design the programmes, assess their progress, suggest new ways

or efforts, mobilise support for the child at local and district level and so on.

4. professional back-up personnel with whom consultations with regard to the child would be undertaken, including referrals for further examination.

The approach is illustrated in the case of a girl called Yunike.

Case 7.1 Community-based rehabilitation (CBR) in a Zambian community

---

Yunike was an eight-year-old girl who had severe intellectual disability and a history of one epileptic fit which marked her disability. She lived in a rural village of the eastern province of Zambia about five kilometres from a rural health centre. She lived with her mother and her elder sister of about 19 years of age. A medical doctor diagnosed brain damage which probably occurred in the first year of life, but found no physical signs of illness requiring treatment. Her physical coordination was good and she was reported as cooperative when being dressed. She also showed some representation and play.

The intervention action plan included home visits by the DRT to identify agents and local supervisors and supply them with training packages (simplified manuals) to help in a selected learning programme in self-help skills like toileting, dressing and feeding, while also building in some language development. The team would then monitor the progress of the programme. Six months after the programme design, the DRT visited Yunike's home and revealed no toileting and feeding problems. However, she needed training in dressing and language development. The mother reported that she was hyperactive and had got into the habit of wandering off somewhere. The team advised closer monitoring of her activities and supplied training packages focusing on hearing and/or speech/communication; training children in dressing themselves; and dealing with strange behaviour. The mother was identified as the agent for speech development and training in dressing, while the uncle was to supervise the programme with the support of a local health care worker.

At the time of impact evaluation a year later, the mother had taken the responsibility of teaching the child simple day-to-day activities in which the older sister occasionally took part. The mother often took Yunike with her wherever she went, especially to the fields. The uncle was reported to have been helpful in teaching the child basic things but had since left the village. The mother reported no more aimless wandering (perhaps due to a closer eye on her), but the impact of the mother and uncle's efforts at training self-help skills was not immediately visible. Yunike still had problems in communication (speech), self-help (still needed help in dressing) and learning new tasks. However, the family had clearly taken a keen interest in stimulating her development. Also they were not only more tolerant of Yunike, but also more appreciative of even very small achievements apparently made by her. The mother maintained that she understood simple instructions but admitted that she could not be said to learn much that way. She was confident of her own ability to teach Yunike to do certain things but was also aware that most achievements would be of a lower age level. Her view was that Yunike would be expected to learn most things through interactions with friends and through imitation if she were developing normally but that in this case extra coaching was necessary. She felt that it was only her (as the mother) who could really provide such teaching properly since she understood her condition best.

Children's health in context

The health status of children varies enormously worldwide. Physical and mental health and developmental difficulties all interact in relation to context. Thus developmental pathways generally diverge in relation to varying resources that are largely economic, but may also be sociocultural and psychological in nature. Brown (1991) illustrated clearly the systemic nature of most, if not all, conditions in different environments and cultures. Brown suggests that the more adverse or limiting the environment, the greater the number of potentially negative factors that can intervene and interact to promote further difficulties. An example is cited of a child who may face a greater array of negative and interacting causative factors within a developing country. The child could be female with phenylketonuria (PKU), and born in a Muslim family where there are already several other children. Such a child is less likely to be identified as suffering from PKU at birth, if born in a rural environment of a developing country rather than a modern urban hospital in a developed country. In the former case, treatment may be delayed or non-existent, partly due to lack of services but also because of the different value attached to female compared with male offspring within the society. Yet in the first place, Brown points out, the precipitating situation can result from marriage amongst related family members.

Brown's example illustrates three interacting causes (environment, attitudes and cultural practices). In developed countries, other but similar factors may also interact to account for a disabling condition. It has been pointed out that even in such settings it tends to be the poorer and less developed communities that are often most affected by disability.

Parenting practices

As described in previous chapters, parenting practices can have implications for both the incidence and prevalence of aspects of atypical development, particularly conduct disorders and child physical abuse. For example, the control of children's behaviour is an important dimension of socialisation in all cultures. However, the specifics of this vary. The disciplining of children is one example which involves social-emotional and physical dimensions in all cultures. However, cultures differ in the extent to which physical chastisement of children is an approved practice, as Bronfenbrenner showed in his comparison of parenting in the USSR and USA in the 1960s (Bronfenbrenner, 1970). The important question of the possible relationship between approval of physical punishment of children and the extent of child abuse in a culture remains a current debate (Leach, 1993).

Similarly, parental negativity has been implicated in the other main areas of atypical development – learning and emotional and behavioural difficulties – considered in this text. Belsky et al. (1998) discussed the evidence that externalising problem behaviour in children is linked to aspects of parenting behaviour. For example, a study found that mother–child conflict at 20 months was associated with reports by mothers of problems when their children were 28–36 months of age (Leadbeater et al., 1996); another study indicated that high levels of negative control by mothers at age four predicted higher externalising problems at age nine (Campbell et al., 1996). In addition, high levels of maternal responsiveness have been associated with lower incidences of externalising problems, especially for boys (Shaw et al., 1994).

An ecological-transactional approach

The 'ecological-transactional' (ET) approach is a more recent perspective that combines both the ecological and transactional approaches to child development (Lynch and Cicchetti, 1998). This approach, which was introduced in Chapter 3, can be useful in providing an explanation of a wide range of circumstances of atypical development. Consideration will be given here to two of the most important issues in atypical child development facing societies today:

- aggression in children in relation to violence in society and neighbourhood
- the satisfaction of basic physiological needs, such as having enough to eat, which is necessary before the other developmental needs such as security and self-esteem can be realised. Such consideration is consistent with LeVine's (1974) notion of the universal goals of child-rearing.

Both of these are intimately related to fundamental aspects of parenting, that is, feeding as a key component of nurturing and discipline as an important aspect of finding the right balance between control and the encouragement of developing autonomy in the child. Part of this means parents allowing their children enough freedom to show their developing sense of responsibility and also opportunities to explore, have excitement and adventure, free from adult supervision. At the same time parents need to supervise their children sufficiently to ensure their safety. The relative balance of these competing needs will vary greatly depending on the environment. For example, greater freedom is likely to be allowed in a rural compared with an urban setting. The relationship between child-rearing practices and environmental settings was clearly illustrated in an elaboration of the notion of the developmental niche by Super and Harkness (1986), referred to earlier in this chapter.

With regard to nutrition, much research has been conducted on an epidemiological scale by organisations such as the UN to establish the effects of social and ecological factors. At the same time, smaller scale psychological studies have revealed major long-term effects of malnutrition in relation to cognitive impairment and learning difficulties (see Chapter 2). Other aspects of development particularly affected are the social and emotional domains, described in Chapter 5. The work described in this section throws light on the important issue of 'sensitive' periods in development. The social relevance of these issues is emphasised.

Violence and aggression in neighbourhoods and families in relation to child maltreatment

Following on from the earlier ideas of Bronfenbrenner, Cicchetti and Lynch in particular have been centrally influential in developing the ET approach over the past 10 years or so. This has been particularly in terms of relationships between violence in society and community and the abuse of children. Their work in the USA is used here to illustrate also the 'interplay' between child maltreatment, children's internalising and externalising behaviour problems and risk factors for other developmental problems. Therefore this example particularly links concepts and empirical findings introduced in Chapter 2 on developmental risk, Chapter 3 on child abuse and Chapter 4 on emotional and behavioural difficulties.

As was described in Chapter 3, the ET approach was successfully used by Lynch and Cicchetti (1998) to explain their findings as to the consequences of child abuse involving a group of children in summer camp in the USA. Cicchetti et al. (2000) have operationalised/conceptualised the ET approach in the model shown in Figure 7.1.

A more complete explanation of child maltreatment incorporates evidence from studies of attachment theory at the microsystem level of the ET model. If a child has a secure attachment relationship with an adult, this can be viewed as a compensatory factor in situations of abuse. On the other hand, the various forms of insecure attachment relationship are potentiating factors for abuse. Studies (see Howe et al., 1999) have implicated the adult's working model of attachment and his attachment history with abusive behaviours towards his own child. So, for example, some adults cannot cope with the needs of others, so withdraw and become emotionally unavailable when faced with a dependent infant (Main, 1995). The more violent

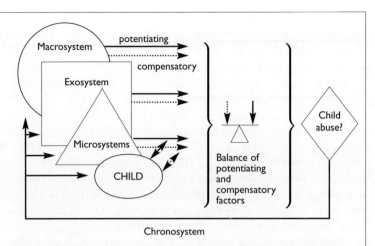

Figure 7.1 illustrates a model of child maltreatment which incorporates the transactional approach of Sameroff and Chandler (1975) and the ecological systems approach introduced by Bronfenbrenner (1977). It shows the systems within the child and the contexts he inhabits which contribute to the likelihood of the occurrence of child abuse. The model can also be applied to other forms of child maltreatment such as community violence. Risk factors for abuse can be present at each level of the ecology (Belsky, 1980) (that is, micro-, exo- and macrosystems) and within the child (ontogenetic characteristics such as difficult temperament and insecure attachments). These factors exert reciprocal influences over time (the chronosystem) influencing child development. Factors in the systems of the environment and child may constitute potentiating factors for abuse (contextual factors include domestic violence, social isolation and social acceptance of violence) or compensatory factors (such as easy infant temperament, secure attachment, positive family relations, supportive social network). The presence of potentiating factors makes abuse more likely and the presence of compensatory factors makes it less likely. The balance of potentiating and compensatory factors will determine the likelihood of the occurrence of child abuse, maltreatment only occurring when potentiating factors outweigh compensatory ones.

Figure 7.1 An ET model of child abuse
(based on Cicchetti et al., 2000)

the parents' own experiences of childhood, the more violent and intrusive they are in relationships with their own children. Thus the incidence of the disorganised pattern of attachment is 80 per cent in maltreated children (Hobbs et al., 1998). Such patterns of relationships highlight the significance of the developmental perspective in the genesis of child maltreatment. Analogous patterns can be seen in the development of aggression in children.

The development of aggression in children

A number of specific processes may be involved in the possible association between attachment and the development of conduct problems. Many of the disruptive behaviours observable in young children such as aggression and non-compliance are precursors of conduct problems. These behaviours can be viewed in the context of attachment as ways of eliciting attention from a caregiver who otherwise would ignore the child. Secondly, the working model of relationships, which develops in the context of an unresponsive, cold or rejecting parent will be characterised by negative emotions of mistrust, fear, anxiety and anger and insecure attachment. Expectations of hostility from others – 'negative attributional biases' – can then lead to displays of aggression by the child. The pattern of attachment which a particular child develops will also contribute to the child's motivations in social situations. Again, insecure attachments will be linked with less self-discipline, autonomy and reciprocity, so that relationships will be immature and negative, testing the limits of those with whom the child is involved. Problems in conduct may result from all these workings of the attachment relationship.

The evidence linking attachment processes with later externalising problems is mixed. Early measures of insecure attachments in infancy show that these are linked with negative behaviours and poor peer relationships in the preschool years (Sroufe, 1983). But, associations between early attachment status and later externalising problems are only significant for high-risk groups of children who are exposed to risk factors, such as family stresses, in addition to insecure attachment (Erickson et al., 1998). The relationship between attachment and antisocial behaviour is stronger for boys than for girls, while there is generally a non-significant relationship for low-risk samples. DeKlyen and Speltz suggest that the findings are consistent with the view that secure attachment may operate as a protective factor in high-risk environments and that insecure attachment combined with family adversity may contribute to later behaviour problems. (2001, p328)

Thus, recent research evidence provides some support for links between different attachment types and atypical development as originally suggested by Bowlby (1944).

Another perspective on the development of aggression in children can be seen in the work of Dodge and his associates from the 1980s onwards. Dodge provides an analysis of aggression at the microsystem level but emphasises social cognitive processing by those involved in social interactions (Crick and Dodge, 1994). Dodge's information-processing explanation can incorporate the ontogenetic development of the child. He explains how the individual child interprets information about social cues in his social environment. A child's behaviour is an outcome of his interpretation of cues in the immediate environment. In turn, this serves as a cue of others' response to the child in question. Dodge emphasised that it is not the social information as such that is important but that different children may interpret the same situation in different ways. It has been shown that children who are aggressive may interpret social cues and information differently from other children (Dodge and Frame, 1982) (Figure 7.2).

The relationship between social cognitive development and behaviour has been applied to children with learning disabilities (Nabuzoka, 2000). Understanding of the processes involved in such relationships can be furthered by comparing the development of social understanding in typically and atypically developing children. Such comparisons exemplify the use of the developmental psychopathological approach. However, the application of the ET approach goes beyond this. Here, while the impact of social cognitive difficulties is acknowledged, other more ecological factors are recognised as potentially interacting with these to create further difficulties for children who may, for example, have developmental difficulties (Nabuzoka and Empson, 2002). The ET approach therefore illustrates the dynamic, flexible, reciprocal nature of development which does not necessarily imply pathology.

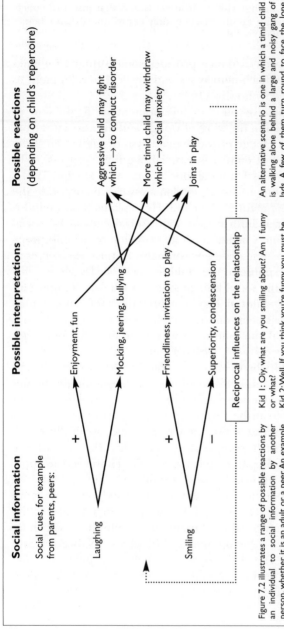

Social information

Social cues, for example from parents, peers:

Laughing + → Enjoyment, fun

Laughing − → Mocking, jeering, bullying

Smiling + → Friendliness, invitation to play

Smiling − → Superiority, condescension

Possible interpretations

Possible reactions
(depending on child's repertoire)

Aggressive child may fight
which → to conduct disorder

More timid child may withdraw
which → social anxiety

Joins in play

Reciprocal influences on the relationship

Kid 1: Oiy, what are you smiling about? Am I funny or what?
Kid 2: Well. If you think you're funny you must be.
Kid 1: Funny peculiar or funny ha-ha?
You can imagine how this exchange can escalate into verbal insult and perhaps physical fighting. This kind of interaction may be habitual and mean that aggression becomes a regular reaction to what could have been initially a positive behaviour.

Figure 7.2 illustrates a range of possible reactions by an individual to social information by another person, whether it is an adult or a peer. An example might occur when secondary school kids come out of school and make their way home in rival groups, pairs of friends and some on their own. There is boisterous activity, joshing and talking face to face or on mobile phones as they wend their way homewards. Kids 1 and 2 are from rival gangs and engage in the following interaction.

An alternative scenario is one in which a timid child is walking alone behind a large and noisy gang of lads. A few of them turn round to face the lone child; they are laughing. The timid child thinks they are laughing at him because he is on his own. He interprets this as evidence of his social inadequacy and lags further behind to avoid any further contact. This may be a persistent feature of this child's negative interpretations of positive or neutral behaviours by others.

Figure 7.2 A microsystem analysis of aggression in the child (based on Dodge, 1986)

Sociocultural factors in malnutrition

Another area where the ET approach may be clearly illustrated concerns the availability of resources in relation to the nourishment of children. Child malnutrition in the context of cultural variations in diet and feeding practices can have major developmental effects on children. Sameroff and Chandler, in a key paper in 1975, placed emphasis on poor diet as part of the 'continuum of care-taking casualty'. As discussed in Chapter 2, diet is crucially important in pregnancy and early life. Behaviours such as smoking and drinking to excess and in the lifestyles of drug addicts can be implicated in the dietary deficiencies of parents and/or their children. There is also, of course, a close link between poverty and poor diet. In developing countries, there is an added problem whereby established dietary practices are being changed rapidly by globalisation, for example the introduction of powdered milk. At another level, people in many countries are experiencing starvation on the scale of famine, sometimes because of physical factors such as climatic changes but also because of sociopolitical factors such as wars. All these factors have implications for the developmental paths of individual children.

Worldwide, the most common diseases of infancy are those associated with malnutrition and they are a common cause of developmental abnormality. Early studies suggested that if malnutrition is severe and sustained for the first two years of a child's life, it may have a 'critical period' effect. This was thought to be because of the effects of reduced production of DNA and RNA (the basis of genetic material) on the number and size of the brain cells being irreversible (Dobbing and Smart, 1974). The early weeks following birth appear to be crucial as the brain is growing so quickly. Even if nutritional status improves in later childhood, this does not eliminate the effects of early severe malnutrition, such as smaller head circumference, height and weight, lower intelligence and poorer perceptual–motor functioning (Stoch et al., 1982).

It is also possible that malnutrition early in life can have adverse effects much later. Prentice (1997) related the nutritional state of mothers during foetal development to the ability of their children as adults to fight infection some decades later. The study was done in The Gambia, where there are two seasons, a harvest season when food is plentiful and a wet, 'hungry' season when food is scarce and adults each lose 6 kg in weight on average. Records had been kept in three villages since 1949 and a comparison of the births in the two seasons showed that the infant death rate was the same. However, by the age of 15 the mortality of those nutritionally deprived in later foetal development and born in the 'hungry' season was four times that of those born in the harvest season who had had adequate nutrition in the last trimester of pregnancy. By the age of 25 this had increased to ten times the mortality rate. Prentice suggested that there is a 'sensitive period' in gestation when the immune system is permanently 'programmed', making it better or worse at fighting infection as the years go by.

In developed countries, inappropriate nutrition of children often results in a different health hazard – obesity. Obesity is now a pandemic – the most important health problem for 20 years. It has arisen as a result of rapid change in diets in wealthy nations. In 2002, Prentice, speaking at the annual Conference of the British Association for the Advancement of Science, argued that the implications of this are that 20 per cent of the population may lose nine years from their lifespan as the result of being obese, which may reverse the 'progress that has been made in the last century in terms of health and longevity' (reported in Radford, 2002, p3).

Additional evidence from a range of sources demonstrates that malnutrition damages essential physiological functions and renders the child vulnerable to many other illnesses. For example, vitamin A deficiency, which affects about 100 million young children worldwide, when present, even to a mild extent, impairs the immune system, reducing children's resistance to illnesses such as diarrhoea, which kills 2.2 million children a year (Bellamy, 1998).

Generally, the earlier in life that malnutrition occurs, the more severe and permanent are the effects, with maximal sensitivity to malnutrition during pregnancy leading to poor physical growth, impaired neurological and intellectual development. However, the effects are not always predictable; a study of four nations experiencing an improvement in nutrition found that children were stunted in growth and overweight (Popkin et al., 1996). These findings contradict the expected improvement in height and weight.

Malnutrition in infancy and early childhood affects development through a dynamic interaction between biological status and interpersonal functioning over time, again supporting an ecological-transactional explanation of development. The experience of kwashiorkor illustrates this.

Kwashiorkor is severe malnutrition of infants and young children, resulting from a dietary deficiency of protein. It is associated with sustained apathy and depressed mental performance. Such apathy in infants can lead to less interaction between mother and child, lack of stimulation and deterioration in the mother–child relationship. Infants also interact less with other aspects of their environment. Thus a cycle is set up which restricts intellectual development in the child (see Bellamy, 1998). If malnutrition continues, this can result in a progressive deterioration in the child's reactions and a spiral of negative interaction with the environment. Galler et al. (1990) found long-term effects of kwashiorkor on educational performance.

There is evidence for a catch-up in growth following the removal of a child from a situation of malnutrition to a favourable environment. The effect is most marked and may be complete if the later life circumstances are really good; also if the change occurs within the first couple of years of life. This is shown in Rutter et al.'s (1998b) study of adopted Rumanian children (described in Chapter 1). This study also found that although the children were very small and underweight when they were first adopted, there was considerable physical as well as cognitive catch-up following adoption. In addition, initial weight was not a predictor of status at age four, suggesting that the degree of under-nutrition had no major continuing effect on cognitive performance, provided that *adoption together with adequate nutrition occurred before the age of two years*. The duration of early privation and especially the lack of social and emotional stimulation were probably more influential on continuing difficulties.

The evidence that Rutter and others found for catch-up growth in physical and mental aspects of development supports Clarke and Clarke's (1998) view of a 'self-righting tendency' in development. This constitutes a powerful force towards normal development, which can overcome the distorting influences for adverse development exerted by risk factors, unless these are major and long-lasting.

The question of whether intrauterine development and the early months of life constitute a particularly sensitive period for the effects of malnutrition on later cognitive development remains an open one. Some studies have shown more damaging effects of malnutrition in the early months (for example Skuse et al., 1994) while a recent replication (Drewett et al., 2001) failed to support Skuse's finding. Factors that might explain these discrepant findings are different causes of the malnutrition or changes in growth rate, the possible contribution of other physical differences in the various groups taking part and the different environmental conditions in which the children are growing up in the different studies. The implications of the involvement of such diverse factors will be discussed further in the next section.

Research and practical implications

The application of the ET approach has a number of research and practical implications for those concerned with the welfare of children with developmental difficulties. In the first instance, it requires recognition of the multifaceted nature of the aetiology, incidence and prevalence of atypical development. It requires appreciation of variability on these dimensions depending on the type of atypical development and the contexts within which it occurs. Thus, similar factors may impact differently on individual children to account for learning difficulties, emotional and behavioural difficulties, vulnerability to abuse and so on. Traditionally, research has sought to explain developmental difficulties in terms of biological and environmental factors in interaction. The approach discussed in this chapter is more recent and emphasises a transactional and dynamic perspective. This has implications for the type of research questions that need to be addressed as well as interventions that need to be put in place to address the needs of the children affected.

One of the more obvious areas of focus includes the identification and elucidation of ways in which child and contextual variables interact longitudinally to account for positive as well as negative outcomes for children at risk for various forms of atypical development. For example, the question as to why there seems to be a greater vulnerability for developmental difficulties in males as compared with females needs to be fully addressed. Questions have arisen as to whether developmental processes may differ for males and females, from conception onwards, in physical terms and also in psychological terms such as reactions to stresses. There are also other questions relating to the impact of cultural factors. The cultural relativity of the incidence, prevalence and manifestation of various forms of atypical development is generally accepted. However, the processes involved in various forms of developmental outcomes need to be more clearly identified.

Similarly, and in terms of practical applications, the consideration of the ET approach entails implementation of intervention programmes that are multidisciplinary both in their design and execution. Thus, cognitive-behavioural intervention based on challenging interpretations of social messages and self-beliefs of families in difficulty may be useful and have been shown to be effective. However, the effectiveness of such interventions relies upon taking into account the child's developmental niche so that the physical and social settings, parenting practices as well as the beliefs that accompany them are addressed in the intervention. Such an approach entails not only accounting for the general cultural context of the child's functioning, but also more specific aspects such as the social context of the immediate neighbourhood and community. Such an approach was illustrated in the community programmes for children with disabilities in Zambian communities (Nabuzoka, 1993).

Sources of cohesion in families and communities are a crucial point at which intervention/facilitation should begin. This means listening to the people who live there. As Damon (1998) showed, it is important not just to know whether or not neighbours agree with each other, but what they agree about. It is now widely recognised that taking into account the individual perspectives of all those involved may be a crucial ingredient in the success of intervention programmes that require community participation. Failure to acknowledge that may explain why traditional top-down interventions have been relatively ineffective. Any intervention strategy that pays due attention to what the people are telling the professionals will be time consuming and costly. However, the bottom-up approach is perhaps the best way forward for changing society and enhancing the efficacy of intervention programmes aimed at the amelioration of atypical conditions in children. Such an approach entails that those professionals involved in hands-on work with children with developmental difficulties should have a direct input in policy decisions affecting such children.

Conclusion

Atypical development in children is now generally recognised as arising as a result of a complex interplay between many variables at different levels in both the individual and the environment. Within-child variables are widely categorised as essentially biological, cognitive and socio-emotional, although to separate these domains entirely is problematic (Keil, 1999) as they mutually influence each other. Individual child variables and environmental ones, including social-ecological factors, may not in themselves be sufficient in determining the course of individual development. In interaction however, they should be considered as significant and necessary and thus be incorporated into efforts aimed at the amelioration of atypical child development. The possible specific variables in the environment of the child must be specified and measurable for the purposes of research and intervention, but are so numerous that we are only part of the way towards identifying which are the most relevant to different circumstances, contexts and individuals. Nonetheless some progress has been made in the right direction.

Our conception of development has changed over the years from a primarily linear one, guided by the idea of changes occurring over time and interactions between child and environment, to a dynamic, transactional and systemic view of the child living in an increasingly wide range of contexts as he grows up. The child who is developing well is seen as a person who actively contributes to and increasingly influences his family, playgroup, school and neighbourhood with positive relationships, an enquiring mind, good educational progress, successful achievement of developmental tasks and prosocial attitudes and behaviours. The child whose development is usually viewed as atypical by society is one who has difficulty in one or more of the following areas: achieving developmental milestones; living in a family experiencing difficulties; experiencing hostility, negativity and a lack of encouragement; and functioning ineffectively in the wider environment, notably the school. These examples represent diverging pathways associated with different manifestations of the processes of socialisation.

The personal and interpersonal resources of family members, which transact over time with their views of the world and their position in society, can be understood in relation to their biological make-up, physical and mental state of health and opportunities for the future. It is the goal of socialisation to realise the potential of all of society's members. We hope that the increased understanding of atypical development will in some ways help to achieve that end. Researchers and participants in the research process have, of course, given their time and energy to provide the evidence, which has enabled progress to be made. This area of psychology is one of the most challenging and difficult (Hobson, 1999), but at the same time most rewarding to study.

Although the main orientation is from the perspective of developmental psychology, specifically child development, it informs and is informed by personality theory, abnormal, cognitive and social psychology. Advances in explaining atypical development can throw light on processes in all these areas. In addition, this area of psychology has especial relevance to current social issues. We have tried to illustrate this particularly in terms of learning disability, maltreatment and the development of aggression and other emotional and behavioural problems in children. Similarly, problems can be identified in relation to malnutrition and obesity, alcohol consumption and other kinds of drug-taking. We hope that this book has stimulated, informed and encouraged readers to find out more about how and why children develop so variably as well as being such fascinating and special human beings.

Discussion topics

1. Discuss the role of sociocultural factors in understanding atypical development.
2. What processes may be involved in the development of aggression?
3. How may parenting practices be implicated in the aetiology of some forms of atypical development?
4. How useful is the ET approach in explaining why children develop atypically?

Recommended reading

Lerner, R.M. (ed.) (1998) Theoretical models of human development. In Damon, W. (ed.), *Handbook of Child Psychology* (5th edn). Chichester: J. Wiley & Sons.

Lynch, M. and Cicchetti, D. (1998) An ecological–transactional analysis of children and contexts: The longitudinal interplay among child maltreatment, community violence and children's symptomatology. *Development and Psychopathology*, **10**, 235–57.

Lytton, H. (2000) Toward a model of family-environmental and child-biological influences on development. *Developmental Review*, **20**, 150–79.

Plomin, R., DeFries, J.C., McClearn, G.E. and McGuffin, P. (2001) *Behavioural Genetics* (4th edn). New York: Worth.

Glossary

ADHD: attention deficit/hyperactivity disorder; A disorder characterised by inattention and symptoms of hyperactivity-impulsivity to a degree that is maladaptive and inconsistent with developmental level, evident before the age of seven years, with clear evidence of clinically significant impairment in social, academic or occupational functioning.

Anxiety disorders: Disorders involving anxiety or phobic avoidance, including panic disorder, obsessive-compulsive disorder, post-traumatic stress disorder, social phobia, specific phobias, and generalised anxiety disorder.

Attachment: An emotional bond between people that is usually powerful and long-lasting. The term is used particularly about the relationship between an infant and mother, from which the infant derives security.

Atypicality: Developmental patterns, or emotional or behavioural symptoms, that are significantly divergent from the population norm, with reference to the person's chronological age and cultural group.

Child abuse: A large and complex group of human behaviours involving a caregiver (or other(s) in a position of responsibility) and a child, that constitute interactions which are often traumatic for the child. A less obviously abusive, but nonetheless harmful situation, is any interaction between 'family' members which results in non-accidental harm to the child. All abuse is relative to sociocultural and historical context.

Child-centred intervention: Involvement of a professional person in order to prevent or ameliorate behavioural or developmental problems in the child, by focusing on the child without reference to the needs of significant others in the child's life.

Chromosomes: These are located in the nucleus of every cell in the body, are threadlike, in pairs, and are composed of deoxyribonucleic acid (DNA). DNA is the material which constitutes the genetic code.

Cognitive-behavioural intervention: Intervention which attempts to modify the child's belief systems and thought processes in order to change affect or behaviour. It is based on the assumption that the child has irrational, maladaptive beliefs that require cognitive restructuring.

Conduct disorder (CD): Conduct disorders are characterised by a repetitive and persistent pattern of antisocial, aggressive or defiant conduct, amounting to major violations of age-appropriate social expectations, more severe than ordinary childish mischief or adolescent rebelliousness. Isolated antisocial or criminal acts are not in themselves grounds for the diagnosis, which implies an enduring pattern of behaviour.

Critical period: A limited time in the development of the person (or other creature) during which he or she is susceptible to influences which bring about specific and permanent changes.

Deficiency: Limitation in psychological functioning.

Deficit: A limitation or shortcoming in an area or domain of psychological or biological functioning.

Development: Long-term changes in a person's capacities and behaviour, including physical growth and skills, feelings, patterns of thinking and social relationships.

Developmental lag: A delay in acquisition or attainment of developmental milestones in one or more domains of psychological (such as language development) or physical functioning (such as a child learning to walk).

Ecological: This refers to the interconnecting social and/or physical environments within which the individual is living. It includes also the relationships between individuals and their environments or contexts.

Ecological-transactional: An approach to explaining development which incorporates a longitudinal dimension as well as a number of contexts, with varying degrees of proximity to the individual. It incorporates many interacting variables which transact over time.

Emotional abuse: This involves cognitive, affective and interpersonal aspects. Through the relationship between 'caregiver' and child, the 'adult' conveys to the child that he or she is worthless, unwanted, and of value only in meeting the needs of others.

Externalising disorders: Disorders involving excessive acting-out or undercontrolled behaviour including conduct disorder, ADHD, or oppositional-defiant disorder.

Family-focused intervention: An intervention which attempts to change family dynamics, relationships among family members or the behaviour of family members, in order to address the child's disorder. This contrasts with child-centred intervention.

Family cohesion: The degree of separation or connection of family members to the family. There are four levels of family cohesion ranging from extreme low cohesion to extreme high cohesion: disengaged, separated, connected, and enmeshed.

Gene: A segment of DNA that contains the code for producing a particular protein. Specific genes may be associated with particular characteristics or conditions in individuals.

Home environment: The domestic setting in which a child lives, usually with his or her family.

Intellectual disability: Difficulty that involves psychological processes by which individuals learn and think about their environment. It includes a limitation in processes by which an individual acquires knowledge, methods of thinking or gaining knowledge about the world.

Intelligence quotient (IQ): For children, this is a score obtained from an intelligence test by dividing the mental age (MA) on that test by the chronological age (CA) and multiplying by 100. The norm (or average) IQ is 100, where MA = CA.

Internalising disorders: A group of disorders of childhood characterised by social withdrawal and which includes depression, anxiety, or somatic problems.

Interpersonal processes: The underlying changes within and between individuals in the course of social interaction and the development of relationships.

Learning: A relatively permanent change in behaviour with experience; it involves social and/or cognitive processes which result in the acquisition of knowledge and other forms of understanding. It can be differentiated from temporary states such as those arising from fatigue or drug-induced conditions.

Learning disability: Difficulty in mastering a specific academic skill such as reading or arithmetic (as defined in the USA and other countries such as Australia; in the UK this is defined as in intellectual disability above).

Maintenance: The extent to which the change in the child's functioning, resulting from intervention, continues after all or part of the intervention has been discontinued.

Maturation: A genetically determined sequence of changes in growth and acquisition of skills which are common to all children across different societies and cultures. This constrains environmental influences and is somewhat variable in different contexts. It provides a readiness to learn specific skills at particular ages.

Models of abuse: Representations that operationalise theories, or parts of theories, to provide an explanation of particular processes, and specify more precise relationships between variables, in relation to child abuse.

Mood disorders: Disorders characterised by the experience of extremes of emotion in both intensity and duration. There are several types of mood disorder including major depression and bipolar disorder (also known as manic depression).

Neglect: This is the persistant failure by caregiver(s) to meet a child's physical and/or psychological needs, such as failing to provide adequate food and clothing or responding to the child's emotional needs. It must be seen in context.

Ontogeny: The development of the individual during his or her lifetime.

Parental conflict: Discord between primary caregivers, which may be characterised by persistent disagreements over key issues, aggressive verbal exchanges or physical violence.

Perinatal: The period around and including birth.

Perpetrator characteristics: Characteristics, such as particular personality traits, of the person who abuses.

Physical abuse: The intentional use of physical force or non-accidental failure to protect a child by a parent or other caregiver, in the course of their relationship. Such behaviours are aimed at hurting, injuring or destroying the child.

Prevention: Providing early intervention, when risk factors have been identified, in order to reduce the probability of manifestation of the disorder.

Protective factor: Any characteristic, condition or circumstance that offsets the effect of a risk factor.

Psychopathology: Clinical term meaning abnormal behaviour, condition or pattern of development.

Psychosocial factor: A characteristic, condition or circumstance that is psychological (personal) and social (interpersonal) in nature.

Risk factor: Any characteristic, condition or circumstance that increases the likelihood of some disorder.

Scientist-practitioner: A professional who applies critical thought to practice, uses proven treatments, and evaluates client progress, and whose practice is informed by the literature.

Sensitive period: A period in development when the individual is particularly susceptible to influences that have a great effect upon his or her development, although these are not irreversible.

Sexual abuse: This is the involvement of children and adolescents in sexual activities that, because of their developmental immaturity, they do not fully understand and cannot give informed consent to.

Social learning theory: A theory of learning which explains development in terms of the interaction between the individual and his or her social environments. Its basic principle is that observational learning is crucial to a child's development.

Social validation: Determination of the extent to which intervention goals are socially meaningful, intervention methods are socially acceptable, and intervention effects are socially significant.

Sociocultural context: A setting defined by its social and cultural characteristics, including a shared way of life of a group of people with their artefacts (such as social institutions, and technology), and symbols (such as communications and beliefs).

Stress: This is the condition that results when transactions between the person and the environment lead the individual to perceive a discrepancy (whether real or not) between the demands of a situation and his or her resources – biological, psychological and social – to deal effectively with it.

Teratogen: A substance in the environment that can cause abnormalities in prenatal development.

Transactional: Processes of reciprocal and mutual influence on development across time.

Treatment: An intervention, applied to either the child or the family, after the problem is already occurring.

Universal domains: Areas or realms of psychological functioning that are deemed to be of importance and present in all societies or cultures. These may be manifested in different ways in different societies.

References

Achenbach, T.M. and McConaughy, S.H. (1992) Taxonomy of internalizing disorders of childhood and adolescence. In W.M. Reynolds (ed.), *Internalizing Disorders in Children and Adolescents* (pp. 19–60). New York: Wiley.

Achenbach, T.M., McConaughy, S.H. and Howell, C.T. (1987) Child adolescent behavioural problems: Implications of cross-informant correlations for situational specificity. *Psychological Bulletin*, **102**, 213–32.

Ainsworth, M.D.S. and Wittig, B.A. (1969) Attachment and the exploratory behaviour of one-year-olds in a strange situation. In B.M. Foss, (ed.), *Determinants of Infant Behaviour,* Vol. 4. London: Tavistock.

Ainsworth, M.D.S., Bell, S. and Stayton, D. (1971) Individual differences in strange-situation behaviour of one-year-olds. In H.Schaffer (ed.), *The Origins of Human Social Relations.* New York: Academic Press.

Ainsworth, M.D.S., Blehar, M., Aters, E. and Wall, S. (1978) *Patterns of Attachment: A Psychological Study of the Strange Situation.* Hillsdale, NJ: Lawrence Erlbaum.

Amato, P.R. and Keith, B. (1991) Parental divorce and the well-being of children: a meta-analysis. *Psychological Bulletin*, **110**, 26–46.

American Academy of Pediatrics (1982) The Doman-Delacato treatment of neurologically handicapped children. *Pediatrics*, **70**, 810–12.

American Psychiatric Association (1994) *Diagnostic and Statistical Manual of Mental Disorders* (4th edn). Washington, DC: American Psychiatric Association.

Anderson, J.C., Williams, S., McGee, R., and Silva, P.A. (1987) DSM-III disorders in preadolescent children. *Archives of General Psychiatry*, **44**, 69–76.

Anderson, S.R., and Romanczyk, R.G. (1999) Early intervention for young children with autism: Continuum-based behavioral models. *Journal of the Association for Persons with Severe Handicaps*, **24**, 162–73.

Aries, P. (1962) *Centuries of Childhood.* New York: Vintage Books.

Atkinson, R.C. and Shiffrin, R.M. (1968) Human memory: A proposed system and its control processes. In K.W. Spence and J.T. Spence (eds), *The Psychology of Learning and Motivation*, Vol. 2. New York: Academic Press.

Baker, B.L. (1996) Parent training. In J.W. Jacobson and J.A. Mulick (eds), *Manual of Diagnosis and Professional Practice in Mental Retardation* (pp. 289–99). Washington, DC: American Psychological Association.

Bancroft, D. and Carr, C. (eds) (1995) *Influencing Children's Development*. Milton Keynes: Open University Press.

Bandura, A. (1965) Influence of model's reinforcement contingencies on the acquisition of imitative responses. *Journal of Personality and Social Psychology*, 1, 589–95.

Bandura, A. (1977) *Social Learning Theory*. Englewood Cliffs, NJ: Prentice Hall.

Barkley, R.A. (1990) *Attention Deficit Hyperactivity Disorder: A Handbook for Diagnosis and Treatment*. New York: Guilford.

Barkley, R.A. (1998) *Attention Deficit Hyperactivity Disorder: A Handbook for Diagnosis and Treatment* (2nd edn). New York: Guilford.

Barkley, R.A., Anastopolous, A.D., Guevremont, D.C. and Fletcher, K.E. (1991) Adolescents with ADHD: Patterns of behavioural adjustment, academic functioning and treatment utilisation. *Journal of the American Academy of Child and Adolescent Psychiatry*, **30**, 752–61.

Barrett, P.M., Dadds, M.R. and Rapee, R.M. (1996) Family treatment of childhood anxiety: A controlled trial. *Journal of Consulting and Clinical Psychology*, **64**, 333–42.

Becker-Lausen, E., Sanders, B. and Chinsky, J.M. (1995) Mediation of abusive childhood experiences: depression, dissociation and negative life outcomes. *American Journal of Orthopsychiatry*, **65**(4), 560–73.

Beckman, P.J., Robinson, C. Rosenberg, S. and Filer, J. (1994) Family involvement in early intervention: the evolution of family-centered services. In. L.J. Johnson, R.J. Gallagher, M.J. LaMontagne, J.B. Jordan, J.J. Gallaher, P.L. Hutinger and M.B. Karnes (eds), *Meeting Early Intervention Challenges: Issues from Birth to Three* (pp. 13–32). Baltimore, MD : Paul H. Brookes.

Behan, J. and Carr, A. (2000) Oppositional defiant disorder. In A. Carr (ed.), *What Works with Children and Adolescents: A Critical Review of Psychological Interventions with Children, Adolescents and their Families* (pp. 102–30). London: Routledge.

Bellamy, C. (1998) *The State of the World's Children 1998*. Oxford: Oxford University Press, Published for UNICEF.

Belsky, J. (1980) Child maltreatment: An ecological integration. *American Psychologist*, **35**, 320–35.

Belsky, J. (1993) Etiology of child maltreatment: A developmental-ecological analysis. *Psychological Bulletin*, **114**, 413–34.

Belsky, J., Hsieh, K.H., and Crnic, K. (1998) Mothering, fathering, and infant negativity as antecedents of boys' externalizing problems and inhibition at age 3 years: Differential susceptibility to rearing experience? *Development and Psychopathology*, **10**(2), 301–19.

Belsky, J., Youngblade, L., Rovine, M. and Volling, B. (1991) Patterns of marital change and parent–child interaction. *Journal of Marriage and the Family,* **53**, 487–98.

Bender, L. (1957) Specific reading disability as maturation lag. *Bulletin of the Orton Society,* **7**, 9–18.

Berk, L.E. (1996) *Child Development* (5th edn). Needham Heights, MA: Allyn & Bacon.

Berk, L.E. (2003) *Child Development* (6th edn). Boston, MA: Allyn & Bacon.

Berry, J.O. and Hardman, M.L. (1998) *Lifespan Perspectives on the Family and Disability.* Boston, MA: Allyn & Bacon.

Bettison, S. (1996) The long-term effects of auditory training on children with autism. *Journal of Autism and Developmental Disorders,* **26**, 361–74.

Biederman, J., Faraone, S.V., Hirshfeld-Becker, D.R., Friedman, B.A., Robin, J.A., Rosenbaum, D. and Jerrold, F. (2001) Patterns of psychopathology and dysfunction in high-risk children of parents with panic disorder and major depression. *American Journal of Psychiatry,* **158**, 49–57.

Biklen, D. (1990) Communication unbound: autism and practice. *Harvard Educational Review,* **60**, 291–314.

Birnbrauer, J.S. and Leach, D.J. (1993) The Murdoch Early Intervention program after 2 years. *Behaviour Change,* **10**, 63–74.

Bowlby, J. (1944) Forty-four juvenile thieves: their character and home lives. *International Journal of Psycho-analysis,* **25**, 19–52.

Bowlby, J. (1951) *Maternal Care and Mental Health.* Geneva: World Health Organization.

Bowlby, J. (1969) *Attachment and Loss: Vol I. Attachment.* New York: Basic Books.

Bowlby, J. (1980) *Attachment and Loss, Vol III: Loss, Sadness and Depression.* London: Hogarth Press.

Boyd, R.D. and Bluma, S.M. (1977) *Parent Readings: Portage Parent Program.* Portage, WI: Co-operative Educational Service Agency No. 12.

Boyd, R.D., Stauber, K.A. and Bluma, S.M. (1977) *Instructor's Manual: Portage Parent Program.* Portage, WI: Co-operative Educational Service Agency No. 12.

Brandt, B.R. (1996) Impaired tactual perception in children with Down's Syndrome. *Scandinavian Journal of Psychology,* **37**, 312–16.

Brassard, M.R. and Hardy, D.B. (1997) Psychological maltreatment. In M.E. Helfer and R.S. Kempe (eds), *The Battered Child.* Chicago: Chicago University Press.

Bronfenbrenner, U. (1970) *Two Worlds of Childhood: USA and USSR.* London: Russell Sage Foundation, Allen & Unwin.

Bronfenbrenner, U. (1977) Toward an experimental ecology of human development. *American Psychologist,* **32**, 513–31.

Bronfenbrenner, U. (1979) *The Ecology of Human Development: Experiments by Nature and by Design.* Cambridge, MA: Havard University Press.

Bronfenbrenner, U. and Morris, P.M. (1998) The ecology of developmental processes. In Lerner, R.M. (ed.), *Theoretical Models of Human Development,* Vol 1. In Damon, W. (ed.), *Handbook of Child Psychology* (5th edn). Chichester: John Wiley & Sons.

Brooks-Gunn, J. and Duncan, G.J. (1997) The effects of poverty on children. *Futures of Children,* **7**(2), 55–71.

Brooks-Gunn, J., Britto, P.R. and Brady, C. (1999) Struggling to make ends meet. Poverty and child development. In M.E. Lamb (ed.), *Parenting and Child Development in 'Non-traditional' Families.* Mahwah, NJ: Lawrence Erlbaum.

Browder, D.M. and Snell, M.E. (1993) Daily living and community skills. In M.E. Snell (ed.) *Instruction for Students with Severe Disabilities* (4th edn) (pp. 480–525). New York: Merrill.

Brown, G. and Harris, T. (1978) *Social Origins of Depression.* London: Tavistock.

Brown, R.I. (1991) Changing the concepts of disability in developed and developing communities. In D. Mitchell and R.I. Brown (eds), *Early Intervention Studies for Young Children with Special Needs.* London: Chapman & Hall.

Bruder, M.B. (2000) Family-centered early intervention: Clarifying values for the new millennium. *Topics in Early Childhood Special Education,* **20**, 105–15.

Burgess, R.L. and Conger, R.D. (1978) Family interaction in abusive, neglectful and normal families. *Child Development,* **49**, 1163–73.

Campbell, S.B. (1995) Behaviour problems in preschool children. *Journal of Child Psychology and Psychiatry,* **36**, 113–49.

Campbell, S.B., Pierce, E.W., Moore, G., Marakovitz, S. and Newby, K. (1996) Boys' externalizing problems at elementary school age: Pathways from early behaviour problems, maternal control and family stress. *Development and Psychopathology,* **8**, 701–19.

Cannon, W.B. (1928) The mechanism of emotional disturbance of bodily function, *New England Journal of Medicine,* **198**, 877–92.

Cannon, W.B. (1929) *Bodily Changes in Pain, Hunger, Fear and Rage.* New York: Appleton & Co.

Carr, A. (2000a) Introduction. In A. Carr (ed.), *What Works with Children and Adolescents: A Critical Review of Psychological Interventions with Children, Adolescents and their Families* (pp. 1–16). London: Routledge.

Carr, A. (2000b) Conclusions. In A. Carr (ed.), *What Works with Children and Adolescents: A Critical Review of Psychological Interventions with Children, Adolescents and their Families* (pp. 300–22). London: Routledge.

Carr, E.G., Levin, L., McConnachie, G., Carlson, J.L., Kemp, D.C. and

Smith, C.E. (1994) *Communication-based Intervention for Problem Behavior: A User's Guide for Producing Positive Change*. Baltimore, MD: Paul H. Brookes.

Ceci, S.J. (1990) *On Intelligence, More or Less*. Engelwood Cliffs, NJ: Prentice Hall.

Chase-Lansdale, P.L. and Brooks-Gunn, J. (1994) Correlates of adolescent pregnancy and parenthood. In C.B. Fisher and R.M. Lerner (eds), *Applied Developmental Psychology* (pp. 207–36). New York: McGraw-Hill.

Chomsky, N. (1969) *The Acquisition of Syntax in Children from Five to Ten*. Cambridge, MA: MIT Press.

Chorpita, B.F. (2002) The tripartite model and dimensions of anxiety and depression: An examination of structure in a large school sample. *Journal of Abnormal Child Psychology*, **30**, 177–90.

Christopoulos, C., Cohn, D.A, Shaw, D.S., Joyce, S., Sullivan-Hanson, J., Kraft, S.P. and Emery, R.E. (1987) Children of abused women: I Adjustment at time of shelter residence. *Journal of Marriage and the Family*, **49**(3), 611–19.

Cicchetti, D. (1984) The emergence of developmental psychopathology. *Child Development*, **55**, 1–7.

Cicchetti, D. (1989) How research on child maltreatment has informed the study of child development: perspectives from developmental psychopathology. In D. Cicchetti and V. Carlson (eds), *Child Maltreatment*. Cambridge, MA: Cambridge University Press.

Cicchetti, D. and Carlson, V. (eds) (1989) *Child Maltreatment*. Cambridge: Cambridge University Press.

Cicchetti, D. and Rizley, R. (1981) Developmental perspectives on the etiology, intergenerational transmission and sequelae of child maltreatment. *New Directions for Child Development*, **11**, 32–59.

Cicchetti, D. and Rogosh, F.A. (1997) The role of self-organization in the promotion of resilience in maltreated children. *Development & Psychopathology*, **9**, 797–815.

Cicchetti, D. and Toth, S.L. (1995) A developmental psychopathology perspective on child abuse and neglect. *Journal of the American Academy of Child and Adolescent Psychiatry*, **34**, 541–65.

Cicchetti, D., Toth, S.L. and Maughan, A. (2000) An ecological-transactional model of child maltreatment. In A.J. Sameroff, M. Lewis, and S.M. Miller (eds), *Handbook of Developmental Psychopathology* (2nd edn) (pp. 689–722). New York: Kluwer Academic/ Plenum.

Clarke, A.M. and Clarke, A.D.B. (1976) *Early Experience: Myth and Evidence*. London: Open Books.

Clarke, A.M and Clarke, A.D.B. (1998) Early experience and the life path. *The Psychologist*, **11**, 433–6.

Clarke, A.M. and Clarke, A.D.B. (2000) *Early Experience and the Life Path*. London: Jessica Kingsley.

Clarke-Stewart, K.A. and Fein, G.G. (1983) Early childhood programmes. In M.M. Haith and J.J. Campos (eds), *Infancy and Developmental Psychobiology*, Vol. 2 of P.H. Mussen (ed.), *Handbook of Child Psychology* (4th edn). New York: Wiley.

Clarke-Stewart, A., Perlmutter, M. and Friedman, S. (eds) (1988) *Lifelong Human Development*. Chichester: Wiley.

Cloninger, C.R. and Gottesman, I.I. (1987) Genetic and environmental factors in antisocial behaviour disorders. In S.A. Mednick, T.E. Moffitt and S.A. Stack (eds), *The Causes of Crime: New Biological Approaches*. New York: Cambridge University Press.

Cockett, M. and Tripp, J. (1994) Children living in reordered families. *Social Policy Research Findings*, 45. York: Joseph Rowntree Foundation.

Cohen, P. and Brook, J. (1995) The reciprocal influence of punishment and child behaviour disorder. In J. McCord (ed.), *Coercion and Punishment in Long-term Perspectives*. Cambridge: Cambridge University Press.

Corby, B. (1993) *Child Abuse: Towards a Knowledge Base*. Milton Keynes: Open University Press.

Corby, B. (2000) *Child Abuse. Towards a Knowledge Base* (2nd edn). Milton Keynes: Open University Press.

Creighton, S. and Noyes, P. (1989) *Child Abuse Trends in England and Wales 1983–1987*. London: NSPCC.

Crick, N.R. and Dodge, K.A. (1994) A review and reformulation of the social information processing mechanisms in children's social adjustment. *Psychological Bulletin*, 115, 74–101.

Crossley, R. and Remington-Gurney, J. (1992) Getting the words out: facilitated communication training. *Topics in Language Disorders*, 12, 29–45.

Culp, R., Heide, J. and Richardson, M. (1987) Maltreated children's developmental scores: Treatment versus non-treatment. *Child Abuse and Neglect*, 11, 29–34.

Culp, R., Little, V., Letts, D. and Lawrence, H. (1991) Maltreated children's self-concept: effects of a comprehensive treatment program. *American Journal of Orthopsychiatry*, 61, 114–21.

Damon, W. (ed.) (1998) *Handbook of Child Psychology* (5th edn). Chichester: J. Wiley & Sons.

Davis, G.E. and Leitenberg, H. (1987) Adolescent sex offenders. *Psychological Bulletin*, 101(3) 417–27.

Dawson, G. and Osterling, J. (1997) Early intervention and autism. In M.J. Guralnick (ed.), *The Effectiveness of Early Intervention* (pp. 307–27). Baltimore, MD: Paul H. Brookes.

Deater-Deckard, K. (2001) Annotation: recent research examining the role of the peer relationships in the development of psychopathology. *Journal of Child Psychology and Psychiatry*, 42, 565–79.

Deater-Deckard, K., Dodge, K.A., Bates, J.E. and Pettit, G.S. (1996) Physical discipline among African American and European American mothers: links to children's externalizing behaviours. *Developmental Psychology,* **32**, 1065–72.

Deater-Deckard, K., Dodge, K.A., Bates, J.E. and Pettit, G.S. (1998) Multiple risk factors in the development of externalizing behaviour problems: group and individual differences. *Development and Psychopathology,* **10**, 469–93.

Dechillo, N., Koren, P.E. and Schultze, K.H. (1994) From paternalism to partnership: family and professional collaboration in children's mental health. *American Journal of Orthopsychiatry,* **64**, 564–76.

DeKlyen, M. and Speltz, M.L. (2001) Attachment and conduct disorder. In J. Hill and B. Maughan (eds), *Conduct Disorders in Childhood and Adolescence.* Cambridge: Cambridge University Press.

Dempsey, I. and Foreman, P. (2001) A review of educational approaches for individuals with autism. *International Journal of Disability, Development and Education,* **48**, 103–16.

Department for Education and Employment (1999) *The Revised Guidance of the Gifted and Talented Strand of Excellence in Cities.* London: DfEE.

Department of Education and Science (1989) *Discipline in Schools* (the Elton Report). London: HMSO.

Department of Health (2000) *Working Together to Safeguard Children: A Guide to Interagency Working to Safeguard and Promote the Welfare of Children.* London: Stationery Office.

Dobbing, J. and Smart, L.L. (1974) Vulnerability of developing brain and behaviour. *British Medical Bulletin,* **30**, 164–8.

Dockrell, J. and McShane, J. (1993) *Children's Learning Difficulties: A Cognitive Approach.* Oxford: Blackwell.

Dodge, K.A. (1986) A social information processing model of social competence in children. In M. Perlmutter (ed.), *Cognitive Perspectives on Children's Social and Behavioural Development. The Minnesota Symposia on Child Psychology.* **18**, 77–125, Hillsdale, NJ: Lawrence Erlbaum.

Dodge, K.A. (1991) Emotion and social information processing. In J. Garber and K.A. Dodge (eds), *The Development of Emotion Regulation and Dysregulation.* Cambridge: Cambridge University Press.

Dodge, K.A. and Frame, C.L. (1982) Social cognitive biases and deficits in aggressive boys. *Child Development,* **53**, 620–35.

Dowling, E. and Osborne, E. (1994) *The Family and the School: A Joint Systems Approach to Problems with Children* (2nd edn). London: Routledge.

Drewett, R., Wolke, D., Asefa, M., Kaba, M. and Tessema, F. (2001) Malnutrition and mental development: is there a sensitive period? A nested control study. *Journal of Child Psychology and Psychiatry,* **42**(2), 181–7.

Dumas, J.E. and Gibson, J.A. (1990) Behavioural correlates of maternal depressive symptomatology in conduct-disordered children: II

Systemic effects involving fathers and siblings. *Journal of Consulting and Clinical Psychology*, **59**, 877–81.

Duncan, G.J. and Brooks-Gunn, J. (eds) (1997) *Consequences of Growing Up Poor*. New York: Russell Sage Foundation Press.

Dunn, J. (1988) *The Beginnings of Social Understanding*. Oxford: Blackwell.

Dunn, J.F. and Plomin, R. (1986) Determinants of maternal behaviour toward three-year-old siblings. *British Journal of Developmental Psychology*, **4**, 127–37.

Dunn, M.E., Burbine, T., Bowers, C.A. and Tantleff-Dunn, S. (2001) Moderators of stress in parents of children with autism. *Community Mental Health Journal*, **37**, 39–52.

Durand, V.M. (1993) Problem behaviour as communication. *Behaviour Change*, 10, 197–207.

Duwa, S.M., Wells, C. and Lalinde, P. (1993) Creating family-centred programs and policies. In D.M. Bryant and M.M. Graham (eds), *Implementing Early Intervention: From Research to Effective Practice* (pp. 92–123). New York: Guilford Press.

Eamon, M.K. (2001) The effects of poverty on children's socioemotional development: an ecological systems analysis. *Social Work*, **46**, 256–66.

Edgeworth, J. and Carr, A. (2000) Child abuse. In A. Carr (ed.), *What Works with Children and Adolescents: A Critical Review of Psychological Interventions with Children, Adolescents and their Families* (pp. 17–48). London: Routledge.

Egeland, B. and Jacobvitz, D. (1984) Intergenerational continuity of parental abuse: Causes and consequences. Paper presented at the Conference on Biosocial Perspectives in Abuse and Neglect. York, Maine.

Eiden, R. Das., Chavaz, F. and Leonard, K.E. (1999) Parent–infant interactions among families with alcoholic fathers. *Development and Psychopathology*, 11(4), 745–62.

Elmer, E. (1986) Outcome of residential treatment for abused and high-risk infants. *Child Abuse & Neglect*, **10**, 351–60.

Emerson, E. (2001) *Challenging Behaviour: Analysis and Intervention in People with Severe Intellectual Disabilities* (2nd edn). Cambridge: Cambridge University Press.

Emery, J.L. (1989) Family violence. *American Psychologist*, **44**(2), 321–8.

Empson, J. (2001) Problematising Development: Concepts and Conceptions of Normality. In K. Dunn (ed.) *Child Development and Education. Different Experiences, New Voices*, pp. 26–44. Sheffield: Philip Armstrong Publications.

Empson, J.M. and McGlaughlin, A. (1979) Stress Factors in the Lives of Disadvantaged Children. Paper given to the BPS Developmental Section Annual Conference. Bulletin BPS, **32**, 204.

Engfer, A. (1988) The interrelatedness of marriage and the

mother–child relationship. In R.A. Hinde and J. Stevenson-Hinde (eds), *Relationships within Families*. Oxford: Clarendon.

Erickson, M.T. (1998) *Behaviour Disorders of Children and Adolescents: Assessment, Etiology and Intervention* (3rd edn). Upper Saddle River, NJ: Prentice Hall.

Erickson, M.F., Egeland, B. and Pianta, R. (1989) The effects of maltreatment on the development of young children. In D. Cicchetti and V. Carlson (eds), *Child Maltreatment: Theories and Research on the Causes and Consequences of Child Abuse and Neglect*. Cambridge University Press.

Erikson, E.H. (1963) *Childhood and Society*. London: Norton.

Fantuzzo, J. and Holland, A. (1992) Resilient peer training: Systematic investigation of a treatment to improve the social effectiveness of child victims of maltreatment. In A.W. Burgess (ed.), *Child Trauma 1: Issues and Research*. New York: Garland.

Fantuzzo, J., Sutton-Smith, B., Atkins, M. and Meyers, R. (1996) Community-based resilient peer treatment of withdrawn, maltreated pre-school children. *Journal of Consulting and Clinical Psychology*, **64**, 1377–86.

Feehan, M., McGee, R. and Williams, S.M. (1993) Mental health disorders from age 15 to age 18 years. *Journal of the American Academy of Child and Adolescent Psychiatry*, **32**, 1118–26.

Finkelhor, D. (1983) Common features of child abuse. In D. Finkelhor, R. Gelles, G. Hotaling and M. Straus (eds), *The Dark Side of Families: Current Family Violence Research*. Thousand Oaks, CA: Sage.

Finkelhor, D. (1984) *Child Sexual Abuse: New Theories and Research*. New York: Free Press.

Finkelhor, D. (1986) *A Sourcebook on Child Sexual Abuse*. London: Sage.

Finkelhor, D. (1995) The victimization of children: a developmental perspective. *American Journal of Orthopsychiatry*, **65**(2), 177–93.

Finn, C.A. and Sladeczek, I.E. (2001) Assessing the social validity of behavioral interventions: a review of treatment acceptability measures. *School Psychology Quarterly*, **16**, 176–206.

Fischer, M., Barkley, R.A., Fletcher, K.E. and Smallish, L. (1993) The adolescent outcome of hyperactive children: Predictors of psychiatric, academic, social and emotional adjustment. *Journal of the American Academy of Child and Adolescent Psychiatry*, **32**, 324–32.

Fisher, D. (2000) *Fairness and Flexibility: LEA Strategies to Reduce the Need for SEN Statements*. Slough: National Foundation for Educational Research.

Flannery-Schroeder, E. and Kendall, P.C. (1996) *Cognitive-behavioral Therapy for Anxious Children: Therapist Manual for Group Treatment*. Ardmore, PA: Workbook Publishing.

Fogel, A. (1991) *Infancy. Infant, Family and Society*. St Paul, MN: West.

Folstein, S. and Rutter, M. (1977) Infantile autism: a genetic study of 21 twin pairs. *Journal of Child Psychology and Psychiatry*, **18**, 297–321.

Freud, S. (1954) *Collected Papers*, Vol. 1. London: Hogarth Press.

Frost, N. (1990) Official intervention and child protection: the relationship between state and family in contemporary Britain. In The Violence against Children Study Group *Taking Child Abuse Seriously.* London: Routledge.

Fuchs, D. and Fuchs, L.S. (1994) Inclusive school movement and the radicalization of school reform. *Exceptional Children,* **60**, 294–309.

Galler, J.R., Ramsey, C.F., Morley, D.S., Archer, E. and Salt, P. (1990) The long-term effects of early Kwashiorkor compared with Marasmus. IV. Performance on the National High School Entrance Examination. *Pediatric Research,* **28**, 518–23.

Garbarino, J. (1982) *Children and Families in the Social Environment.* Chicago: Aldine.

Garbarino, J., Guttman, E. and Seeley, J.W. (1988) *The Psychologically Battered Child.* San Francisco: Jossey-Bass.

Garmezy, N. and Rutter, M. (1988) *Stress, Coping, and Development in Children.* Baltimore: Johns Hopkins University Press.

Garmezy, N., Masten, A.S. and Tellegen, A. (1985) The study of stress and competence in children: a building block for developmental psychopathology. *Child Development,* **55**, 97–111.

Gelfand, D.M., Jenson, W.R. and Drew, C.J. (1988) *Understanding Child Behaviour Disorders: An Introduction to Child Psychopathology* (2nd edn). New York: Holt, Rinehart & Winston.

George, C. (1996) A representational perspective of child abuse and prevention: internal working models of attachment and caregiving. *Child Abuse and Neglect,* **20**(5), 411–24.

Gesell, A. (1950) *The First Five Years of Life: A Guide to the Study of the Preschool Child.* London: Methuen.

Gesell, A. and Ilg, F.L. (1943) Infant and child in the culture of today. In A. Gesell and F.L. Ilg (eds), *Child Development.* New York: Harper & Row (1949).

Gesell, A. and Ilg, F.L. (1946) The child from five to ten. In A. Gesell and F.L. Ilg (eds), *Child Development.* New York: Harper & Row.

Gesell, A. and Thompson, H. (1929) Learning and growth in identical twins: an experimental study by the method of co-twin control. *Genetic Psychology Monographs,* **6**, 1–124.

Gil, D.G. (1970) *Violence Against Children: Physical Child Abuse in the United States.* Cambridge, MA: Harvard University Press.

Gillberg, C., Johansson, M., Steffenburg, S. and Berlin, O. (1997) Auditory integration training in children with autism: Brief report of an open pilot study. *Autism,* **1**, 97–100.

Gillis, J.J., Gilger, J.W., Pennington, B.F. and DeFries, J.C. (1992) Attention deficit disorder in reading disabled twins: evidence for genetic etiology. *Journal of Abnormal Child Psychology,* **20**, 303–15.

Giovannoni, J. and Becerra, R. (1979) *Defining Child Abuse.* New York: Free Press.

Goldenberg, R.L. (1994) The prevention of low birthweight and its sequelae. *Preventive Medicine,* **23**(5), 627–31.

Goodyer, I.M. (1990) *Life Experiences, Development and Childhood Psychopathology.* Chichester: Wiley.

Grandin, T. (1992) An inside view of autism. In E. Schopler and G. Mesibov (eds), *High Functioning Individuals with Autism.* New York: Plenum.

Green, G. (1996) Evaluating claims about treatments for autism. In C. Maurice, G. Green, and S.C. Luce (eds), *Behavioral Intervention for Young Children with Autism: A Manual for Parents and Professionals* (pp. 15–28). Austin, TX: Pro-ed.

Green, G., and Shane, H.C. (1994) Science, reason, and facilitated communication. *Journal of the Association for Persons with Severe Handicaps,* **19**, 151–72.

Gunter, N. and LaBarbera, R. (1980) The consequences of adolescent childbearing on postnatal development. *International Journal of Behavioural Development,* **3**, 191–214.

Guralnick, M.J. and Groom, J.M. (1988) Peer interactions in mainstreamed and specialised classrooms: a comparative analysis. *Exceptional Children,* **54**, 415–25.

Hack, M., Klein, N.K. and Taylor, H.G. (1995) Long-term developmental outcomes of low birth weight babies. *The Future of Children,* **5**(1), 176–96.

Hagen, J.W., Barclay, C.R. and Schwethelm, B. (1982) Cognitive development of the learning-disabled child. *International Review of Research in Mental Retardation,* **11**, 1–41.

Hallahan, D.P. and Kauffman, J.M. (1976) *Introduction to Learning Disabilities: A Psychobehavioural Approach.* Englewoods, Cliffs, NJ: Prentice Hall.

Hallahan, D.P. and Kauffman, J.M. (1977) Labels, categories, behaviours: ED, LD, and EMR reconsidered. *Journal of Special Education,* **11**, 139–49.

Harris, S., Kasari, C. and Sigman, M. (1996) Joint attention and language gains in children with Down syndrome. *American Journal of Mental Retardation,* **100**, 608–18.

Hartman, C.R. and Burgess, A.W. (1989) Sexual abuse of children: causes and consequences. In Cicchetti, D and Carlson, V. (eds), *Child Maltreatment.* Cambridge: Cambridge University Press.

Hauser-Cram, P., Warfield, M.E., Shonkoff, J.P. and Krauss, M.W. (2001) Children with disabilities. *Monographs of the Society for Research in Child Development,* **66** (3, Serial No 266)

Hayes, S.C., Barlow, D.H. and Nelson-Gray, R.O. (1999) *The Scientist Practitioner: Research and Accountability in the Age of Managed Care* (2nd edn). Needham Heights, MA: Allyn & Bacon.

Heath, E. and Kosky, R. (1992) Are children who steal different from those who are aggressive? *Child Psychiatry and Human Development,* **23**, 9–18.

Helfer, M.E., Kempe, R.S. and Krugman, R.D. (eds) (1997) *The Battered Child* (5th edn). Chicago: Chicago University Press.

Hinde, R.A. (1963) The nature of imprinting. In B.M. Foss (ed.), *Determinants of Infant Behaviour,* Vol. 2. London: Methuen.

Hinshaw, S.P., Henker, B., Whalen, C.K. and Erhaardt, D. (1989) Aggressive, prosocial and nonsocial behaviour in hyperactive boys: Dose effects of methylphenidate in naturalistic settings. *Journal of Consulting and Clinical Psychology,* **57**, 636–43.

Hinsliff, G. (2003) How private trade in babies spawned a public tragedy. *Observer,* 26 January, pp. 10–11.

HM Inspectorate (1990) *Portage Projects: A Survey of 13 Projects Funded by Education Support Grants (1987–1989).* Stanmore, Middlesex: Department of Education and Science.

Hobbs, C. (1990) Signs and symptoms of child sexual abuse. Newsletter of the Asociation of Child Psychology and Psychiatry.

Hobbs, C.J., Hanks, H.G.I. and Wynne, J.M. (1998) *Child Abuse and Neglect: A Clinician's Handbook* (2nd edn). London: Churchill Livingstone.

Hobson, R.P. (1999) Developmental psychopathology: revolution and reformation. In M. Bennett (ed.), *Developmental Psychology.* Hove, Sussex: Taylor & Francis.

Hodges, J. and Tizard, B. (1989) IQ and behavioural adjustment of ex-institutional adolescents. *Journal of Child Psychology and Psychiatry,* **30**, 53–76.

Holder, H.B. and Kirkpatrick, S.W. (1991) Interpretation of emotion from facial expressions in children with and without learning disabilities. *Journal of Learning Disabilities,* **24**, 170–7.

Horne, M. (1990) Is it social work? In The Violence against Children Study Group *Taking Child Abuse Seriously.* London: Routledge.

Horner, R.H., O'Neill, R.E. and Flannery, K.B. (1993) Effective behavior support plans. In M.E. Snell (ed.), *Instruction for Students with Severe Disabilities* (4th edn) (pp. 184–214). New York: Merrill.

Howe, D., Brandon, M., Hinings, D. and Schofield, G. (1999) *Attachment Theory, Child Maltreatment and Family Support.* Basingstoke: Macmillan – now Palgrave Macmillan.

Howlin, P. (1998) Practitioner review: Psychological and educational treatments for autism. *Journal of Child Psychology and Psychiatry,* **39**, 307–22.

Howlin, P. and Moore, A. (1997) Diagnosis in autism: a survey of over 1200 patients in the UK. *Autism,* **1**, 135–62.

Hudson, A., Melita, B. and Arnold, N. (1993) A case study assessing the validity of facilitated communication. *Journal of Autism and Developmental Disorders,* **23**, 165–73.

Hunt, N. (1967) *The World of Nigel Hunt: The Diary of a Mongoloid Youth.* New York: Garrett Publications.

Hunter, R. and Kilstrom, N. (1979) Breaking the cycle in abusive families. *American Journal of Psychiatry,* **136**, 1320–2.

Illingworth, R.S. (1987) *The Normal Child: Some Problems of the Early Years and their Treatment* (9th edn). Edinburgh: Churchill Livingstone.

Illsley, R. and Mitchell, R.G. (1984) *Low Birthweight: A Medical Psychological and Social Study.* Chichester: Wiley.

Iwata, B.A., Vollmer, T.R. and Zarcone, J.R. (1990) The experimental (functional) analysis of behavior disorders: methodology, applications, and limitations. In A.C. Repp and N.N. Singh (eds), *Perspectives on the Use of Nonaversive and Aversive Interventions for Persons with Developmental Disabilities* (pp. 301–30). Sycamore, IL: Sycamore.

James, J.J., Furukawa, T.P., James, N. and Mangelsdorf, A.D. (1984) Child abuse and neglect reports in the United States Army Central Registry. *Military Medicine,* **149**, 205–6.

Jekielek, S.M. (1998) Parental conflict, marital disruption and children's emotional well-being. *Social Forces,* **76**(3), 905–35.

Jenkins, J.R., Odom, S.L. and Speltz, M.L. (1989) Effects of social integration on preschool children with handicaps. *Exceptional Children,* **55**, 420–8.

Johnson, C.F. and Cohn, D.S. (1990) The stress of child abuse and other family violence. In L.E. Arnold (ed.), *Childhood Stress.* New York: Wiley.

Johnson, H.D., LaVoie, J.C. and Mahoney, M. (2001) Interparental conflict and family cohesion: predictors of loneliness, social anxiety, and social avoidance in late adolescence. *Journal of Adolescent Research,* **16**, 304–18.

Jordan, R., Jones, G. and Murray, D. (1998) *Educational Interventions for Children with Autism: A Literature Review of Recent and Current Research.* London: Department for Education and Employment.

Kagan, J. (1983) Stress and coping in early development. In N. Garmezy and M. Rutter (eds), *Stress, Coping and Development in Children* (pp. 191–216). New York: McGraw-Hill.

Kanner, A.D., Coyne, J.C., Schaefer, C. and Lazarus, R.S. (1981) Comparison of two modes of stress measurement: Daily hassles and uplifts versus major life events. *Journal of Behavioural Medicine,* **4**, 1–39.

Kasari, C., Freeman, S., Mundy, P. and Sigman, M.D. (1995) Attention regulation by children with Down Syndrome: coordinated joint attention and social referencing looks. *American Journal on Mental Retardation,* **100**, 128–36.

Kaslow, N.J., and Thompson, M.P. (1998) Applying the criteria for empirically supported treatments to studies of psychosocial interventions for child and adolescent depression. *Journal of Clinical Child Psychology,* **27**, 146–55.

Kaufman, J. and Zigler, E. (1987) Do abused children become abusive parents? *American Journal of Orthopsychiatry,* **57**, 186–92.

Kazdin, A.E. (1997) Practitioner review: psychosocial treatments for conduct disorder in children. *Journal of Child Psychology and Psychiatry*, **38**(2), 161–78.

Kazdin, A.E. (1998) Psychosocial treatments for conduct disorder in children. In P. Nathan, and J. Gorman (eds), *A Guide to Treatments that Work* (pp. 65–89). New York: Oxford University Press.

Keenan, K. and Shaw, D. (1997) Developmental and social influences on young girls' early problem behaviour. *Psychological Bulletin*, **121**, 95–113.

Keil, F.C. (1999) Cognition, content and development. In M. Bennett (ed.), *Developmental Psychology*. Hove, Sussex: Taylor & Francis.

Keisner, J., Dishion, T.J. and Poulin, F. (2001) A reinforcement model of conduct problems in children and adolescents: advances in theory and intervention. In J. Hill and B. Maughan (eds), *Conduct Disorders in Childhood and Adolescence*. Cambridge: Cambridge University Press.

Kempe, H. and Kempe, R. (1978) *Child Abuse*. Cambridge, MA: Harvard University Press.

Kempe, C.H., Silverman, F., Steele, B., Droegmueller, W. and Silver, H. (1962) The battered child syndrome. *Journal of the American Medical Association*, **181**, 17–24.

Kendall, P.C. and Treadwell, K.H. (1996) Cognitive-behavioral treatment for childhood anxiety disorders. In E.D. Hibbs and P.S. Jensen (eds), *Psychosocial Treatments for Child and Adolescent Disorders* (pp. 169–84). Washington, DC: American Psychological Association.

Kendler, K.S., Myers, J. and Prescott, C.A. (2002) The etiology of phobias: an evaluation of the stress-diathesis model. *Archives of General Psychiatry*, **59**, 242–8.

Kendler, K.S., Myers, J., Prescott, C.A. and Neale, M.C. (2001) The genetic epidemiology of irrational fears and phobias in men. *Archives of General Psychiatry*, **58**, 257–65.

Kendler, K.S., Walters, E.E., Neale, M.C., Kessler, R.C., Heath, A.C. and Eaves, L.J. (1995) The structure of the genetic and environmental risk factors for six major psychiatric disorders in women: phobia, generalized anxiety disorder, panic disorder, bulimia, major depression, and alcoholism. *Archives of General Psychiatry*, **52**, 863–70.

Kezuka, E. (1997) The role of touch in facilitated communication. *Journal of Autism and Developmental Disorders*, **27**, 571–93.

King, N.J. and Ollendick, T.H. (1998) Empirically validated treatments in clinical psychology. *Australian Psychologist*, **33**, 89–95.

King, N.J., Hamilton, D.I. and Ollendick, T.H. (1988) *Children's Phobias: A Behavioural Perspective*. Chichester: John Wiley.

Kirk, S.A. (1962) *Educating the Exceptional Children*. Boston: Houghton Miffin.

Kirk, S.A. (1963) Behavioural diagnosis and remediation of learning disabilities. In *Proceedings of the Annual Conference on Exploration into the Problems of the Perceptually Handicapped* (pp. 1–7). Evanston, IL: Fund for Perceptually Handicapped Children.

Kolko, D.J. (1996) Individual cognitive behavioral treatment and family therapy for physically abused children and their offending parents: a comparison of clinical outcomes. *Child Maltreatment,* **1**, 322–42.

Kopp, C.B. and Parmelee, A. (1979) Prenatal and perinatal influences on infant behaviour. In J. Osofsky (ed.), *Handbook of Infant Development* (2nd edn). New York: Wiley.

Koppitz, E. (1973) Special class pupils with learning disabilities: A five-year follow-up study. *Academic Therapy,* **8**, 133–40.

Korbin, J. (ed.) (1981) *Child Abuse and Neglect: Cross-cultural Perspectives.* Berkeley: University of California Press.

Korbin, J.E., Coulton, C.J., Chard, S., Platt-Houston, C. and Su, M. (1998) Impoverishment and child maltreatment in African American and European American neighbourhoods. *Development and Psychopathology,* **10**, 215–33.

Koren, G., Koren, T. and Gladstone, J (1996) Mild maternal drinking and pregnancy outcome: perceived versus true risks. *Clinica Chimica Acta,* **246**(1–2), 155–62.

Kovacs, M. and Devlin, B. (1998) Internalising disorders in childhood. *Journal of Child Psychology and Psychiatry,* **39**, 47–63.

Kumar, V. (1993) *Poverty and Inequality in the UK: The Effects on Children.* London: National Children's Bureau.

Lahey, B.B. and Loeber, R. (1991) Attention-deficit/hyperactivity disorder, oppositional defiant disorder, conduct disorder, and adult antisocial bahaviour: A life span perspective. In J. Garber and K.A. Dodge (eds), *The Development of Emotional Regulation and Dysregulation: Cambridge Studies in Social and Emotional Development.* New York: Cambridge University Press.

Last, C.G., Perrin, S., Hersen, M. and Kazdin, A.E. (1992) DSM-III-R anxiety disorders in children: sociodemographic and clinical characteristics. *Journal of the American Academy of Child and Adolescent Psychiatry,* **31**, 1070–6.

Lavigne, J.V., Arend, R., Rosenbaum, D., Binns, H.J., Christoffel, K.K. and Gibbons, R.D. (1998) Psychiatric disorders with onset in the preschool years: I. Stability of diagnoses. *Journal of the American Academy of Child and Adolescent Psychiatry,* **37**, 1246–54.

Lazarus, R.S. (1999) *Stress and Emotion: A New Synthesis.* London: Free Association Books.

Leach, P. (1993) Should parents hit their children? *The Psychologist,* **6**, 216–20.

Leadbeater, B., Bishop, S. and Rave, C. (1996) Quality of mother–toddlers interactions, maternal depressive symptoms, and behaviour problems in preschoolers of adolescent mothers. *Developmental Psychology,* **32**, 280–8.

Lerner, J. (1993) *Learning Disabilities: Theories, Diagnosis, and Teaching Strategies.* Boston: Houghton Mifflin.

LeVine, R.A. (1974) Parental goals: A cross-cultural view. In H.J. Leichter (ed.), *The Family as Educator.* New York: Teachers College Press.

Levy, F., Hay, D.A., McStephen, M., Wood, C. and Waldman, I. (1997) Attention-deficit hyperactivity disorder: A category or a continuum? Genetic analysis of a large-scale twin study. *Journal of the Americal Academy of Child and Adolescent Psychiatry,* **36**, 737–44.

Lipman, E.L., Offord, D.R. and Boyle, M.H. (1996) What if we could eliminate child poverty? The theoretical effect on child psychosocial morbidity. *Social Psychiatry Epidemiology,* **31**, 303–7.

Llewellyn, G., McConnell, D. and Bye, R. (1998) Support and service needs of parents with intellectual disability: Perspectives of parents, their significant others and service providers. *Research in Developmental Disabilities,* **19**, 245–60.

Llewellyn, G., McConnell, D., Cant, R. and Westbrook, M. (1999) Support network of mothers with an intellectual disability. *Journal of Intellectual and Developmental Disability,* **24**, 7–26.

Loeber, R. and Farrington, D.P. (eds) (1998) *Serious and Violent Juvenile Offenders: Risk Factors and Successful Intervention.* London: Sage.

Lovaas, O.I. (1987) Behavioral treatment and normal educational and intellectual functioning in young autistic children. *Journal of Consulting and Clinical Psychology,* **55**, 3–9.

Luckasson, R., Coulter, D.L., Polloway, E.A., Reiss, S., Schalock, R.L., Snell, M.E., Spitalnik, D.M. and Stark, J.A. (1992) *Mental Retardation: Definition, Classification and Systems of Supports.* Washington, DC: American Association on Mental Retardation.

Luiselli, J.K., Cannon, B.O., Ellis, J.T. and Sisson, R.W. (2000) Home-based behavioural intervention for young children with autism/pervasive developmental disorder: A preliminary evaluation of outcome in relation to child age and intensity of service delivery. *Autism,* **4**, 426–38.

Luker, K. (1996) *Dubious Conceptions: The Politics of Teenage Pregnancy.* Cambridge, MA: Harvard University Press.

Luthar, S.S. and Cushing, G. (1997) Substance use and personal adjustment among disadvantaged teenagers: a six-month prospective study. *Journal of Youth and Adolescence,* **26**, 353–72.

Lutzker, J.R., and Campbell, R. (1994) *Ecobehavioral Family Interventions in Developmental Disabilities.* Pacific Grove, CA: Brooks/Cole.

Lutzker, J.R., Bigelow, K.M., Doctor, R.M., Gershalter, R.M. and Greene, B.F. (1998) An ecobehavioral model for the prevention and treatment of child abuse and neglect: History and applications. In J.R. Lutzker (ed.), *Handbook of Child Abuse Research and Treatment* (pp. 239–66). New York: Plenum.

Lynch, M. and Cicchetti, D. (1998) An ecological-transactional analysis of children and contexts: the longitudinal interplay among child maltreatment, community violence and children's symptomatology. *Development and Psychopathology*, **10**, 235–57.

Lynn, R., Hampson, S. and Magee, M. (1983) Determinants of education achievement at 16+: Intelligence, personality, home background and school. *Personality and Individual Differences*, **4**(5), 473–81.

Lytton, H. (2000) Toward a model of family-environmental and child-biological influences on development. *Developmental Review*, **20**, 150–79.

Maccoby, E.E. (1980) *Social Development: Psychological Growth and the Parent–Child Relationship*. New York: Harcourt, Brace Jovanovich.

Machel, G. (1996) *The Impact of Armed Conflict on Children*. New York: United Nations.

McClure, E.B., Brennan, P.A., Hammen, C. and Le Brocque, R.M. (2001) Parental anxiety disorders, child anxiety disorders, and the perceived parent–child relationship in an Australian high-risk sample. *Journal of Abnormal Child Psychology*, **29**, 1–10.

McConnell, D., Llewellyn, G. and Bye, R. (1997) Providing services for parents with intellectual disability: parent needs and service constraints. *Journal of Intellectual and Developmental Disability*, **22**, 5–17.

McEachin, J.J., Smith, T. and Lovaas, O.I. (1993) Long-term outcome for children with autism who received early intensive behavioural treatment. *American Journal on Mental Retardation*, **4**, 359–72.

McGee, R., Feehan, M., Williams, S. and Anderson, J. (1992) DSM-III disorders from age 11 to age 15 years. *Journal of the American Academy of Child and Adolescent Psychiatry*, **31**, 50–9.

McGlaughlin, A. and Empson, J.M. (1979) Early child development and the home environment. Paper given to the BPS Developmental Conference, Bulletin BPS, **32**, 148.

McLoyd, V.C. (1990) The impact of economic hardship on black families and children: Psychological distress, parenting, and socioemotional development. *Child Development*, **61**, 311–46.

MacMillan, D.L., Gresham, F.M. and Bocian, K.M. (1998) Discrepancy between definitions of learning disabilities and school practices: an empirical investigation. *Journal of Learning Disabilities*, **31**, 314–26.

MacTurk, R., Vietze, P., McCarthy, M., McQuiston, S. and Yarrow, L. (1985) The organization of exploratory behaviour in Down Syndrome and non-delayed infants. *Child Development*, **56**, 573–87.

McWilliam, R.A. (1999) Controversial practices: The need for a reacculturation of early intervention fields. *Topics in Early Childhood Special Education*, **19**, 177–88.

Main, M. (1995) Recent studies in attachment: overview, with selected implications for clinical work. In S. Goldberg, R. Muir and J. Kerr (eds), *Attachment Theory: Social, Developmental and Clinical Perspectives*. Hillside, NJ: Analytic Press.

Main, M. and Solomon, J. (1986) Discovery of an insecure-disorganized/

disoriented attachment pattern. In T. Brazelton and M. Yogman (eds), *Affective Development in Infancy*. Norwood, NJ: Ablex.

Mallick, S.K. and McCandless, B.R. (1966) A study of catharsis of aggression. *Journal of Personality and Social Psychology*, **4**, 591–6.

Maser, J.D. and Cloninger, C.R. (1990) *Comorbidity in Mood and Anxiety Disorders*. Washington, DC: American Psychiatric Press.

Mash, E.J. and Wolfe, D.A. (1999) *Abnormal Child Psychology*. Belmont, CA: Brooks/Cole.

Maughan, B. (2000) Conduct disorders in context. In J. Hill and B. Maughan (eds), *Conduct Disorders in Childhood and Adolescence*. Cambridge: Cambridge University Press.

Maughan, B., Ouston, J., Pickles, A. and Rutter, M. (1990) Can schools change? I. Outcomes at six London secondary schools. *School Effectiveness and School Improvement*, **1**, 188–210.

Maxwell, W. (1994) Special educational needs and social disadvantage in Aberdeen city school catchment zones. *Educational Research*, **36**(1), 25–37.

Mazzocco, M.M.M., Nord, A.M., van Doorninck, W., Green, C.L., Kovar, C.G. and Pennington, B.F. (1994) Cognitive development among children with early-treated phenylketonuria. *Developmental Neuropsychology*, **10**, 133–51.

Melton, G.B., Goodman, G.S., Kalichman, S.C., Levine, M., Saywitz, K.J. and Koocher, G.P. (1995) Empirical research on child maltreatment and the law. *Journal of Clinical Child Psychology*, **24**, 47–77.

Mesman, J., Bongers, I.L. and Koot, H.M. (2001) Preschool developmental pathways to preadolescent internalising and externalising problems. *Journal of Child Psychology and Psychiatry*, **42**, 679–89.

Meezan, W. and O'Keefe, M. (1998) Evaluating the effectiveness of multifamily group therapy in child abuse and neglect. *Research in Social Work Practice*, **8**, 330–53.

Moffitt T.E. (1993a) The neuropsychology of conduct disorder. Special issue: Toward a developmental perspective on conduct disorder. *Development and Psychopathology*, **5**, *1-2*, 135–51.

Moffitt, T.E. (1993b) Adolescence-limited and life-course-persistent antisocial behaviour: a developmental taxonomy. *Psychological Review*, **100**, 674–701.

Moore, K.L. and Persaud, T.V.N. (1998) *Before we are Born* (5th edn). Philadelphia: Saunders.

Moore, M. and Carr, A. (2000) Anxiety disorders. In A. Carr (ed.), *What Works with Children and Adolescents: A Critical Review of Psychological Interventions with Children, Adolescents and their Families* (pp. 178–202). London: Routledge.

Morris. R. and Kratochwill, T. (1991) Childhood fears and phobias. In T. Kratochwill and R. Morris (eds), *The Practice of Child Therapy* (2nd edn) (pp. 76–114). New York: Pergamon Press.

Nabuzoka, D. (1993) How to define, involve and assess the care unit?

Experiences and research from a CBR programme in Zambia. In H. Finkenflügel (ed.), *The Handicapped Community: The Relation Between Primary Health Care and Community-based Rehabilitation* (pp. 73–87). Amsterdam: VU University Press.

Nabuzoka, D. (2000) *Children with Learning Disabilities: Social Functioning and Adjustment.* Leicester: BPS/Blackwell.

Nabuzoka, D. and Empson, J.M. (2002) Social cognitive development of children with learning difficulties. *Educational and Child Psychology,* **19**, 16–26.

Nabuzoka, D. and Smith, P.K. (1993) Sociometric status and social behaviour of children with and without learning difficulties. *Journal of Child Psychology and Psychiatry,* **34**, 1435–48.

Nabuzoka, D. and Smith, P.K. (1995) Identification of expressions of emotions by children with and without learning disabilities. *Learning Disabilities Research and Practice,* **10**, 91–101.

Nabuzoka, D. and Smith, P.K. (1999) Distinguishing serious and playful fighting by children with learning disabilities and non-disabled children. *Journal of Child Psychology and Psychiatry,* **40**, 883–90.

National Joint Committee on Learning Disabilities (1994) *Collective Perspectives on Issues Affecting Learning Disabilities:* Position papers and statements. Austin, TX: Pro-ed.

National Society for the Prevention of Cruelty to Children (2003) Someone to turn to: an effective child protection system fot the 21st century. Discussion Paper at www.nspcc.org.uk/publicaffairs/.

Newberger, C.M. and Cook, S. (1983) Parental awareness and child abuse: a cognitive-developmental analysis of urban and rural samples. *American Journal of Orthopsychiatry,* **53**, 512–24.

Newberger, E.H. (1973) The myth of the battered child syndrome. In R. Bourne and E.H. Newberger (eds), *Critical Perspectives on Child Abuse.* Lexington, MA: Lexington Books.

Newman, R.S. and Hagen, J.W. (1981) Memory strategies in children with learning disabilities. *Journal of Applied Developmental Psychology,* **1**, 297–312.

Nixon, E. (2001) The social competence of children with attention deficit hyperactivity disorder: a review of the literature. *Child Psychology and Psychiatry Review,* **6**, 172–80.

Oates, J. (1994) First relationships. In J. Oates (ed.), *The Foundations of Child Development.* Oxford: Blackwell.

Ollendick, T.H. and King, N.J. (1994) Diagnosis, assessment, and treatment of internalizing problems in children: The role of longitudinal data. *Journal of Consulting and Clinical Psychology,* **62**, 918–27.

Ollendick, T.H. and King, N.J. (1998) Empirically supported treatments for children with phobic and anxiety disorders: current status. *Journal of Clinical Child Psychology,* **27**, 156–67.

O'Neill, R.E., Horner, R.H., Albin, R.W., Storey, K. and Sprague, J.R.

(1990) *Functional Analysis of Problem Behavior: A Practical Assessment Guide.* Sycamore, IL: Sycamore.

Parkes, C.M., Stevenson-Hinde, J. and Marris, P. (eds), (1991) *Attachment Across the Life Cycle.* New York: Tavistock/Routledge.

Parton, N. (1990) Taking child abuse seriously. In The Violence against Children Study Group *Taking Child Abuse Seriously.* London: Routledge.

Patterson, G.R. (1982) *Coercive Family Interactions.* Eugene, OR: Castalia Press.

Patterson, G.R. and Capaldi, D.M. (1991) Antisocial parents: unskilled and vulnerable. In P.A. Cowan and E.M. Hetherington (eds), *Family Transitions.* Hillsdale, NJ: Lawrence Erlbaum.

Patterson, G.R., Dishion, T.J. and Chamberlain, P. (1993) Outcomes and methodological issues related to treatment of antisocial children. In T.R. Giles (ed.), *Effective Psychotherapy: A Handbook of Comparative Research.* New York: Plenum.

Peagam, E. (1994) Special needs or educational apartheid? The emotional and behavioural difficulties of Afro-Caribbean children. *Support for Learning,* **9**(1), 33–8.

Pearlin, L.I. and Schooler, C. (1978) The structure of coping. *Journal of Health and Social Behaviour,* **19**(1), 2–21.

Pelton, L. (1978) Child abuse and neglect: the myth of classlessness. *American Journal of Orthopsychiatry,* **48**(4), 608–17.

Perlmutter, B.F. (1986) Personality variables and peer relations of children and adolescents with learning disabilities. In S.J. Ceci (ed.), *Handbook of Cognitive, Social and Neuropsychological Aspects of Learning Disabilities,* Vol. 1. London: Lawrence Erlbaum.

Peterson, L. and Brown, D. (1994) Integrating child injury and abuse–neglect research: common histories, etiologies, and solutions. *Psychological Bulletin,* **116**, 293–315.

Phillips, O.P. and Elias, S. (1993) Prenatal genetic counseling issues in women of advanced reproductive age. *Journal of Women's Health,* **2**, 1–5.

Piaget, J. (1952) *The Origins of Intelligence in Children.* New York: International University Press.

Piaget, J. (1960) *The Child's Conception of the World.* London: Routledge.

Piaget, J. (1970) *The Science of Education and Psychology of the Child.* New York: Grossman.

Plomin, R., DeFries, J.C., McClearn, G.E. and McGuffin, P. (2001) *Behavioural Genetics* (4th edn). New York: Worth.

Pogge, D.L. (1992) Risk factors in child abuse and neglect. *Journal of Social Distress and the Homeless,* **1**(3/4), 237–48.

Polansky, N.A., Hally, C. and Polansky, N.F. (1976) *Profile of Neglect: A Survey of the State of Knowledge of Child Neglect.* Washington, DC: US Department of HEW.

Polloway, E.A., Patton, J.R., Smith, T.E.C. and Buck, G.H. (1997) Mental retardation and learning disabilities: conceptual and applied issues. *Journal of Learning Disabilities*, **30**(3), 297–308.

Popkin, B.M., Richards, M.K. and Montiero, C.A. (1996) Stunting is associated with overweight in children of four nations that are undergoing nutrition transition. *Journal of Nutrition*, **126**, 3009–16.

Prentice, A. (1997) *Nature*, **338**, 434 see G. Vines Eating for two, *New Scientist*, 2.8.97, p. 4.

Pringle, M.K. (1971) *The Needs of Children*. London: Hutchinson.

Pritchard, D.G. (1963) *Education of the Handicapped, 1760–1960*. London: Routledge & Kegan Paul.

Putnam, F.W. (1991) Dissociative disorders in children and adolescents: a developmental perspective. *Psychiatric Clinics of North America*, **14**, 519–31.

Putnam, F.W. and Trickett, P.K. (1993) Child sexual abuse: A model of chronic trauma. In D. Reiss, J.E. Richters and M. Radke-Yarrow (eds), *Children and Violence*. New York: Guilford Press.

Quinton, D. (1988) Urbanism and child mental health. *Journal of Child Psychology and Psychiatry*, **29**, 11–20.

Quinton, D., Rutter, M. and Liddle, C. (1984) Institutional rearing, parenting difficulties and marital support. *Psychological Medicine*, **14**, 107–24.

Quinton, D., Rutter, M. and Gulliver, L. (1991) Continuities in psychiatric disorders from childhood to adulthood in the children of psychiatric patients. In L. Robins and M. Rutter (eds), *Straight and Devious Pathways from Childhood to Adulthood*. Cambridge: Cambridge University Press.

Radford, T. (2002) Slavish eating, child obesity, and green bananas: what other researchers found. *Guardian*, 10.9.02, p. 3.

Rapee, R.M. (1997) Potential role of childrearing practices in the development of anxiety and depression. *Clinical Psychology Review*, **17**, 47–67.

Reppucci, N.D., Britner, P.A. and Woolard, J.L. (1997) *Preventing Child Abuse and Neglect Through Parent Education*. Baltimore, MD: Paul H. Brookes.

Rice, F., Harold, G. and Thapar, A. (2002) The genetic aetiology of childhood depression: a review. *Journal of Child Psychology and Psychiatry*, **43**, 65–79.

Roberts, J. (1988) Why are some families more vulnerable to child abuse? In K. Browne, C. Davies and P. Stratton (eds), *Early Prediction and Prevention of Child Abuse*. Oxford: Wiley.

Roberts, R.N., Rule, S. and Innocenti, M.S. (1998) *Strengthening the Family–Professional Partnership in Services for Young Children*. Baltimore, MD: Paul H. Brookes.

Robertson, C.M.T., Finer, N.N. and Grace, M.G.A. (1989) School performance of survivors of neonatal encephalopathy associated with birth asphyxia at term. *Pediatrics,* **76**, 753–60.

Rodgers, B. and Pryor, J. (1998) *Divorce and Separation: The Outcomes for Children.* York: Joseph Rowntree Foundation.

Rosett, H.L. (1980) The effects of alcohol on the fetus and offspring. In O.J. Kalant (ed.) *Research Advances in Alcohol and Drug Problems: Vol. 5 Alcohol and Drug Problems in Women.* New York: Plenum.

Rothbaum, F. and Weisz, J. (1994) Parental caregiving and child externalising behaviour in nonclinical samples: a meta-analysis. *Psychological Bulletin,* **116**, 55–74.

Rourke, B. (1989) *Nonverbal Learning Disabilities: The Syndrome and the Model.* New York: Guilford Press.

Rourke, B.P. and Del Dotto, J.E. (1992) Learning disabilities: a neuropsychological perspective. In C.E. Walker and M.C. Roberts (eds), *Handbook of Clinical Child Psychology* (2nd edn). New York: Wiley.

Russell, D. (1983) The incidence and prevalence of intrafamilial and extrafamilial sexual abuse of female children. *Child Abuse and Neglect,* **7**, 133–46.

Rutter, M. (1979) Protective factors in children's responses to stress and disadvantage. In M.W. Kent and J.E. Rolf (eds), *Primary Prevention of Psychopathology,* Vol. 3, *Social Competence in Children.* Hanover, NH: University Press of New England.

Rutter, M. (1982) Epidemiological longitudinal approaches to the study of development. In W.A. Collins (ed.), *The Concept of Development. Minnesota Symposium on Child Psychology,* Vol. 15. Hillsdale, NJ: Erlbaum.

Rutter, M. (1985a) Resilience in the face of adversity: protective factors and resistance to psychiatric disorder. *British Journal of Psychiatry,* **147**, 598–611.

Rutter, M. (1985b) Family and school influences on cognitive development. In R.A. Hinde, A. Perret-Clermont and J. Stevenson-Hinde (eds), *Social Relationships and Cognitive Development.* Oxford: Clarendon Press.

Rutter, M. (1987) Psychosocial resilience and protective mechanisms. *American Journal of Orthopsychiatry,* **57**, 316–31.

Rutter, M. (1989a) Intergenerational continuities and discontinuities in serious parenting difficulties. In D. Cicchetti and V. Carlson (eds), *Child Maltreatment.* Cambridge: Cambridge University Press.

Rutter, M. (1989b) Pathways from childhood to adult life. *Journal of Child Psychology and Psychiatry,* **30**(1), 23–51.

Rutter, M. (1990) *Helping Troubled Children* (2nd edn). London: Penguin.

Rutter, M. (1991) A fresh look at maternal deprivation. In P. Bateson (ed.), *The Development and Integration of Behaviour.* Cambridge: Cambridge University Press.

Rutter, M. (1996) Developmental psychopathology as an organising research construct. In D. Magnusson (ed.), *The Lifespan Development of Individuals*. Cambridge: Cambridge University Press.

Rutter, M. and Madge, N. (1976) *Cycles of Disadvantage: A Review of Research*. London: Heinemann.

Rutter, M., Giller, H. and Hagekk, A. (1998a) *Antisocial Behaviour by Young People*. New York: Cambridge University Press.

Rutter, M. and the English and Romanian Adoptees (ERA) study team (1998b) Developmental catch-up, and deficit, following adoption after severe global early privation. *Journal of Child Psychology and Psychiatry*, **39**, 465–76.

Rutter, M., Bolton, P, Harrington, R., Le Couteur, A., Macdonald, H. and Simonoff, E. (1990a) Genetic factors in child psychiatric disorders – I. A review of research strategies. *Journal of Child Psychology and Psychiatry*, **31**, 3–37.

Rutter, M., Macdonald, H., Le Couteur, A., Harrington, R., Bolton, P. and Bailey, A. (1990b) Genetic factors in child psychiatric disorders – II. Empirical findings. *Journal of Child Psychology and Psychiatry*, **31**, 39–83.

Sameroff, A.J. (1987) The social context of development. In N. Eisenberg (ed.), *Contemporary Topics in Developmental Psychology*. New York: Wiley.

Sameroff, A.J. (1991) The social context of development. In M. Woodhead, R. Carr and P. Light (eds), *Becoming a Person*. London: Routledge/Open University.

Sameroff, A.J. and Chandler, M.J. (1975) Reproductive risk and the continuum of caretaking casualty. In F.D. Horowitz, M. Hetherington, S. Scarr-Salapatek and G. Siegal (eds), *Review of Child Development Research*, Vol. 4. Chicago: University of Chicago Press.

Schaffer, H.R. (1996) *Social Development*. Oxford: Blackwell.

Schaffer, H.R. (2000) The early experience assumption: Past, present and future. *International Journal of Behavioural Development*, **24**, 5–14.

Schechter, M. and Roberge, L. (1976) Child sexual abuse. In R. Helfer and C. Kempe (eds), *Child Abuse and Neglect: the Family and the Community*. Cambridge, MA: Ballinger.

Schopler, E. and Mesibov, G. (1995) Language and cognition in autism. In E. Schopler and G. Mesibov (eds), *Current Issues in Autism*. New York: Plenum.

Schwartz, I.S. (1999) Controversy or lack of consensus? Another way to examine treatment alternatives. *Topics in Early Childhood Special Education*, **19**, 189–93.

Serketich, W. and Dumas, J.E. (1996) The effectiveness of behavioral parent training to modify antisocial behavior in children: a meta-analysis. *Behavior Therapy*, **27**, 171–86.

Serpell, R. (1983) Cross-culturally universal domains for the assessment of severe intellectual handicap. A discussion paper. Lusaka: Institute for African Studies, University of Zambia.

Serpell, R. (1988) Assessment criteria for severe intellectual disability in various cultural settings. *International Journal of Behavioural Development*, **1**(1), 117–44.

Serpell, R. and Nabuzoka, D. (1985) Community-based rehabilitation for disabled children in Vulamkoko Ward: A follow-up study. Paper presented at the Workshop on the International Pilot Study of Severe Childhood Disability at the IASSMD Congress in New Delhi, India, April 1985.

Serpell, R. and Nabuzoka, D. (1989) Assessment as a guide to meeting the needs of rural Zambian families with a disabled child. Paper presented at the 10th Biennial Meeting of the International Society for the Study of Behavioural Development. Jyvaskyla, Finland: 9–13 July 1989.

Serpell, R., Mariga, L. and Harvey, K. (1993) Mental retardation in African countries: Conceptualisation, services and research. *International Review of Research in Mental Retardation*, **19**, 1–39.

Shaw, D., Keenan, K. and Vondra, J. (1994) Developmental precursors of externalizing behaviors: Ages 1 to 3. *Developmental Psychology*, **30**, 355–64.

Shochet, I.M., Dadds, M.R., Holland, D., Whitefield, K., Hartnett, P.H., and Osgarby, S.M. (2001) The efficacy of a universal school-based program to prevent adolescent depression. *Journal of Clinical Child Psychology*, **30**, 303–15.

Silver, L.B. (1995) Controversial therapies. *Journal of Child Neurology*, **10**(1), 96–100.

Silverman, W.K. and Kurtines, W.M. (1996) *Anxiety and Phobic Disorders: A Pragmatic Approach*. New York: Plenum Press.

Silwamba, S. (1990) The Impact of Mental Handicap on Families in Zambia. Dissertation for the Certificate in the Further Education and Training of Mentally Handicapped People. Hull: Humberside College of Higher Education.

Siqueland, L., Kendall, P.C. and Steinberg, L. (1996) Anxiety in children: perceived family environments and observed family interaction. *Journal of Clinical Child Psychology*, **25**, 225–37.

Skuse, D., Reilly, S. and Wolke, D. (1994) Psychosocial adversity and growth during infancy. *European Journal of Clinical Nutrition*, **48** (Suppl. 1), S113–30.

Smith, T. (1996) Are other treatments effective? In C. Maurice, G. Green and S.C. Luce (eds), *Behavioral Intervention for Young Children with Autism: A Manual for Parents and Professionals* (pp. 45–59). Austin, TX: Pro-ed.

Smith, T. and Lovaas, O.I. (1998) Intensive and early behavioral intervention in autism: The UCLA Young Autism Project. *Infants and Young Children*, **10**, 67–78.

Smith, T., Buch, G.A. and Gamby, G.A. and Bamby, T.E. (2000) Parent-directed, intensive early intervention for children with pervasive developmental disorder. *Research in Developmental Disabilities*, **21**, 297–309.

Snell, M.E. (ed.) (1993) *Instruction for Students with Severe Disabilities* (4th edn). New York: Merrill.

Spafford, C.S. and Grosser, G.S. (1993) The social misperception syndrome in children with learning disabilities: social causes versus neurological variables. *Journal of Learning Disabilities*, **26**, 178–89 and 198.

Spitzer, A., Webster-Stratton, C. and Hollinsworth, T. (1991) Coping with conduct-problem children: parents gaining knowledge and control. *Journal of Clinical Child Psychology*, **20**, 413–27.

Sroufe, L.A. (1983) Infant-caregiving attachment and patterns of adaptation and competence. In M. Perlmutter (ed.) *Minnesota Symposia on Child Psychology* Vol. 16. Hillsdale, NJ: Erlbaum.

Sroufe, L.A., Carlson, E. and Shulman, S. (1993) The development of individuals in relationships: From infancy through adolescence. In D.C. Funder, R. Parke, C. Tomlinson-Keesey and K. Widaman (eds), *Studying Lives Through Time: Approaches to Personality and Development*. Washington, DC: American Psychological Association.

Sroufe, L.A., Cooper, R.G. and DeHart, G.B. (1996) *Child Development. Its Nature and Course* (3rd edn). New York: McGraw-Hill.

Stainback, W. and Stainback, S. (1990) *Support Networks for Inclusive Schooling*. Baltimore, MD: Paul H. Brookes.

Steele, B.T. (1997) Psychodynamic and biological factors in child maltreatment. In M.E. Helfer, R.S. Kempe and R.D. Krugman (eds), *The Battered Child* (5th edn). Chicago: University of Chicago Press.

Stoch, M.B., Smythe, P.M., Moodie, A.D. and Bredshaw, D. (1982) Psychosocial outcome and CT findings after growth undernourishment during infancy: a 20-year developmental study. *Developmental Medicine and Child Neurology*, **24**, 419–36.

Sullivan, P.F., Neale, M.C. and Kendler, K.S. (2000) Genetic epidemiology of major depression: review and meta-analysis. *American Journal of Psychiatry*, **157**, 1552–62.

Sulzer-Azaroff, B. and Mayer, G.R. (1991) *Behavior Analysis for Lasting Change*. Fort Worth, TX: Holt, Rinehart & Winston.

Sunday Times Insight Team (1979) *Suffer the Children. The Story of Thalidomide*. London: Andre Deutsch.

Super, C.M. (1981) Behavioural development in infancy. In R.H. Munroe, R.L. Munroe, and B.B. Whiting (eds), *Handbook of Cross-cultural Human Development* (pp. 181–270). New York: Garland.

Super, C.M. and Harkness, S. (1986) The developmental niche: a conceptualization at the interface of child and culture. *International Journal of Behavioral Development*, **9**, 545–69.

Swenson, C.C. and Hanson, R.F. (1998) Sexual abuse of children: Assessment, research, and treatment. In J.R. Lutzker (ed.), *Handbook of Child Abuse Research and Treatment* (pp. 475–99). New York: Plenum.

Sykes, D.H., Hoy, E.A., Bill, J.M., McClure, B.G., Halliday, H.L. and Reid, M. McC. (1997) Behavioural adjustment in school of very low birth weight children. *Journal of Child Psychology and Psychiatry*, **38**(3), 315–25.

Szatmari, P., Saigal, S., Rosenbaum, P. and Campbell, D. (1993) Psychopathology and adaptive functioning among extremely low birthweight children at eight years of age. *Development and Psychopathology*, **5**, 345–57.

Tapasak, R.C. and Walther-Thomas, C.S. (1999) Evaluation of a first-year inclusion program. *Remedial and Special Education*, **20**, 216–25.

Terr, L.C. (1983) Chowchilla revisited: The effects of psychic trauma four years after a school-bus kidnapping. *American Journal of Psychiatry*, **140**, 1543–50.

Terr, L.C. (1991) Childhood traumas: an outline and overview. *American Journal of Psychiatry*, **148**, 10–20.

Thapar, A. and McGuffin, P. (1995) Are anxiety symptoms in childhood heritable? *Journal of Child Psychology and Psychiatry*, **36**, 439–47.

Thapar, A., Holmes, J., Poulton, K. and Harrington, R. (1999) Genetic basis of attention deficit and hyperactivity. *British Journal of Psychiatry*, **174**, 105–11.

The Violence against Children Study Group (1990) *Taking Child Abuse Seriously*. London: Routledge.

Thomas, A. and Chess, S. (1977) *Temperament and Development*. New York: Bruner-Mazel.

Thomas A., Chess, S. and Birch, H.G. (1968) *Temperament and Behaviour Disorders in Children*. New York: New York University Press.

Tizard, B. (1977) *Adoption: A Second Chance*. London: Open Books.

Tizard, B. (1985) Social relationships between adults and young children, and their impact on intellectual functioning. In R.A. Hinde, A. Perret-Clermont and J. Stevenson-Hinde (eds), *Social Relationships and Cognitive Development*. Oxford: Clarendon Press.

Tizard, B. and Hughes, M. (1984) *Young Children Learning: Talking and Thinking at Home and at School*. London: Fontana.

Turnbull, A.P., Blue-Banning, M., Turbiville, V. and Park, J. (1999) From parent education to partnership education: a call for a transformed focus. *Topics in Early Childhood Special Education*, **19**, 164–72.

Valentine, C.W. (1956) *The Normal Child and Some of his Abnormalities*. London: Penguin.

van IJzendoorn, M.H., Goldberg, S., Kroonenberg, P. and Frankel, O. (1992) The relative effects of maternal and child problems on the quality of attachment: a meta-analysis of attachment in clinical samples. *Child Development*, **63**, 840–58.

Warnock, H.M. (1978) *Special Educational Needs.* Report of the Committee of Enquiry into the Education of Handicapped Children and Young People. London: HMSO.

Waterhouse, L., Wing, L. and Fein, D. (1989) Re-evaluating the syndrome of autism in the light of empirical research. In G. Dawson (ed.) *Autism: Nature, Diagnosis and Treatment.* New York: The Guildford Press.

Waters, E., Wippman, J. and Sroufe, L.A. (1979) Attachment, positive affect and competence in the peer group: two studies in construct validation. *Child Development,* **50,** 821–9.

Waters, E., Posada, G., Crowell, J. and Keng-Ling, L. (1993) Is attachment theory ready to contribute to our understanding of disruptive behaviour problems? *Development and Psychopathology,* **5,** 215–24.

Webster-Stratton, C. (1993) Strategies for helping early school-aged children with oppositional defiant disorders and/or conduct disorders: The importance of home-school connections. *School Psychology Review,* **22,** 437–57.

Webster-Stratton, C. (1997) From parent training to community building. *Families in Society,* **78,** 156–71.

Webster-Stratton, C. (1998) Preventing conduct problems in Head Start children: Strengthening parenting competencies. *Journal of Consulting and Clinical Psychology,* **66,** 715–30.

Webster-Stratton, C. and Herbert, M. (1993) *Troubled Families – Problem Children.* Chichester: John Wiley & Sons.

Webster-Stratton, C. and Herbert, M. (1994) *Troubled Families, Problem Children: Working with Parents, A Collaborative Process.* Chichester: John Wiley & Sons.

Webster-Stratton, C., Reid, J. and Hammond, M. (2001) Social skills and problem solving training for children with early-onset conduct problems: Who benefits? *Journal of Child Psychology and Psychiatry,* **42,** 943–52.

Weinert, F.E. and Weinert, S. (1998) History and systems of developmental psychology. In A. Demetriou, W. Doise, and C. van Lieshout (eds), *Life-span Developmental Psychology.* Chichester: Wiley.

Weisberg, P. (1992) Education and enrichment approaches. In C.E. Walker and M.C. Roberts (eds) *Handbook of Clinical Child Psychology* (2nd edn). New York: Wiley.

Weisz, J.R., Sigman, M., Weiss, B. and Mosk, J. (1993) Parental reports of behavioural and emotional problems among children in Kenya, Thailand and the United States. *Child Development,* **64,** 98–109.

Werner, H. (1957) The concept of development from a comparative and organismic point of view. In D.B. Harris (ed.), *The Concept of Development.* Minneapolis, MN: University of Minnesota Press.

Whiting, B.B. and Edwards, C.P. (1988) *Children of Different Worlds: The Formation of Social Behaviour.* Cambridge MA: Harvard University Press.

Whitman, T.L., Scherzinger, M.F. and Sommer, K.S. (1991) Cognitive instruction and mental retardation. In P.C. Kendall (ed.), *Child and Adolescent Therapy: Cognitive-behavioral Procedures* (pp. 276–315). New York: Guilford Press.

Whitney, I., Nabuzoka, D. and Smith, P.K. (1992) Bullying in schools: Mainstream and special needs children. *Support for Learning*, **7**(1), 3–7.

Whitten, D. (1996) Fetal alcohol risk: A current perspective. In A.L. Waterhouse and J.M. Rantz (eds), Conference proceedings. *Wine in Context: Nutrition-Physiology-Policy*, Reno, NV.

WHO (1983) *Training the Disabled in the Community: A Manual on Community-based Rehabilitation for Developing Countries* (Prepared by Einar Helander, Padmani Mendis and Gunnel Nelson) Geneva: World Health Organization.

WHO (1985) *Mental Retardation: Meeting the Challenge*. Geneva: World Health Organization. Offset publication No. 86.

WHO (1993) *The ICD-10 Classification of Mental and Behavioural Disorders. Diagnostic Criteria for Research*. Geneva: World Health Organization.

Wichstrom, L., Skogen, K. and Oia, T. (1996) Increased rate of conduct problems in urban areas: what is the mechanism? *Journal of the American Academy of Child and Adolescent Psychiatry*, **35**, 471–9.

Williams, L.M. and Finkelhor, D. (1995) Paternal caregiving and incest: test of biosocial model. *American Journal of Orthopsychiatry*, **65**(1), 101–13.

Wilson, B.A. (1999) Inclusion: Empirical guidelines and unanswered questions. *Education and Training in Mental Retardation and Developmental Disabilities*, **34**, 119–33.

Wilson, W.J.O. (1987) *The Truly Disadvantaged: The Inner City, the Underclass and Public Policy*. Chicago: University of Chicago Press.

Wolf, M. (1978) Social validity: The case for subjective measurement, or how behavior analysis is finding its heart. *Journal of Applied Behavior Analysis*, **11**, 203–14.

Woodhead, M. (1995) Disturbing behaviour in young children. In P. Barnes (ed.), *Personal, Social and Emotional Development of Children* (pp. 41–82). Oxford/Milton Keynes: Open University/Blackwell.

Zelazo, P.R. (1983) The development of walking: new findings and old assumptions. *Journal of Motor Behaviour*, **15**, 99–137.

Zigler, E. (1980) Controlling child abuse: Do we have the knowledge and/or the will? In G. Gerbner, L. Ross and E. Zigler (eds), *Child Abuse: An Agenda for Action*. New York: Oxford University Press.

Zigler, E. and Hall, N.W. (1989) Physical child abuse in America: Past, present and future. In D. Cicchetti and V. Carlson (eds), *Child Maltreatment*. Cambridge: Cambridge University Press.

Author Index

Subject Index